A Life Spent Changing Places

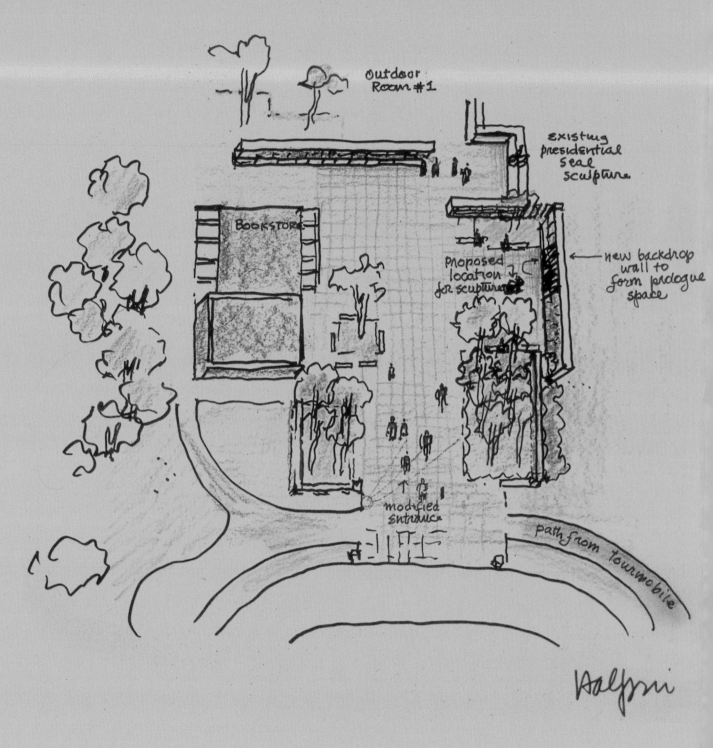

outdoor
Room #1

existing
presidential
seal
sculpture

BOOKSTORE

Proposed
location
for sculpture

← new backdrop
wall to
form prologue
space

modified
entrance

path from Tourmobile

Penn Studies in Landscape Architecture

John Dixon Hunt, Series Editor

This series is dedicated to the study and promotion of a wide variety of approaches to landscape architecture, with special emphasis on connections between theory and practice. It includes monographs on key topics in history and theory, descriptions of projects by both established and rising designers, translations of major foreign-language texts, anthologies of theoretical and historical writings on classic issues, and critical writing by members of the profession of landscape architecture. The series was the recipient of the Award of Honor in Communications from the American Society of Landscape Architects, 2006.

A Life Spent Changing Places | Lawrence Halprin

PENN

University of Pennsylvania Press

Philadelphia

Publication of this volume was aided by generous gifts from the following institutions: Foundation for Landscape Studies; Furthermore: A Program of the J. M. Kaplan Fund; Getty Foundation; Richard and Rhoda Goldman Fund; University of Pennsylvania Graduate School of Design.

All images not otherwise cited are courtesy of the University of Pennsylvania Architectural Archives.

Published by

University of Pennsylvania Press

Philadelphia, Pennsylvania 19104-4112

www.upenn.edu/pennpress

Printed in Canada on acid-free paper

10 9 8 7 6 5 4 3 2 1

Library of Congress Cataloging-in-Publication Data

Halprin, Lawrence.

   A life spent changing places / Lawrence Halprin. — 1st ed.

      p. cm. — (Penn studies in landscape architecture)

   Includes index.

   ISBN 978-0-8122-4263-8 (hardcover : alk. paper)

   1. Halprin, Lawrence   2. Architects—California—San Francisco Bay Area—Biography.   I. Title.   II. Series: Penn studies in landscape architecture.

   NA737.H27A2 2011

   720.92—dc22

   [B]   2010053546

Facing title page: Forecourt, FDR Memorial, Washington, D.C. (Figure 170).

Part I title page: Wailing Wall (Figure 8).

Part II title page: Yosemite Falls entrance (Figure 174).

To my dear Uncle Sydney,

whose wise counsel I treasured

Contents

Lawrence Halprin was a great landscape architect. He was also a strong advocate for community, sociability, cities, and nature. The remark that "Every great artist inhabits a genre, and remakes it" could find no better proof than in his life and work. He produced a series of masterpieces of iconic stature: Ghirardelli Square in San Francisco; Sea Ranch on the north California coast; the Lovejoy and Ira Keller Fountain sequence in Portland, Oregon; Freeway Park in Seattle, Washington; the Franklin Delano Roosevelt Memorial in Washington, D.C.; and Stern Grove Theater in San Francisco, to name some of the best known. He knew plants horticulturally and could use them architecturally. Many of his greatest works were executed with humble, ordinary building materials: concrete, asphalt, stucco, wood, soil, and plants. As he matured and whenever he could, he utilized natural stone and water.

Between 1949 and 1961, long before he produced the works for which he is known today, he designed more than three hundred residential gardens in the San Francisco Bay region. Two of these were major steps in his development and have entered the canon of midcentury American landscape design. The first was at his own house (1952) designed by William Wurster, an architect he'd met as a student at Harvard. A key element was a detached redwood dance deck made for his wife. On this nonrectangular platform she developed many of her avant-garde works, with a number of young dancers who were to become future leaders in the field such as Merce Cunningham. Anna Halprin credited its free shape and multilevels with helping her to explore space, the body, its senses, and its perceptions. In turn Halprin has credited his experience with her work as having had a major influence in developing his ideas of movement and sequence in spatial terms. The other generative early project, the McIntyre garden in Hillsborough, California (1959), he designed with Joseph Esherick, another architect with whom he was to work later—most importantly at the Sea Ranch. In it one can see Halprin beginning to survey and reflect upon the history of landscape design and see that he was trying his hand at materials both contemporary and timeless, particularly masonry and water, with ideas drawn from well-known historical works to see how he measured up.

By the late 1950s, with a large body of domestic-scale projects behind him, his practice began to expand to take on commercial work such as shopping centers with architects Richard Marsh Bennett outside Chicago and Eero Saarinen near Dallas. Aspects of these commercial developments anticipate the important civic plans and spaces, fountains and plazas he was to design later. In these early suburban malls we see his use of concrete, stepped levels, and angular shapes; sequences of spaces that

Foreword

Laurie Olin

narrow, swell, change direction; fountains; and idiosyncratic custom furnishing. These projects, like some of his finest later work, have unfortunately been so heavily copied and thoroughly absorbed into the vernacular of late twentieth-century urban development that they now appear as cliché. At the time, however, he and his staff were designing and building a new kind of public space, flowing free-form pedestrian ways between shops in the new marketplaces of America.

The period from 1956 to 1961 was one of enormous personal, intellectual, artistic, and professional growth, during which he began taking trips to the high Sierras, hiking, sketching, and photographing the mountains, rocks, and vegetation, and especially the water in all its moods and situations. Although he had drawn for pleasure and amusement since college days it was in this period that he began regularly keeping sketchbooks for drawing, recording his observations and making studies and notes for projects. A fierce appetite for experience and persistent observation recorded directly on the spot honed his visual acuity and fed his design repertoire. This graphic skill became an important tool in Halprin's design process, contributing significantly to his success.

In the summer of 1961 Halprin took a trip with his daughter Daria to Europe and Israel largely to study their cities, streets, plazas, waterfronts, great gardens, and classical sites. One outcome was the book *Cities*, published two years later. This survey and meditation on the character of both ordinary and outstanding furnishings of European civic spaces almost immediately fed directly into a sequence of commissions in which he explored and experimented with urban design typologies. These were to include Ghirardelli Square, Embarcadero Plaza, and Market Street in San Francisco; Nicollet Mall in Minneapolis; the Seattle World's Fair site; and a pedestrian mall in Charlottesville, Virginia. In this work Halprin developed experimental processes he called *scores* and *motation*, personal and somewhat idiosyncratic systems to graphically record, study, and script human movement through sequences of space and topography and to describe the particular character of the each space.

The Ghirardelli development (1965) shows Halprin revisiting the ideas and character of his earlier suburban shopping centers through the filter of his recent European experience. When asked for ideas regarding the site of an abandoned nineteenth-century chocolate factory above Fisherman's Wharf in San Francisco, he suggested that rather than clearing the buildings for new development, which was (and often still is) the habit of the day, he suggested the project should save most of the brick structures, while at the same time cutting into them so as to open views to the bay below and creating a series of stairs and ramps linking their levels and the adjacent streets to a collection of shops around several small plazas. It was a brilliant and pioneering example of adaptive reuse producing a form of urban theater within commercial development.

Another typology he challenged in this period was that of the traditional street as it had evolved, choked with automobiles, in twentieth-century America. His experiment with a transit mall in Minneapolis intrigued designers all over while it terrorized engineers and puzzled businessmen. His proposal asked why couldn't the road or bus-way wander sinuously within the right-of-way, like a river, creating varying and more generous widths alternately on either side for pedestrians instead of the habitual narrow straight sidewalks. This arrangement would allow for amenities such as bus shelters, art, fountains, planting, and seating (all of which he also designed) along the course of the street that simply would not fit on the normal twelve- to sixteen-foot-wide walks of most American streets. Nicollet Mall set in motion several decades of experiment and street improvement projects in the core of American cities and towns.

Halprin's plan for the five-thousand-acre Sea Ranch project was a innovation in twentieth-century American design. Spending a great amount of time on the site, Halprin, walking, drawing, and studying it, proposed to preserve the character of a former sheep ranch with ten miles of rugged coastline, hedgerows, and meadows. His response to and exploitation of the wind, rocks, spaces, and views prefigured subsequent ecological planning a decade later.

Working with the Portland, Oregon, Redevelopment Authority in 1965, Halprin proposed an open-space system consisting of three one-acre parks linked by pedestrian lanes. The resultant squares, Lovejoy Plaza, Pettigrove Park, and the Auditorium Forecourt (now known as the Ira Keller Fountain), brought together Halprin's creative energy and one of his deepest inspirations, that of a particular group of streams and waterfalls in Yosemite National Park. The first plaza contained a representation of a mountain, an abstract one in concrete, sharp edged, with a waterfall coming from its top that tumbled and fell into a calm pool with stepping-stones below, inviting people to participate. It was like nothing else in America at the time in its palette, forms, or imagery. Pettigrove Park in the middle of the development is quiet and green, a stunning contrast to Lovejoy Plaza, consisting of a series of mounds, trees, paths, low walls, and benches. The canopy and green surfaces that rise above one's head and fill the visual field form an oasis, a refuge that is as unexpected as the waterfall at Lovejoy. The strength and pure forms of the mounds is striking even today. The culmination of the Portland sequence is the giant Auditorium Forecourt fountain plaza. Here tons of water fall with a roar from an upper plaza to a sunken basin eighteen feet below. As at Lovejoy the elements are concrete, water, and plants. It is a pure landscape. There are no benches, no lights, and no furnishings. The cubic forms of concrete are superb, with an aggregate of different sizes exposed in the various parts. Some of the plaza is fine and delicate, barely more than a sand finish, some pebbly, while other areas have large river cobbles. It is a splendid abstraction of a glaciated mountain landscape.

With the Portland projects Halprin changed the course of landscape architecture by reintroducing representation and reference as content in design. His early postwar gardens, like those of his mentor Thomas Church and contemporaries Robert Royston and Garrett Eckbo, were skillful in their expression of an evolving western lifestyle. They solved problems and created particular spaces and zones for activities such as automobile parking, children's play, swimming, barbecuing, adult social gathering, and sunbathing. They were the epitome of functionalism and exemplars of a relatively new version of suburban life, often possessing striking geometric form. In Portland, Halprin took the forms and technique he had acquired and produced a work of art that was as representational as any figurative painting could be about a western

regional landscape. He retrieved one of the most powerful aspects of historic landscape design without the trappings of neoclassical iconography. It was abstract, modern, and powerful. People responded to it.

Halprin lived with contradictions in ways that for him were complementary rather than oppositional. He loved cars and driving; he loved to walk and hike; he loved cities; he loved farms; he loved wild nature. He chose to live in the woods next to Mount Tamalpais, in Marin County, north of San Francisco and to have a sequence of offices in the bustling center of the city. He admired both urbanity and highways; writing and publishing books about both while trying to work out ways to plan for each that were equally expressive and logical. Literature and criticism to date in the field of landscape architecture, its history and theory, have focused primarily upon his gardens and urban plazas, and to a large extent have not assessed the many urban planning and design projects he and his office undertook. This may be due partly to the time it takes for such work to bear fruit, partly to their lack of visual panache, and partly to the fate many have eventually suffered.

If one measure of his greatness is the number and quality of handsome and important places he created, another is how he contributed to changes in the practice of landscape architecture and the processes of public works. Larry Halprin managed to do so while rejecting the office practice and business model that evolved during his lifetime and was employed by many of his contemporaries and competitors partly in order to do projects at the scale he frequently worked at. Hideo Sasaki, Garrett Eckbo, Ed Stone Jr., Ian McHarg, Peter Walker, and other contemporaries who began with small practices developed offices that adopted corporate structures, often with large staff, multiple partners, and branches. Halprin approached and backed away from this situation, managing to maintain a studio atmosphere with personal and artistic control of all the work.

Aspects of several of his methods in one guise or another have become accepted and normal, at times even obligatory, public processes throughout America and Europe. Recording and designing events he borrowed an appropriate term from music, the score, while working with artists, psychologists, scientists, and designers and with key assistants and friends to develop what evolved into his RSVP process of workshops in an attempt to resist preconceived forms and ideas, or determinist quasi-scientific methodologies. Halprin strove to work in a way that would allow an open process with feedback that engaged clients, communities, stakeholders, and designers equally through a series of exercises and explorative activities indi-

vidually and as a group. Despite the strong influence of Jungian psychology and a genuine (and generous) liberal political urge to respond to the needs of others, Halprin consistently controlled the design response to this input, maintaining a strong personal artistic expression in form and imagery.

Halprin's first professional public goal-oriented workshop took place in Fort Worth, Texas, in 1979. After putting civic leaders and influential businessmen through orientation and sensitivity exercises in the older heart of the city, he coaxed them through sessions that led to goals, a program and a framework that encompassed public and private transportation, parking, and mixed-use commercial and residential developments, as well as pedestrian ways, public plazas, and parks. This led to an ambitious plan for eight miles of the Trinity River corridor that included drives, parks, and recreation areas reminiscent of some of the best of the WPA projects of the Great Depression, as well as proposals for reshaping portions of the river, landings, and commercial and residential development. With this and other schemes in his office at this period, Halprin was thirty years ahead of his time. Some aspects of the plan were taken up and realized by the business community, albeit only those that facilitated commuters and commerce in the downtown, while few of the civic spaces or park proposals were implemented. It was only after the beginning of the twenty-first century that some of his proposals for the river and its development for residential use and recreation have been revived and one of the only public spaces he managed to realize in Fort Worth, Heritage Plaza, overlooking the Trinity River, derelict at the time of this writing, is in the process of restoration.

Unlike a number of other leading American landscape architects of his generation Halprin had little involvement with academia. For reasons of personality and the pressure of his practice, by the 1970s Halprin had come to avoid the environmental design school at Berkeley, where he had once had close friends, even running a couple of experimental summer studios. His alma mater, Harvard, was far away and didn't seem very welcoming, either. He and Ian McHarg, who had published *Design with Nature* in 1969, were great admirers of each other's work. McHarg managed to persuade him to come to the University of Pennsylvania to spend time with the students in their design studios during the period that he was deeply involved in the Roosevelt Memorial and traveling to the East Coast for periods of time.

In the heart of Portland, Seattle, and Denver Halprin explored and produced bold and original public spaces through the use of abstract imagery, forms, and processes derived from hauntingly beautiful environments of the American West. In his design for the Franklin Delano Roosevelt Memorial in the nation's capital, which followed, his interest shifted from nature to culture, from plants, rocks, and water, to art, language, text, inscription, and figurative sculpture. In this project, begun in 1974 but delayed for more than a decade by difficulties with Congress and funding, he almost single-handedly revived the use of figurative sculpture and the use of words as central elements in an architectural scheme. Banished from architecture and high-style art in the early decades of the twentieth century by Adolf Loos and modernists such Wright, Le Corbusier, and Gropius from whom he'd learned so much, the use of sculpture or any sort of verbal hortatory element on buildings or gardens had become one of the biggest taboos.

The atavistic urge to recall the stone and earthen structures of pre-Columbian America he employed in Denver's Skyline Park gave way in the Roosevelt Memorial to memories of Bronze Age sites and ruins of the old world. As with the Portland and Seattle projects, which have been overly and poorly imitated, this memorial has been so envied by others that it has influenced a number of other narrative-based memorials that tend toward interpretive tableaus, becoming quasi-museums that are not as iconic or fitting as his work may yet become.

Larry Halprin helped to change how landscape architecture is practiced and how it is perceived today. Loving nature he chose to work in and on cities, and in so doing he invented ways of working with communities that resulted in open-ended processes for their involvement in formulating public design. Unlike his talented contemporaries whose projects frequently remained (regardless of how successful) works either of formal, social, or ecological performance, his work embraced all of these aspects while restoring the power of narrative and representation to landscape design. Larry Halprin's work is thoroughly grounded in the classical and ancient past, while no more copying or mimicking it than the natural world he so loved, thereby offering a profound lesson for students and professionals alike.

Invited to a conference at Harvard in 1991 entitled "Urban Ground" and focused upon design criticism regarding the landscape of cities, something Halprin had concerned himself with for most of his life, he was direct and spoke in a way rarely heard in academic circles. He began talking about Jungian notions of things we all experience and have in common: sex, food, love, and sequences of movement—of entry, processional, and arrival. While interested in and accepting that there is such a thing referred to as "Common Ground," he

bluntly asserted that it isn't an "image." "It is about time not space." For him the two were nevertheless linked. Closing he said simply, "If one moves differently through space in time it is very different. The act of being in love takes time irrespective of space." Despite having made a series of unforgettable physical creations, he was devoted to process to the end.

As my name was called I jumped to my feet and raised my arms in victory. I was on stage with the president and vice president of the United States and flanked by senators and dignitaries from near and far. It had taken me twenty-three years to bring the Franklin Delano Roosevelt Memorial design to fruition and on that warm May day in 1997 I was exuberant, joyful, relieved, and very proud. I gave the president and First Lady a personal tour and then stood for hours shaking hands and enjoying perhaps the most satisfactory day of my life. I knew there were parties to attend as friends gathered to share in the celebration but I wasn't ready to leave. I wanted to watch the memorial serve its purpose and produce the results I had envisioned for so many years. It was the pinnacle of my career and a personal homage to a man I considered our greatest president. I wanted to stay and savor the moment.

In 1916, when I was born, FDR was thirty-three years old. By the time I became aware of politics he was governor of New York and then the thirty-second president of the United States. I listened to his fireside chats and followed his social programs. He was my commander in chief when I was a young naval ensign. I was on a destroyer in the South Pacific when I heard he had died in Warm Springs, Georgia, during his fourth term as president. As the tough sailors on our ship cried over the loss of a great leader, it was unimaginable that I would some-day build a memorial to honor him.

I began this book by reviewing how I started down my life path and became that man on the podium as well as the man I am today at ninety-two. I looked at the resources I was born with, and the manner in which family, school, and my own internal motivations initially gave me direction. I sorted through the important recurring themes in my life and looked at how I've modified and recycled them. In fact, this is the way I begin all of my projects. It is part of the RSVP Cycles process that I use for designing, problem solving, and decision making. I am not surprised to find that I can also use it to see how I have invented and reinvented my life. It was originally my intention to write down my life for the benefit of my grandchildren so they would know where I came from genetically and culturally as well as how I migrated geographically from the East Coast to the West. Somewhere along the way, however, the book became a much larger project, and I hope it will be interesting to a much larger audience.

My life, and probably my very nature, has led me to be process oriented. To study form making in nature you need to understand the physical forces that are at work. To begin a community design project you need to understand the physical and human forces that are at work, and to understand a person you must also understand the many forces that formed them. I hope this autobiography reveals the process that made me who I am.

Preface

PART I

As a young boy I had a secret hiding place in the woods near my parents' house in Brooklyn, New York. I often escaped to it, sometimes with my friends but usually by myself. In that hidden landscape I felt very safe, whole, and unthreatened. It was far from all the complexities of my life at home and all the growing-up problems of everyday life. There were trees and small animals, plants and good natural smells, snakes and birds. It was a complete little universe that I could inhabit. It was a place where I could be myself. I could dream. I could play games. I could fantasize. Perhaps most important it felt nonjudgmental. I didn't feel I had to change myself to fit anyone else's ideas or demands.

That place in the woods has remained with me all my life. I suppose what I have been doing as an adult is trying to find the basic meaning of my relationship to that place. Through that search I have hoped to discover the elements of people's inherent connections to the landscape so that they could serve as a guide for design principles.

Although it now seems impossible to imagine, back in the early 1920s our part of Brooklyn was still mostly open space. Our house, at the corner of Twenty-fourth and Avenue K was in the Flatbush neighborhood and had been the first of several houses on the block. Most of the area was wooded with native cherry trees and other forest trees. My parents had moved here in 1920.

My mother, Rose Luria, was the eldest of eight children and grew up in the cramped quarters of Manhattan's Lower East Side. Following the trend of upward mobility for ethnic minorities, the family moved to Borough Park, then a kind of suburb in Brooklyn that had good public schools. Still later they moved again and settled in the Bronx. Although I was born in the Bronx, my parents moved to Flatbush when I was four and thereby in my mind established Brooklyn as my hometown.

In those early formative days, I felt very close to my mother's family in Borough Park. It was not far from our house in Flatbush and very often we would drive over to my grandparents' house on Friday nights for Sabbath. Of course, we had to appropriately acknowledge the ritual edict against driving on Sabbath, so we parked our car around the corner. Then we would walk to Grandma's house and arrive in a way that implied we had not violated the Sabbath ritual but had walked all the way.

To this day I remember the wonderful smell of Friday night cooking, of matzoh-ball soup and gefilte fish, and the delicious aroma of chicken. I can't remember now what we had for dessert, but the meal was always satisfying and all of my aunts and uncles were there to join with us. Since my mother was the eldest, most of my aunts and uncles seemed more like sisters and brothers to me, especially since we often slept over. As a result, I formed close

1
Family and
Tribal Heritage

Figure 1

At Camp Greylock I was known for my pitching and I learned that I enjoyed being really good at something. The first entry in my scrapbook was an issue of the *Greylock Beacon* heralding my pitching: under the headline "Larry Halprin's Great Pitching," the story explained, "All this while, Larry was holding the Cayuga batters with his tantalizing curve and his remarkable control. Only in the last inning did he waver. Cayuga scored once, and advanced the tying runners to second and third; but Larry bore down and struck out the last batter, giving Greylock a hard-won 7-5 victory. That 'brought home the bacon,' as the boys sang all the way back to Becket. But there were still two hurdles to an undefeated season: the return game with Chester High School, and the Dalton Y.M.C.A. game." Photography courtesy the Halprin family.

relationships, particularly with my uncle Sydney and aunt Blanche, who were just a few years older than I was. They remained very close to me all of my life.

The next day on Sabbath I would walk over to the synagogue with my grandfather Phillip. On the way he would say "good shabbas" to everyone. His seat was on a bench halfway along the right side of the synagogue. Sometimes Uncle Sydney would have gotten there before us. All the girls in the family would be up on the balcony since in those days women were separated from the men. In Orthodox synagogues they still are today. Grandpa would put on his *talis* (prayer shawl), kiss the fringes on the ends, sit down, and start *davening* (praying). By now that ritual seems terribly medieval but in retrospect the quality of that experience had a profound effect on me. I loved it and that feeling of being part of a community remains with me to this day. The intense quality of that Orthodox experience was never replicated even during the years that I spent in a kibbutz in Israel. Today, as I read about the Muslim madrases and the hold that they have on our neighbors in the Middle East, I can somewhat understand the source of their extremism and the intense effects of extreme religious faith. I confess that I abhor it, just as I abhor similar fanaticism in my own religion. I think that in order to avoid fanaticism, outdated rituals need to be redefined in relationship to contemporary culture and values. Because they provide such basic and strong binding elements in human life, we should replace these rituals with others when the original ones are no longer appropriate.

My grandfather Phillip Luria was twenty-one years old when he left the small village of Kurenitz located near Vilna, the capital of Lithuania. Together with his father, Eliezer Luria, they passed through Ellis Island in the mid-1880s as part of a great wave of Russian Jews escaping from the pogroms. My name, Larry, is an anglicized version of Eliezer (short version is Lazer) and translates from the Hebrew as "my God helps."

My great-grandfather Lazer Luria settled first in Connecticut, home of the great International Silver Company. The enormous influx of Orthodox Jews created a large market for silverware since every family required eight sets of dishes to fulfill the amount in duplicate for Sabbath, Passover, meat, and milk. The International Silver Company hired my great-grandfather to advise them on these special religious requirements. He became successful and later moved to New York's East Side, where he founded L. Luria & Son. That is where my mother was born, in an area of Manhattan that is now Chinatown.

My own neighborhood in Flatbush was primarily Irish and so were most of my friends. I can't remember any problems that arose over our different religions but I do remember the feeling of envy I had every year when Christmas rolled around.

My friends had wonderful Christmas trees in their houses, lots of presents, and Santa Claus climbing down the chimney. We had Chanukah, of course, but in those days it didn't compare to their extravaganza. For that reason alone I was delighted that our neighbors were Catholic, and I spent as much time as possible during the holidays at their houses.

My early growing-up years in Brooklyn were quite simple—I played stickball in the street after school, and on Saturdays I went to the movies, which were silent in those days with organ music providing the only sound. When I was eight, our family grew to include my sister, Ruth. Because of the big difference in our ages Ruth and I never really were able to play together. By the time she was four I was already a teenager devoted to sports and other "manly" pursuits. In the summers my parents sent me to summer camp—first to Maine and then for many years to Camp Greylock in Massachusetts (Figure 1). There I learned to swim and boat and play sports. Sports, particularly baseball, came very naturally to me, so naturally in fact that when I graduated to prep school I made varsity right away.

I remember very little about my school experiences until I reached high school. But I do recall that my main interest beside sports seemed always to be art. In those early days art classes mostly involved the teacher handing out sheets with black and white drawings and telling us to fill them in with colors.

The emphasis was always that we had to "stay within the lines." How odd that seemed to me even back then. I also remember when I was about six years old my mother enrolled me in a class devoted to creative dance and music. At that time it was an unusual pursuit for a young boy but I rather enjoyed it. In retrospect that seems remarkably prophetic, particularly in light of the fact that all my early girlfriends turned out to be dancers—culminating in my most important creative relationship with my wife, Anna.

My father, Samuel William Halprin, like many Jewish men, was in the garment industry. He manufactured, designed, and sold women's clothes. One of the reasons for our move to Brooklyn from the Bronx was that the new subway extension allowed him to take the train to and from work every day. Dad was doing very well and when I was six we bought a car. I remember sitting on his lap and driving on a lonely road where we could speed along without being caught by the police. On occasion he would take me to work with him and I still remember that each day he stopped in at the barbershop on the ground floor of his office building. Then I watched as my father had his nails manicured and got a shave. These were the days before the safety razor became a common household item.

Mother, who was about thirty years old at this time, was teaching Hebrew at the Educational Alliance. Gradually she became interested in Hadassah,

the American Jewish women's medical organization that supported hospitals in Jerusalem. She was also involved with several book clubs as well as a group interested in Greek classics and literature. My fondest memories were our trips into Manhattan together on weekends. She would shop at Macy's and Gimbel's and then we would walk uptown on Fifth Avenue to the Metropolitan Museum of Art. On the way to the museum we would stop at Schrafft's on Fifth Avenue and have the most delicious ice-cream sodas. At the Met I learned more than anyone thought that I should about female anatomy, but it was also my earliest instruction in composition and the great art of the Renaissance. It would be a very full day and I remember being exhausted when we got home.

Mother was a wonderful mentor throughout my growing-up years and introduced me to all the cultural attributes I would need as a young man. She continually encouraged my appreciation of the arts, dance, and music. On weekends we often went to the young people's symphony concerts at Carnegie Hall conducted by Walter Damrosch. It was long before Lenny Bernstein's superstar concerts, and I remember carefully watching and listening to all of the instruments being played.

Besides encouraging me in the arts, my mother also wanted me to learn Hebrew. European Jews had always been a people with two languages. Yiddish was the secular, everyday language spoken conversationally in the shtetl and in the ghetto. It had developed a rich anecdotal color and forged a brilliant literary background. Its calligraphy used the ancient Hebrew script and the words were a basic German mixed with some Russian, with an additional mixture of Hebrew thrown in. Hebrew was the other language, the language of the Bible, used only for prayers as a way of communicating with God. As immigrants flocked to America fleeing the pogroms and the massacres of nineteenth-century Jews under the tsar, they brought with them their everyday primary language, Yiddish. That was the language of my grandfather Phillip and all of his brothers and sisters. They never spoke Hebrew, but they prayed in Hebrew.

But the next generation, the generation of my mother and father, was born in America. Their first language was English, and they often rejected Yiddish because for them it represented the disagreeable memories of the ghetto. They preserved the idea of Hebrew as the ideal biblical language for Zionism. This struggle for the "right" language went on for years and finally Hebrew was agreed on as the official language for the state of Israel.

The years passed quickly and by the time I was eleven and a half years old I was approaching my bar mitzvah, the ritual of adulthood. The most important reason for me to become proficient in Hebrew was so that I could read my section in the Torah fluently at the ceremony. The best place to study Hebrew was in a Hebrew school in the Bronx. My parents were concerned that it was too far for me to travel alone, but a new subway line opened under the East River and ended up in the Bronx right at the door of my Hebrew school. I just loved the trip and made the journey twice a week after my regular school. The people on the train were fascinating to watch and I made up stories about each one of them. I soon found out that the best place to ride was in the front of the first car. There I could open the window a crack and feel the wind blowing in my face and watch the engineer drive the train.

2

The Grand Tour

By the time I was twelve and a half I had graduated from elementary school, having skipped two years. I was ready for high school, but my mother had other ideas. She pushed my father to consider taking what was then called "The Grand Tour." She was eager to expand all our horizons and perhaps even wanted my father to think of other business pursuits beyond the making of women's dresses. My father was doing extremely well in the business. It was a time of great prosperity for the country in general. So my father agreed to go, sold his dress business to his partners at the height of its value, and took the family (including my uncle Sydney, who had just graduated from college) for a year-long grand tour.

In December 1928 we left on the *Europa* in first class. My mother's steamer trunk had so many dresses in it that she would not be seen at dinner twice in the same dress. My father and Sydney dressed in formal black-tie apparel every night. We spent the first six weeks in Paris. I was delighted to have Sydney along but it soon became clear why he was included—he was able to watch over my sister, Ruth, and me while my parents gallivanted around.

Sydney took us to Versailles (Figure 2). The train let us off in the village and we had to walk a long way to the gates of Versailles. Ruth rode on Sydney's shoulders most of the time, while I kept on asking to run rather than walk in order to get there faster. That was the first time I ever visited Versailles, and I found it most boring, traveling from room to room to room in the Grand Palais (Figure 3). Sydney, however, made a fuss on the way back to Paris about finding some special books that he was after and couldn't find for some reason. It was years later that I realized that one of the books was Radclyffe Hall's *Well of Loneliness* and the other was Joyce's *Ulysses*. The only way that Sydney was able to get these "dangerous and subversive" books past the U.S. customs officers on the way home was to rip the covers off of them.

The grand tour was to be a cultural passage for our family and so eventually we found ourselves at the Paris Opera House. The guard at the gate refused to let me in because I had come dressed in a sweater. That was the first time I ever saw my mother become irate. To calm her down the guard said he would find a coat and tie for me. I repeated over and over again, "I don't want a coat! I don't even want to go to the opera!" I was terribly embarrassed. The coat finally arrived and we all marched in and I sat down very angrily and listened to people who seemed to be endlessly screaming at each other on the stage.

After Paris we took trains to wonderful cities all over Europe. My favorites were Budapest, with its incredible zoo, and Prague, which, even as young as I was, moved me deeply. The dark medieval streets and spires, black against the gray skies, were like

VERSailles

Ruthanna says she wouldn't
like to live here - too big &
would be lonely - she
wonders what the queen
did all day to amuse
herself..... can't see
eny sky -
Sunday May 1 - 1983..

45

Figure 2

Even at twelve years old I found this garden
too static and formal to interest me.

Figure 3

I was aware that in the United States public art such as these statues and urns would be kept in museums. Seeing them displayed outdoors made a big impression on me.

Statues & urns in Tuileries garden
The pedestals are far more important & well designed than the "objets" they support!

nothing I had ever seen, and the Jewish cemetery had a nightmarish quality. Throughout Europe we stopped to examine cathedral after cathedral. Why, I could never understand. I have changed my mind since then, but still, *every single cathedral*?

We traveled from Prague to Rome, and then to Florence (which is still one of my favorite places), followed by Naples, where we boarded a ship to Egypt. My experiences in Cairo and the ride on camelback to the Sphinx and to the Pyramids began my lifelong connection to the Middle East, which has never faltered in its intensity. The desert was exhilarating for me. The long ride out to the Pyramids by camel was the very essence of romanticism for a young boy and the Bedouin tents on the way out were like the background for a movie (Figure 4). I was enthralled!

My mother's intention to expand our horizons was working. The great examples of art, and particularly the architecture of the cities that I saw, grounded me in a deep acceptance of art and architecture as fundamentals of a culture. It left me also with an enjoyment of cities, streets, plazas, and cafes as part of the art experience and undoubtedly helped lead me inexorably to my chosen profession.

Our final destination was Jerusalem, which was then part of Palestine. On the way we had to change trains at the Suez Canal since the track gauges were different in Egypt from those in Palestine. Egypt was then part of the Ottoman Empire, while Palestine was a British protectorate, and the two governments were enemies during World War I. Maintaining different track gauges was a security device between the two countries. I was awakened by my parents for a moonlight crossing of the Suez Canal and I can still recall the squishing sounds of the boat's oars. After the crossing, we reboarded a train and set off on the last leg of the journey to Jerusalem. It was a slow climb and the train zigzagged through the Sinai and up the Judean hills for several hours before reaching the 2,500-foot-high city of Jerusalem. We arrived at the station at dawn and I felt like I had been holding my breath in anticipation of a great adventure.

We were to stay in Palestine for four months. Shortly after we arrived my family moved into the David Stern house in Talpioth. Sydney began looking up friends who had moved from New York to settle here. Although our bungalow was small, it had a garden and was big enough for our family and Sonya, who was hired to help Mother and take care of Ruth and me. The house looked out over a vast wheat field that seemed to stretch out to the Dead Sea in the east. The small path between our house and the field was a lively trail for many Arab peasants passing north to the city of Jerusalem and south to Bethlehem. People passed continuously on

Figure 4

The romantic, adventurous quality of riding camels to the Pyramids no doubt imprinted itself on my overall feelings for the Middle East.

donkeys, on camels, and on foot—some alone and some in groups, all singing and chattering on their way (Figure 5). At times a sheikh rode by on a lithe prancing horse. The chatter was continuous, and sometimes boys would cry out to me. I would try to answer in Arabic and as the days went by I became more and more fluent and was able to reply.

Early one morning when the wheat was shoulder height and almost ripe I quietly left the house and beat a path into the field. I carefully parted a way between the rows and walked as far as I could until I caught a slight glimpse of the ancient walls of the Old City of Jerusalem. I watched for a long while and as the sun rose behind me I lay back among the sheaves of grain to watch the clouds. Insects flew around me with their beating wings making notes in the air. There was a hum of bees and the air was still. I watched the clouds quietly drifting across the summer sky. I remember being clearly aware of how wonderful I felt. Then, from up high and far away, I thought I heard a voice. It spoke no distinct words but produced a sound like music. I listened for a long time trying to pin it down and wondering what it was. The experience was a kind of epiphany for me. It may well have been a profound religious experience, although to this day I can't explain it.

By the fourth month the wheat ripened and the Arabs' harvest began. First a hole was opened up in the field and a thrashing floor was created. As the work progressed more grain was cut, and donkeys were brought in and tied to wheels that turned around and around, changing the wheat into piles of grain. It was wonderful to watch, and I was allowed to join in. The piles of grain grew larger and larger and higher and higher, and finally all of the field was cut into short golden stubble, and at the end a little ritual dance called a *dubke* was begun by the young Arab men holding hands and dancing in a circle until late in the evening.

I thought that the work was ended and I was quite sad to see them all leave. But the next morning there was a whole new influx of people, mostly young women in beautiful Bethlehem dress carrying babies and followed by young children, boys and girls, all coming along the path and then spreading out to the golden stubble field. They had come to pick up the grain that had fallen on the ground. This was according to the biblical injunction which mandated that all seed that fell to the ground during the harvest was to belong to the poor—for them and them only.

From our home base in Jerusalem we traveled all around the country. We went up to En Harod, the kibbutz at the northern border along Lebanon, to visit my mother's friend Manya Shochat. There we began to get a feeling of the meaning of pioneering in Israel. We visited kibbutzim throughout Palestine and I was completely taken by the utopian vision

The Bedouin ?le in Beersheba
7 AM. Thursday July 7 - 61

they sought. We stopped in the Emek, the great valley in the center of the country, where the farmers were harvesting their crops with tractors. This was the antithesis of the primitive harvest that I had been a part of in the field across from our house in Talpioth. At night we heard singing and joined in to dance the hora. We traveled on to the Dead Sea and everywhere we went there were Palestinian villages, whose residents seemed friendly and mixed with the kibbutz people adjoining them.

Finally we returned to Jerusalem, which was then a smallish city of eighty thousand people. The main street entering the Old City from the new part of Jerusalem was called David Street (Figure 6). Some parts of the street were covered with arcades while other parts were open and it was absolutely crowded with people, donkeys, and camels that were pushing up against the shop fronts. The cries of Arab camel drivers created a maelstrom of noise. Outside the wall of the Old City, the area surrounding the Jaffa Gate was also jam-packed with people and full of enormous clay pots big enough to hide someone. The area was full of Bedouins who would come in from the desert for the day and women in beautiful dresses selling fruits and vegetables. It was all so exciting and so much more interesting than shopping in Macy's back home in New York. As David Street approached the Mosque of Omar, it became narrower and narrower and finally, at the end, there was the Wailing Wall, now called the Western Wall (Figure 7). There, the street was full of people *davening* like my grandfather Phillip.

Coming back to Jerusalem I became much more aware of the British. I had not understood that they were really running the country. The new part of Jerusalem was very different from the ancient city surrounded by its great wall. The new part was much more like parts of Europe that we had been through and it seemed that everywhere we turned there were British police and soldiers in khaki shorts. I much preferred the old city, and I spent as much time as I could wandering through its streets.

Much of my time was spent with a group of friends I had made in Talpioth who weren't that much different from my friends back in Brooklyn. Our biggest problem was that they wanted to practice their English with me and I wanted to practice my broken Hebrew with them. I was initially put off by the fact that they started off teasing me by calling me "an American bluffer." It was a stereotypical term that was later changed to "ugly American." But I did make close friends like Elchanan Klein and Yigael Sukenik (Yadin) and acquired my very first girlfriend, Shoshana, who played the violin much better than I ever could. We have all maintained our friendships over the years.

Soon, too soon for me, it was our last few weeks in Jerusalem and time for my bar mitzvah. It was

Figure 5

Bedouins and their camels constantly passed our house on their travels between Bethlehem and Jerusalem.

Figure 6

An open space at the entrance to David Street was lined with old houses and a coffee bar. From there, pedestrians funneled themselves down into the marketplace.

Figure 7

I had gone to Jerusalem for my bar mitzvah and was therefore overwhelmed by the biblical symbolism of this ancient ruin of a temple built by King Solomon.

Entrance to David St
Old City - Apr 13 78

The wailing wall -
mosque in back.

held in an enormous tent in a hotel garden. During our long stay, my parents had made many friends, including my mother's Hadassah pals, and they all filled the tent until it overflowed. I don't remember much of the ceremony, only that I had to recite the ritual prayer in Hebrew and make a short speech for my parents. I was glad when it was over and also glad that I got a lot of presents. One present that I still treasure is a leather-bound prayer book.

By the time we left Jerusalem my mother had accomplished all her intentions. She had met the famous Henrietta Szold, who had founded Hadassah, and who had designated my mother as her successor. Although I could not exactly have put it into words back then, I had become a young Zionist, which from my point of view included socialism as represented by the kibbutz movement. And Ruth and I could both speak Hebrew.

We left Jerusalem for the port of Haifa in the north and sailed for Genoa. From there we traveled by train to Cherbourg, where we caught the ship that took us back home to New York. It was then late October 1929—the month the stock market crashed and transformed my father from a rich young man to a penniless one.

My father, like many overconfident young men of that time, held all his stocks on margin. As a result, we lost everything! To this day I am astounded to realize that I was completely unaware of the trauma my father must have gone through. All I do remember is the difficult transition of returning from my great adventure of the previous year to the new reality of Brooklyn. Many years later I asked Sydney how it was possible for me to be so unaware and he simply said, "Well, you were young and oblivious." I am still uncertain how my parents were able to afford to send me to private school at Polytechnic Preparatory Country Day School for Boys, known colloquially as Poly Prep. I do know that my mother was determined to give me a good education and Poly Prep was considered far superior to the public high schools in the area.

I loved Poly Prep. The campus was beautiful, with a lake, rolling lawns, trees, and, naturally, brick walls covered with ivy. Students received a classic education, including Latin, and the teachers were excellent. I was happy to attend a boys' school because I was rather shy around girls. On the other hand, I think I may have benefited in my later relationships to women if I had had more of a chance to grow up around them in my teen years.

I was certainly out of my depth socially for the first few years at Poly. I was, after all, a Jewish boy at a gentile school. The number of Jewish students was strictly limited by a quota system and I remember only three or four Jewish boys. All the other students came from elite well-established families, and we began each day by reciting the Lord's Prayer in our small auditorium.

Luckily for me, sports were very important at Poly. That helped me to fit in quickly. We had a great new gym for basketball and lovely green fields for sports like lacrosse, football, and baseball. I didn't know lacrosse, but all my summers at Camp Greylock had prepared me well for everything else. I suppose it's fair enough to say that sports pulled me through my years at Poly and occupied most of my attention. I made the varsity in basketball and was a good forward. I started out as a quarterback in football but my coaches thought I should quit football. They feared that I would hurt my pitching arm and that was my forte. What ended my football career, however, happened in the autumn of my third year. During the last quarter of a game, I broke loose for a touchdown. I was running close to the goal when all of a sudden my legs gave way and I dropped to the ground. Everyone thought I had been tackled, but as I was carried off the field I insisted that it was something else. The doctors eventually reported that I had succumbed to an attack of rheumatic fever. I was ordered to spend three months in bed recovering. During that time my mother bought me a beautifully illustrated

3
Poly Prep

Figure 8

In 1932, as I recovered from rheumatic fever, I produced this charcoal drawing of my younger sister, Ruth.

Image courtesy the Halprin family.

book of modern art and I began copying paintings from it. That three months led me to an appreciation of painting and portraiture, an interest I have to this day (Figure 8).

At Poly Prep I became close friends with Rolf Kaltenborn, whose father was the most important news announcer at that time. Mostly we discussed politics and the need for social change. We both had strong feelings about socialism and supported the ideas of Norman Thomas, who was beginning to run for president. These may seem strange subjects for teenage boys but Rolf's father discussed world affairs on a popular radio show every night. I had already been politicized by my travels, especially the time I spent in Palestine. By now it was 1933. There were already worrisome stirrings of the Nazi movement in Germany, and here at home the Depression grew deeper. President Hoover seemed ever more ineffective and the labor movement was becoming stronger. Change was in the air, and even as kids we knew it.

Despite such foreboding winds of change, life on campus continued normally and near the end of my junior year I was invited to join a fraternity. This was a great surprise and it was considered quite an honor. There were no other Jewish boys in the fraternity. I was obviously receiving this invitation because I was an excellent athlete and in spite of the fact I was Jewish. I wasn't sure whether I should

accept the offer in light of this so I discussed it with my parents and we agreed it would be okay. My parents felt I was already anchored in my Jewish identity and the experiences at Poly Prep were a social education for me.

With my new fraternity status, my social life became pretty exciting. I started to attend Friday night dances, even though I didn't know how to dance. My mother again came to the rescue and sent me to ballroom dancing classes. I didn't like the classes, but I did like the actual dances as the girls were beautiful and smelled so good. The final senior dance was a grand ball in the gymnasium. We all wore tuxedos and danced to the big band music of Eddie Duchin. That dance marked the end of my Poly Prep days and the end of a remarkable and carefree time for me.

The summer of 1933 was a difficult time for me. I was at loose ends. I worked for a time at L. Luria & Son, my grandfather's silverware store, where I was a packer down in the basement. In the evenings I wandered around the streets of our neighborhood in Brooklyn missing my Poly Prep schoolmates. My parents would ask me to go to the movies with them, but for the first time in my life I became impatient with them. All I really wanted was for them to leave me alone. Nothing seemed to be quite right. It was then that I decided to return to Palestine and live there for a while.

I was just sixteen. My parents were worried about letting me go off alone on such a long trip. It was true that I was still very naive and unsophisticated. They were also concerned about how long I would be gone, and I had no answers for them. I just wanted to go. I kept pointing out that I did have friends in Palestine and there were families who would, after all, help keep track of me for them. I had no clear idea of where I would get work to carry me along, but we all knew that work was plentiful in the moshavim or the kibbutzim. They finally extracted a promise from me that I would come back to go to college when the appropriate time came. Then, they agreed, although with trepidation. My mother wired her friend Dr. Yassky, then head of Hadassah Hospital in Jerusalem, who promised to put me up at their house while I was getting acclimated. My father bought tourist-class tickets for me on the boat to Cherbourg, the train to Marseilles, and the boat to Haifa. All was set and I was ready to go.

Before I left, however, my father said he wanted to have a heart-to-heart talk with me. This was something we had never done before and made me very nervous. We took the subway into Manhattan and walked over to Central Park, sat down on a park bench, and I braced myself to hear what he had to say. Finally it started to come out. "Larry, you'll have to have some money to carry you through. This will be a long trip and I'm not sure how you'll get along.

I can't give you a great deal, but here is seventy-five dollars mostly in American Express checks. Please spend it wisely." And then came the punch-line—"Your mother and I are worried about whether you have had any experience with women. You must be aware that there are good women, but also there are bad women who may take advantage of you. Please be careful." That was the extent of our heart-to-heart talk and with that nebulous advice I left for my adventure (Figure 9).

I had been on transatlantic liners four years earlier, but this time it was tourist class. Like most adolescents I prowled around a lot and walked the decks, eventually discovering a way I could easily climb a ladder into second class. There was a lot more room there and a lot more fun. The next day I decided I might as well try it again after breakfast,

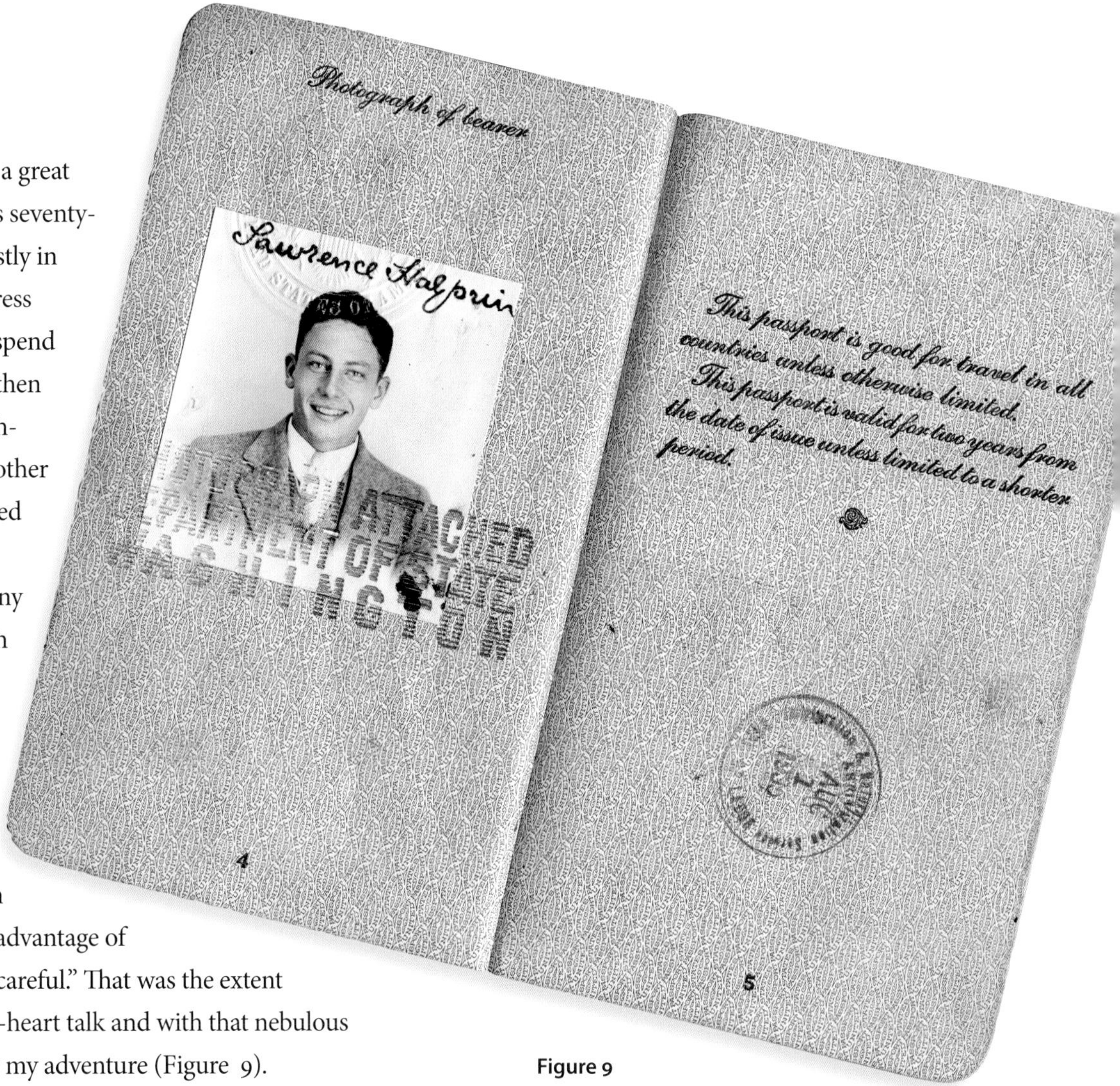

Figure 9

In this 1933 passport photo you see a naive young man setting off on his first solo adventure.

Image courtesy the Halprin family.

and that I did. The decks were empty except in the far distance a girl was playing shuffleboard. I edged my way over and introduced myself. She was as pretty a girl, I thought, as I had ever seen in my life. Soon we started playing shuffleboard together and that went on for the rest of the trip. We ate together and danced together and walked on the deck together. We held hands. Her name was Eve Hoey and I was in love. She told me that she was from New York and was a showgirl on Broadway. She had taken this trip because her producer wanted to have an affair with her and she didn't. It was all very complicated; however, remembering my father's advice I snuck down to her cabin where a steamer trunk did at least verify her name. The next seven days were pure heaven.

When we landed at Cherbourg, Eve asked me to join her in her cabin on the train. I was ecstatic but found I first had to fend off several older men who planned to do the same thing. In Paris I had no idea what was expected of me or even what I wanted to do. We stayed at different hotels, but spent every spare minute together. She had often been to Paris and was far more knowledgeable than I. I had never even drunk wine before and we did do lots of that. We sat on the curb on the Champs-Elysées in the evening and sang to each other. Eventually the time came for me to catch my train to Marseilles. She insisted I go even though I didn't want to. She said that she had to find work because she was out of money. I gave her all I had, and she assured me that she would pay me back. I left Paris brokenhearted.

When I finally got to Jerusalem I did find a room with the Yasskys in a beautiful Jerusalem neighborhood called Rachaviah. I explained to Dr. Yassky that I couldn't pay any rent for the room because I had given it all to a girl in Paris, but I promised that I would soon find work in order to pay him. He smiled at this and said that there was no need and that I was, after all, his guest. Ten days later a check arrived in the mail from Eve Hoey. I was bursting with love and relief. My judgment had fortunately been right and I felt I had to share this victory with someone in the family. I wrote a long letter to Sydney about all that had happened. He went down to Broadway and found a handbill for the show. Sure enough, there was her name, larger than life.

I felt at ease settling into life in Jerusalem again after a four-year absence and immediately tried to contact all of my old friends. Many were in college abroad, either in London or New York. Yigael Yadin, however, was at the Hebrew University in Jerusalem studying archaeology and living with his parents in the Rachaviah neighborhoood near the Yasskys.

There was a different feeling in the air since I had last been in Jerusalem. Now the British were seen as more of an occupying force than a protector. The Haganah, the Hebrew underground, was often meeting in the evenings and after I got acclimated Yigael let me join him there.

I soon got a part-time job in a factory producing potash and fertilizers in the salt flats at the northern end of the Dead Sea. I started as a lab assistant, doing simple chemical analysis of heavy water. At the time the factory was developing into the largest industry in the Middle East and it represented a great advance for the Jewish people. The work was interesting and the ambience was very dramatic and romantic.

I determined the best way for me to travel from my room in Rechaviah to the Dead Sea—1,371 feet below sea level—would be by bicycle. I was riding my bicycle down to the lowest place on Earth. The biking was easy on the way down, but on the way back to Jerusalem I put my bicycle on a bus. Even though it was downhill it was a daunting ride at first. Most of the way I coasted at very high speed. The narrow road twisted down on switchback curves. First I would pass through Arab villages on the outskirts of Jerusalem and then through beautiful rolling hills with black goats cascading down the hillside. Farther down I passed encampments of black Bedouin tents beautifully sited in the crevasses between hills. The tents were surrounded by tethered camels, playful children, and sleek Arab horses. The men sat around smoking water pipes, playing games, and talking. Near the end of the trip there was a magnificent monastery hanging from the cliffs (Figures 10, 11). It was watered by the thin line of an aqueduct that traveled along the side of the canyon like an artery carrying nourishment in the body (Figure 12). That monastery, with its few monks, always seemed magical to me. It was like a statement of determination linking the past to the present and confronting the impossible landscape with faith. This was the gateway to the most awesome cavity on Earth. This was where the Essenes had lived. Later, this was where the Bedouins found the Dead Sea Scrolls. Later yet, my friend Yigael Yadin was the one to determine their significance.

The contrast between the biblical character of the Dead Sea area and the technological presence of the potash factory was jarring. This was where Joshua fought the battle of Jericho, and Moses

4
Return to Palestine

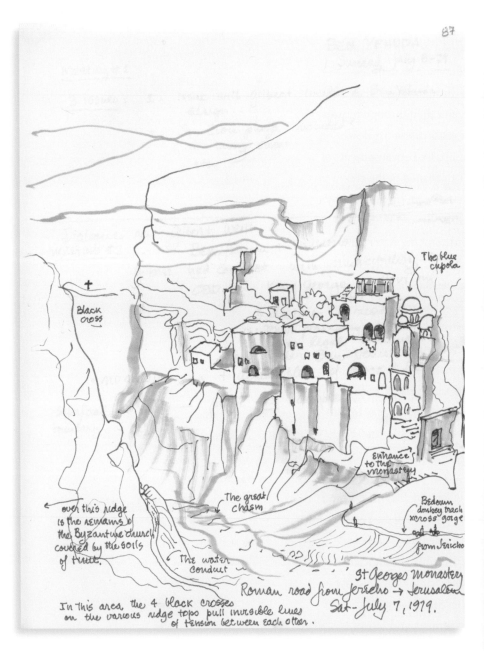

87

Black cross

The blue cupola

Entrance to the monastery

← over this ridge is the remains of the Byzantine church couched by the soils of time.

The great chasm

The water conduit

Bedouin donkey track xcross gorge
↓
from Jericho

St Georges Monastery
Roman road from Jericho → Jerusalem
Sat - July 7, 1979.

In this area, the 4 black crosses on the various ridge tops pull invisible lines of tension between each other.

Figure 10 *(facing page, left)*
When I sketched a scene I knew well,
I always uncovered new feelings and
information.

Figure 11 *(facing page, right)*
I clearly remember hiking down to the
St. George Monastery to ask what they did
and how long they had been there. A monk
let me in but gave me no answers.

Figure 12
I never found the source of this twisting
runnel that carried precious water to
the monastery but that image instilled
knowledge of the importance of water.

Return to Palestine

looked across to the Promised Land. Just to the south was Masada, where Jewish Zealots stood for months against Roman legions. I often passed the Qumran caves where the scrolls were found. The very roots of the Zionist movement were in this landscape. But the potash factory, exporting fertilizer throughout the world, was a modern example and model for all of us who sought the beginning of a Jewish homeland.

On weekends I would visit with friends in Jerusalem. Often Yigael and I would take hikes into the surrounding countryside. We walked to En Karem, home of John the Baptist, and then explored the surrounding hills (Figure 13). One remarkable hike took us into the great cave where David had hidden with his soldiers. The cave was limestone that had been eaten away by the melting of spring waters. Thousands of bats lived there. Yigael knew all the old biblical and Roman routes. Years later Yigael became the first commander in chief of the Israeli Army and I understood exactly what they meant when they said that he depended on his intimate knowledge of the abandoned ancient roads to circumvent enemy forces.

My friends in Jerusalem urged me to travel and learn more about the country. In February, when the orange groves in the coastal flatlands were ripening, I decided it was time for me to leave the Dead Sea, even though I had enjoyed my time

there. I traveled north to Hedera in the heart of the orange groves. When I arrived I jumped off the bus from Jerusalem with only a change of underwear in my backpack. I sat down on the stoop of a small store and waited. Pretty soon someone came along in a pickup truck and greeted me, "Shalom, ha-im atah rotzeh la-avod ba-katif?" By now my conversational Hebrew had improved and I understood, "Do you want to work picking the oranges?" I said, "Of course," and hopped into the back of the truck with a bunch of other young people and we rode off to an orange grove.

I was astonished to learn that my new friends in the grove were a group from America who had come to Palestine to be part of a new kibbutz. They were eagerly waiting for a piece of land that was promised to them by the Keren Kayemeth, the Zionist organization that was at that time in charge of purchasing land from Arabs for distribution to pioneering Jewish groups. As we picked oranges they told me about their hopes. They explained that they were part of a larger group of people from different parts of the world who were committed to forming a Zionist state of Israel. Their name was Shomer Hatzair and their hope for the new state was socialistic and binational; that is, they wished it to include the Arabs then living in Palestine, who numbered about 400,000, as well as the 200,000 Jews who had been there since biblical times.

Figure 13

En Karem, a town on the western edge of Jerusalem, was built around a series of mosques and churches.

Return to Palestine

The kibbutz, to which they were committed, was devoted to working on the land in a style that we would probably call a commune. I was astounded by such absolutely utopian ideas!

At the end of that day Sarah, who had done most of the talking, invited me to stay with their group. After the picking was over we all jumped into their pickup and drove to the commune where I would be staying. It was a temporary community since they did not yet own land, and consisted of a cluster of tents around a few wooden shacks. Sarah said that her tent had room for another person and that I could stay with her and several other kibbutzniks. I was pleased as punch. It turned out to be the beginning of a long and wonderful relationship with the Kibbutz Hashomer movement and particularly with En Hashofeth, the specific group to which Sarah and her future husband, Shimon Avidan, belonged.

That first night, after the long dusty day picking oranges, I was tired and sweaty and needed a shower. Sarah gave me a towel and pointed out the shower room. When I got there I could hear joyful singing and jabbering and walked in. I was shocked to find the showers occupied by men and women in the same room—all bare naked. I turned to leave, but another guy was walking in behind me and he pushed me ahead. "Come on, Larry," he grinned, "you'll get used to it." It took me a long time to "get used to it." Here was a room full of jolly, pretty girls in the nude taking showers and I was supposed to join them? I looked down, not up, closed my eyes as much as possible, showered as fast as I could, and got out of there. It was my first lesson in socialism!

The harvest lasted for weeks and we followed it from orange grove to orange grove. I became more and more adept at picking and earned my keep. I also became increasingly enamored with my new group of friends. Most of them were from the East Coast of the United States and were somewhat older than I—from about twenty-five to thirty years of age. They were a wonderful group, devoted to the future of Zionism in Palestine and to the idea of group living as a vehicle for achieving their goals. Most of them were single but there were a few married couples. Each person had received specialized training in advance for his or her future life in Palestine. Sarah was a shoemaker; Shimon was a tractor driver and mechanic. Some of the women had teaching certificates, some had gone to Cornell to study agriculture, and others were horticulturists.

As the end of the harvest drew near, Sarah began to talk to me about what I should do next. I was unsure so she suggested that if I was interested in the kibbutz movement I would do well to experience life in an established kibbutz, one that had been on the land for a while. There I could see the real thing in action. I agreed and Sarah suggested that I go to Mishmar Haemek, one of the oldest of the shomer-type kibbutzim. She called ahead and advised the administrator that I was coming. It took a day to hitchhike there.

Mishmar was very different from the tent village I had just left. It was the very image of a farming community and was clustered around a real town center that consisted of a large cafeteria (feeding three hundred villagers), library, small museum, school, and a stockroom for everyday needs like clothes, shoes, and hardware. The cafeteria faced a lawn that was surrounded by houses. I was assigned to a small shack called a *tsrif* and shared it with a roommate.

Visitors were required to park their cars outside the center and walk in since cars were not allowed inside the community. This produced a wonderful walking experience within the community. I was also assigned a mentor, Mietiq Bentov, a remarkable man whose specialty on the farm was working with the chickens. He was one of the leaders of Mishmar as well as of the whole kibbutz movement and he was, therefore, a major political figure in the Zionist labor movement. Mietiq knew my mother by name, because by then she had participated in some of the world Zionist meetings in Europe, but he had not as yet met her. He was delighted to have me at the kibbutz; however, he made no allowance

in the work assignments I was given. He never lectured me about Zionism or about how there were two aspects to Zionist socialism, one a political force and the other simply a democratic way of living. For those lessons, he let life at the kibbutz speak for itself. I was bowled over by the political aspect of the kibbutz.

A management committee that was voted into office every few years made work assignments on a daily basis. Work was based simply on ability and training. There were no salaries. All work, whatever its nature, was assumed to have the same value whether it was intellectual, like running the library or teaching in the school, or manual, such as driving tractors or milking the cows. My first work assignment was in the chicken coops with Mietiq but I didn't like and still don't like chickens—they have always seemed stupid to me, and I didn't like preparing them for the kitchen. After a while I was moved over to the dairy farm, which I much preferred.

Health care was provided for everyone by an on-site health clinic staffed with nurses. More serious health problems were taken care of by a kibbutzwide system of doctors who made the rounds of all shomer kibbutzim several times during the week. Everyone's clothing was the same, khaki-type clothes dealt out of the shelves at the clothing shop. Women's dresses for special occasions like holidays or vacations tended to "belong" to each individual. The dresses were simple and each woman had only a few. Meals were eaten in the cafeteria, which also served as a community center for weekly meetings, which everyone in the kibbutz was expected to attend. The room also served as a theater and a Friday night recreation center. People participated in poetry readings, music playing, and serious political discussion.

What puzzled me most at Mishmar were the arrangements for the children. During the week all the children lived in nurseries where they were taken care of by specially trained teachers. They only spent the weekends with their parents. The theory was that since everyone in the kibbutz (men and women alike) worked a full eight-hour day, children were better taken care of in this communal way. The children's schools seemed very much like my own back home. The artwork I saw on the walls was very similar and they played together in much the same way kids do everywhere. What was different, however, was that the kibbutz kids had serious work assignments; they took care of the farm animals and they watered and weeded the vegetable gardens.

For the first time in my life I abandoned drawing and I completely forgot about baseball. I have no idea why. They had always been my obsessions. Perhaps the kibbutz experience was so intense

that it was simply draining all of my energy. My Waspish lifestyle at Poly Prep became a thing of the past and for months on end I barely spoke a word of English. I was sinking deeper and deeper into the life of a kibbutznik. Toward the end of my stay in the kibbutz my work assignment suddenly changed. There had been vandalism in new fields down in the valley and some hay-baling equipment had been pilfered. Assuming that I was an American cowboy, they gave me a horse and asked me to ride around the kibbutz fields from sundown until sunrise. It felt like quite an adventure. In the middle of the night I would stop at the midpoints near some bales of hay, hobble the horse, and take a short nap within the enclave of hay bales. The only mishap that I can remember was one early morning when I allowed the horse to canter back to the barn too quickly for his grain and water. I tried to rein him in near the end, but he stopped so quickly that I ended up unceremoniously flying into the water trough.

During this time I became very tuned into life in the kibbutz, and the utopian idealism was extremely seductive. It combined a productive day-by-day existence with a strong community flavor. In addition I enjoyed the strong social quality of living together without aggressive competitiveness. It was very appealing. In a naive way we hoped that we were creating something that was going to change the whole world for the better while resolving a problem that the Jewish people had faced for centuries—the lack of our own homeland. The kibbutz exemplified this optimistic vision and I wanted to be a part of it.

Back home in New York my parents were also changing. The stock market crash had forced my father to think of other ways to make a living, while my mother had become national president of Hadassah. They decided to move to Jerusalem and asked me to join them there. It was now 1935. Dad arrived in Palestine as a representative for Dodge cars. The company was called Dodge and Seymore, and they had offices in a beautiful old Ottoman building on Mamillah Road near the Jaffa Gate entrance to the Old City. Dad's travels selling cars took him throughout the Middle East—to Egypt, Jordan, Syria, Iraq, and Iran. It was an adventurous enterprise and he loved it. Mother had come to fulfill Henrietta Szold's intention and became her successor. In this role she traveled throughout Palestine and also on occasion to Zionist meetings throughout Europe where she represented Hadassah.

After spending a great deal of time looking for a house in the suburbs of Jerusalem, my parents settled on a very nice place in Rechaviah, directly across the street from the Sukeniks. As a result, Yigael and I became neighbors and the proxim-ity gave us more opportunities to reestablish our friendship. We spent a lot of time together wandering around in the Old City, particularly in the Arab section. Yigael was fluent in Arabic, as were most of my friends. I was very envious of their fluency because it was a beautiful language and knowing how to speak it made getting around much easier. In the Old City of Jerusalem we would often stop for coffee and even smoke a bit from a *nargilah*. Yigael was interested in ancient artifacts so we spent time in the shops looking for oil lamps and other treasures. I got somewhat better with my Arabic and thoroughly enjoyed our walks in various parts of the Old City. It was a great history lesson. Yigael had grown up with this history, and he related to me the stories in the Bible as if they were real and had occurred recently, not mythically the way that I had perceived them.

During this period I was able to get a job with a contractor building gardens. Most of our work was in the areas of Rechaviah and Talbiah, the two residential areas around downtown Jerusalem. I wasn't much interested in the local plants and flowers but I did take quickly, almost intuitively, to the stonework in the gardens (Figure 14). The stones for the gardens and the houses were all dug from the local quarries. It was a beautiful pinkish limestone, soft enough to fashion with special hammers. The surfaces of the hammers were made of points that

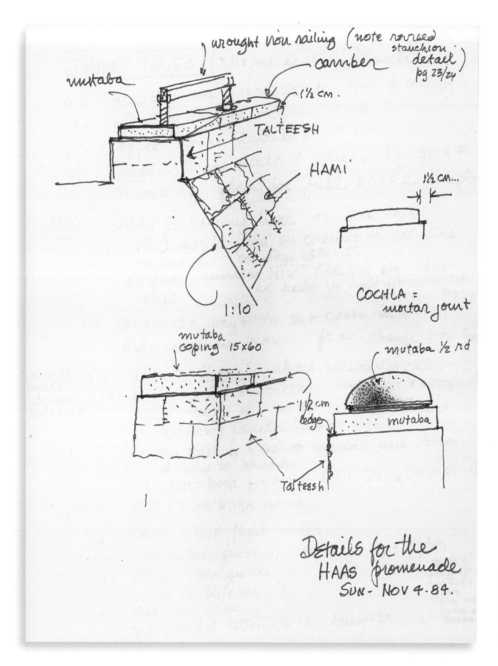

were of various distances from each other, so that when they struck the stone the effects were markedly different. Each type of surface had a specific Arabic name; *talteesh* left a rough surface, and *samsam* left a fine one. I loved building gardens with walls and pathways made of stone.

I had by this time become very used to living on my own and my parents were reminding me that before I left America I had promised them that I would return and go to college. It was extremely difficult for me to think of leaving Jerusalem. After my experience on the kibbutz I wanted to join the young group I had met in the orange groves of Hadera, once they finally acquired their own piece of land. I realized, however, that if I was going to join the kibbutz I would benefit them more if I received more technical training in some form of agriculture.

Figure 14

Stonework details I learned doing construction work in 1934 have served me well throughout my career.

I was nineteen when I returned to New York to fulfill my promise and go to college. I left Palestine with a heavy heart and took the ship home via Genoa. Sydney was waiting for me when I arrived. It was the beginning of summer and my aunt Blanche was by then the headmistress of a summer camp in Maine. As a transition back into life in America, she arranged a camp-counselor job for me. Meanwhile I gathered my qualifications from Poly Prep and applied to Cornell Agricultural School in Ithaca, New York.

While I was waiting to hear from Cornell I kept busy in New York visiting family and museums. One day I went into the subway to go uptown to the Metropolitan Museum of Art. I took my seat and looked around. Across the aisle a man was unfolding his newspaper. Finally he got it open to the front page and there, stretched out in front of me, was a banner headline: "Eve Hoey Commits Suicide." Eve and I had kept up a desultory correspondence while I was in Palestine, but I hadn't heard from her in a long while. I was in shock—I couldn't imagine her committing suicide. She was so full of life and energy. Her beauty lit up everything around her. Finally, I called Sydney and asked him what to do. He tried to calm me down and assured me that the police would do everything necessary to check it out, but I never did learn the circumstances that led to her death.

That summer was a very strange and confusing time for me. The utopian lifestyle on the kibbutz had been very compelling. My experiences in Palestine had had a great impact on me. I saw life in America in a very different light than I had before I left. My value systems had shifted. I was no longer the youngster that had gone to the elite Poly Prep. My reputation as a talented young pitcher seemed like ancient history and no longer seemed the least bit relevant. Though kibbutz life had been joyful, looking back from America it seemed very serious. I felt as if I was on a mission to convince people about the importance of community life and, in particular, the importance of Zionism for the Jews of America. In addition, echoes of stories I'd heard about Nazism and how the Jews were being mistreated plagued me and I somehow felt their impact more in America than I did in Palestine.

This was also the first time I recognized the effects of the Great Depression. Franklin Delano Roosevelt was now president and the New Deal was making a big difference in American society. The labor movement had become far more politically important. And, although the New Deal was far different from socialism, the changes in American society were beginning to be profound. The world seemed in turmoil when I received my acceptance letter and entered Cornell in the fall of 1935.

**5
My College Career**

Cornell

In some ways my first days in Cornell were much like those at Kibbutz Hadera. I had no prior arrangements for housing and had few clothes to pack. I stopped in a restaurant to get a cup of coffee before I walked on campus and ran into a bunch of guys there. I asked if they knew how I could find a room. They asked where I was from and I told them I was from Brooklyn, but that I had just gotten back from several years in Palestine. "Well," they said, "you better come with us, we live in a house just off campus. We're Zionists and we'd be happy to have you join us. Glad to know you." We all lived together for four years after that and remained fast friends throughout our lives.

The house we lived in was at the top of the hill above Ithaca adjacent to the Cornell campus. The address was 717 Beach Street and it was managed by a remarkable housemother by the name of Mrs. Truax. She accepted me immediately as one of the boys and took care of us all with loving care. That included hot tea laced with a toddy of rum whenever we caught cold, which I did quite often, as I remember. The house was typical of the times. It had four floors, and in our case, each of them was devoted exclusively to a particular political point of view. Socialist Zionists occupied the top floor. They were mostly from Jewish families who had been immigrants to America. Butch Furman,

Igal Roodenko, Itzik Hamlin, Sam Friedman, and I all occupied the top floor. The third floor were all Trotskyites, heavily focused on the Russian Revolution. The second floor students were all die-hard Communists. The ground floor were all law students with a variety of viewpoints. The basement was extremely important because it was a common ground where we could come together to drink tea or beer and listen to the football games on the radio on Saturday afternoons. There were also several stores down the block; there was a restaurant and a beer hall where we could go on Saturday nights with our dates. It wasn't the kibbutz, but it sure had some wonderful community qualities that helped make school enjoyable.

The campus was the kind of archetypal place that we all imagine as perfect for study. Brick buildings covered with ivy surrounded the grass rectangle of well-kept lawns shaded by enormous American elms that seemed to dwarf everything. The most dramatic element was the deep gorge that had been cut out of the sedimentary rock by a rushing torrent of water on its way down to Lake Cayuga. A small lake on campus froze over in winter and gave us a place to skate. I also learned to toboggan down onto the lake ice from the surrounding hills. That was even more fun.

Cornell Agricultural School was available at no fee for citizens of New York State. I still, however, had to work to support myself and pay for room, board, books, etc. What I did to earn my way varied over the years. The first year I inherited some trinkets from alumni that I could sell at the football games. I started out selling caps, flags, pins, and that got me into the games for free. I also had a paper route that year and checked coats at the student union on weekends. During my second year I peeled potatoes and washed pans at a fraternity house for some richer students I had met. The food was good and the walk from 717 Beach to the fraternity led me over a scenic swinging bridge that crossed the gorge.

While at Cornell I was becoming more and more interested in the politics of the labor movement. I supported the Socialist Party. The Lincoln Brigade was already in action in Spain and several men who had fought there came to the campus to urge us to enlist. I thought about that very seriously, but I decided to stick with my plan and study for my return to the kibbutz. Because of developments in Europe, there was a terrifying sense of foreboding hanging over everything. Since I had recently returned from Palestine, I became a focus for students interested in the Zionist movement.

Zionism was under attack at school. The Socialists were powerful and both those students and the Communists were violently opposed to what I stood for—which was a socialist form of Zionism. They were outraged because they could not understand the concept of merging the two ideals—the idea that a homeland for the Jews could be based on a liberal socialist format was beyond their comprehension. We argued constantly. It didn't seem to matter that in Palestine the dominant political party was the Labor Party.

In the meantime, the Great Depression was deepening. Labor strikes were everywhere and I often stood in picket lines supporting strikes in Ithaca. Although I don't now remember the particular issues, we traveled down to Pennsylvania to help the strikers in the coal mines. Deer hides hung on lines outside the miners' houses. They were drying the skins after scraping off the meat. There was not enough food and they were desperate, particularly to feed their children. We took some food with us each time we went down but our major contribution was moral support.

Despite all the tension in the air, summers were still enjoyable. As part of my studies in the agriculture school I spent summers working in some related fields of agriculture or forestry. One summer I was with the Works Project Administration (WPA). The Dutch elm disease had just started to do damage to the East Coast native elms and I was sent up into the trees to take samples and cut off suspicious looking branches. What I liked most about the WPA work was the opportunity to see many small towns all over the state. People were kind and

friendly during those days of the Depression and
very welcoming.

I did not, of course, own a car at that time. We
all hitchhiked in some form or another (Figure 15).
Some people hitched on railroad trains though I
usually hitchhiked by car and that is how I made my
way to Fort Wayne, Indiana, and to George Sweet's
vegetable farm. George's farm was several hundred
acres and he specialized in beets, celery, and car-
rots. He was one of those farmers who took appren-
tices from Cornell every summer. George had two
daughters, one very sassy and pretty. I was assigned
to sleep in a tiny trailer that he kept out back of the
house. As George put it, it took him a while to get
accustomed to "having a Jew in his house." George
talked politics a lot—the midwestern Republican
kind. He was antilabor and considered Roosevelt
a kind of socialist, not much to be trusted. My job
at the farm was mostly weeding the fields. It was
tough work and hard on my back. In the evenings
after work I'd go to the house, take a shower, and
have dinner with the family. I learned a lot about the
Midwest and how different people could be in the
same country. They were very friendly and outspo-
ken on the one hand but extremely conservative on
the other. On weekends George would take us all
down to a lake where we would go fishing, and he
would introduce me to his friends as "the college Jew
radical who is staying with us."

Another summer job didn't work out so well.
This time I was sent to a vegetable farm in New
Jersey, a small town outside of Newark. The driver,
who met me in his pickup truck, was carrying a
rifle on his lap and there was a shotgun hanging
in the back of the cab. As we arrived at the farm
we went by a couple of men who searched the cab.
They carried shotguns as well. We drove by a cluster of workers carrying strike placards. I asked what
was going on and the driver said, "Don't worry,
you won't get into any trouble. Just stay away from
those goddam strikers." All of a sudden I realized I
was being brought in as a scab, a strikebreaker. The
next morning I said I had left my gear in town and
hitched right out of there.

The school year was also interspersed with holidays, which gave me a chance to hitchhike to New
York where I always stayed with my uncle Sydney,
who had a nice apartment in Manhattan. I spent a
lot of my time in all of the museums, but I especially
enjoyed the Museum of Modern Art, which had just
recently moved to Fifty-third Street. I had started
drawing and sketching again and I wanted to see
what the "real" artists were doing. My future seemed
unclear to me then. I was enjoying my studies in
botany, particularly the field work that allowed me to
spend time in the out-of-doors collecting and press-
ing specimens. But the basic classes required for my
degree in horticulture didn't spark my creativity. I

wasn't sure what I wanted to do with my life. At the same time the unsettling world atmosphere affected all of us on the fourth floor of 717 Beach Street.

During one of my trips to New York, Sydney asked me why I wasn't playing baseball at Cornell. I explained that I had no time for it since working took up all my time after schoolwork. He was a young lawyer by then and wasn't making a lot of money, but he said he had a little cash left over and asked me how much it would take to allow me to play baseball. I figured it out carefully—room, board, laundry, movies, dates, and even beer. It came out to thirty-five dollars per week. That was what I needed in order to play ball without working. Sydney said he would go for it.

Because this windfall came about very unexpectedly I was late for baseball tryouts. I explained to the coach what had happened and how I had been away for several years. Somehow I convinced him to let me join the squad. I hadn't pitched a ball for six years but I traveled all around the East Coast with the team that year and I was still good enough to play in an exhibition game at Yankee Stadium.

The trips with my team offered me even more opportunity to indulge my new interest in seeing more of America. I was so anxious to get going that I didn't even hang around for graduation. Having received my bachelor of science in horticulture I had been offered an appointment at the University of Wisconsin as a research assistant to a Dr. Roberts. I hurriedly put my gear together, said goodbye to my dear friends Sam, Igal, Itzik, and Butch at number 717, and hitchhiked to Wisconsin. It was the spring of 1939.

University of Wisconsin

When I reported to Dr. Roberts in the horticulture department he introduced me to the research that I would be working on. It had to do with the fruiting mechanism in crop plants, particularly fruit trees. I was to assist him in deciphering what it was that caused fruiting to occur. I already knew that there were several influences: one being temperature, and another the length of days or rather the number of hours of daylight on the tree. The latter was Dr. Roberts's particular interest. The technical term for this is photoperiod. I was entrusted with a microscope and primarily spent my days examining sections of the fruiting cells in the various subject trees.

Dr. Roberts was a hard taskmaster. I was only one of several graduate students who were at various stages in their work for doctorate degrees and, being the last onboard, I was the beginner. In retrospect, I think that the most interesting thing about Dr. Roberts was his unusual interest in dreams as a major element in his creativity. He frequently brought his dreams into the lab and talked about them at length, trying to decipher their meaning. The most impor-

tant things for me at University of Wisconsin were not my studies, however, but rather the fact that the university provided a setting for two events that changed the course of my life.

After I had settled in at school, found myself a room, and started my work with Dr. Roberts, I decided to go to the Friday evening services at Hillel, the Jewish student club. I knew that this would be the quickest way for me to make acquaintances among the Jewish student body. Rabbi Kadushin was giving the sermon on the subject of the treatment of the Jews in Nazi Germany and what President Roosevelt's role should be. There were about fifty people there and as he spoke I glanced around the room. Off in a corner I saw a very attractive girl with a wonderful profile. Her nose fitted charmingly into the socket between her eyebrows and she had a wonderful head full of curly reddish hair. I knew I had to meet her so after the sermon I walked over and asked if I could walk her home. I learned that her name was Anna Schuman, she was studying in the dance department under Professor Margaret H'Doubler, and she came from a suburb of Chicago called Winnetka. By the time we reached her dormitory, I was in love. We dated for about a year, and then one evening on a trail around Lake Mendoza we climbed up the wooden ski jump to watch the full moon. I backed her into the railing, kissed her before she could object, and asked her to marry me.

I was twenty-three and she was nineteen and we have been together ever since.

I soon found, though, that Anna was going to be hard to keep up with (Figure 16). Early in our courtship the Humphrey Weidman dance group arrived for a performance. Charles Weidman was performing a dance called "Lynchtown" about the horrors of lynching in the Deep South. He needed an extra to be the victim. Without asking, Anna volunteered me. My task was simple and required no specific training; "Just let them drag you across the stage," she said, "and remember you've already been lynched and you have no life left in you." As I allowed myself to be dragged across the stage I heard her whisper from the wings, "Keep your butt down."

Another experience was even worse. Anna was taking a class in human dissection. It was an important part of Miss H'Doubler's philosophy. She felt that as part of movement training dancers needed to know everything there was to know about the human body and the best way to know that was to dissect one. Anna thought that as an artist I would be fascinated by this, so she invited me to go to the class with her. I joined her in the class one afternoon. We entered through the zoology department and walked past tanks with snakes hissing and striking against the glass walls, then moved into the area where the cadavers were lying on tables with sheets covering them. Anna moved

Figure 16

Anna and I were drawn together from the first moment we met at the University of Wisconsin.

Image courtesy the Halprin family.

me really close to her cadaver, removed the sheet, and began showing me the incisions she was in the process of making. I managed to watch for a moment, then became dizzy and fainted. All that I remember was lying on the floor of the dissection room and vowing never to return.

We married in September 1940, about a year after we met. The war in Europe had changed from a distant echo to an immediate threat to our own country. The draft had started and we were sending ancient destroyers over to Britain to defend against the U-boats that were trying to sink our ships transporting supplies to England. The Luftwaffe had started bombing London. Churchill and Roosevelt were often on the radio. By then, we were all calling President Roosevelt FDR. He spoke to us in his fireside chats, and everyone was anxious for the information he imparted. At the urging of my grandparents and the rest of the family, my parents decided to leave Palestine and come home for safety's sake. For Anna and me their return was timely because they were able to join us for our wedding. I had told Anna's parents about my mother and father but they had never actually met. Then on the day of the wedding in Winnetka my father stepped into the house and exclaimed, "My god, it's Isadore Schuman, my old acquaintance from the garment-business days!"

We had a traditional Jewish wedding. Two rabbis conducted the service; Rabbi Kadushin represented Anna and me, and Rabbi Shulman served as the link for Anna's parents as the rabbi of their temple. We stood under a *chupa* made of palm branches. Rabbi Kadushin, as per tradition, took me aside and asked me to confirm that I wanted to make this commitment. I said that yes I did—for sure.

After the wedding Anna and I returned to Wisconsin. She continued her dance studio under Miss H'Doubler and I completed my graduate work on photoperiod and began working on my doctorate. Anna was a junior in college. I was earning seven hundred dollars that year as a teaching assistant. Summer rolled around and Anna and I traveled to a small town called Sturgeon Bay on the northern peninsula of Lake Michigan. The university kept a small farm there for research in the agricultural sciences. I was in charge of the cherry trees. I directed a small group of young people who came in to do the picking. The days were full of picking cherries, of chattering, and of singing songs like "You Are My Sunshine, My Only Sunshine." It was a long way from my picking days in Palestine, but carried a lot of the same flavor. Anna and I rented part of a small farmhouse with some locals. She wasn't very happy using someone else's kitchen, but we were fairly close to Green Bay, where Margaret H'Doubler and her artist/architect husband, Wayne Claxton, had built a summerhouse, and we often visited them.

I had never experienced a house like the one Wayne Claxton had designed and built. The house was slung low to the ground with a roof that extended far out from the exterior walls. He called the projections "overhangs." The walls were built of stone, and that I understood from my garden-building days in Jerusalem. But the stones were laid out in a way I had never seen before in thin sheets that reminded me of shelving. Wayne explained that this method echoed the natural configuration of the local stone. The inside of the house was wide open, with only a few walls that he called "partitions."

Back at school Anna and I found a small house to rent and also bought a Chevy coupe with a rumble seat for only seventy-five dollars. The car gave us a great deal of freedom and flexibility to go out and explore the countryside on weekends. However, before we could start our weekend trips I had to overcome one problem—I had never driven a car.

Anna quickly taught me how to drive and one weekend asked if I would enjoy driving with her to a place called Taliesin built by an architect named Frank Lloyd Wright, about thirty miles from Madison. She had heard that Wright was a remarkable architect and that this was a very special place. The road there was lovely, passing through a very midwestern landscape of rolling hills punctuated by white barns and corn silos. It reminded me of paintings by Thomas Hart Benton and Grant Wood. This part of Wisconsin felt much more real to me than Madison and the university campus. I was happy to get out into the country and the farms gave me a joyful feeling of settlement and people's relationship to the land.

As we approached Taliesin I could see from a distance that the roofline was very similar to Wayne Claxton's house and I guessed that Wayne had been influenced by Wright's work. We parked our car and walked through the front entrance. Overhead on the lintel was a sign that read, "What a man does, that he is." At that moment I could almost hear trumpets blowing.

We went further into the house through rooms the like of which I had never experienced. It was somewhat like a symphony with high and low ceilings representing musical notes and walls mixing wood and white plaster feeling like echoes. Eventually we came to a large living room that dropped down several steps. There was a piano there, music was being played, and the atmosphere was like a painting in chiaroscuro by Rembrandt. Wright was sitting there surrounded by a group of young students. The music went on for a long while, sweet and clear. After it stopped we walked over, introduced ourselves to Wright, and left. That trip was to change my life.

On the way back to Madison I said very little but my mind was racing. I was mentally revisiting

Taliesin and remembering a designed place that held community, culture, and music. The idealism of the image resonated with me. It was dusk when we arrived home. After dinner I said to Anna, "If that's what architecture is about, then that's what I want to do." The next day was Sunday so I went to the campus library to look up architecture. There were quite a few books in the architecture section and I glanced through a lot of them until, finally, they merged with a subject called "landscape architecture." There were only a few books in that section, among them a book by Christopher Tunnard called *Gardens in the Modern Landscape*. I riffled through that book and realized that it was speaking my language. There were a number of photographs in Tunnard's book and I particularly remember one of a person sitting in a chair, gazing across a terrace to a long view of a landscape framed by a handsome wooden grid. In the foreground there was a sculpture by Henry Moore. I was struck by the fact that the image harmoniously included all aspects of design—poetry of place, perspective, scale, sculpture, framed view, and light. That picture was followed by photographs of small gardens and then gardens the size of city parks. I noted that they were all designed by landscape architects and realized that I was looking at a three-dimensional art form. Tunnard went on to write about communal gardens and my mind flashed back to the kibbutz. I was overwhelmed by the thought

that there was a profession dedicated to the making of these kinds of places.

The very next day I asked Dr. Roberts if he knew anything about landscape architecture. "Why yes," he said, "it's taught upstairs. Just go up and ask for Professor Longenecker." I rushed upstairs and sure enough there was a department of landscape architecture. Professor William Longenecker guided me to Professor Franz Aust, the head of the department, who was amazingly kind and sympathetic. He suggested that I bring in some of my paintings, which I did the very next day. Then, despite the fact that it was a little late in the semester, he told me that he could squeeze me into one of Professor Longenecker's classes.

From then on things moved so quickly that I sometimes felt absolutely breathless. I took to my design class like a duck takes to water. I remember my very first assignment was to design a small garden as part of a series of row houses. The garden would require a degree of privacy and I decided that had to be accomplished with some kind of fencing. I had never thought of solving three-dimensional design problems before and the challenge excited me. I threw myself into it and came up with a concept that Professor Longenecker liked. Then, for some reason, I decided to take the design a step further and make the fence transparent by using glass blocks. I found that design concepts came to me easily but I spent a lot of time figuring out how to construct them.

Within weeks Professor Aust called me back to his office. He said that I seemed to be a natural as far as landscape architecture was concerned. He felt that if I wanted to drop my work in horticulture he would support that and, in fact, he would strongly recommend it. He went on to say that he felt the landscape architecture department at Madison was too limited for me. He suggested that I go to Harvard and pointed out that Christopher Tunnard was teaching there. He also said that he could almost promise me a scholarship at Harvard for the spring semester, which was about to start in a couple of weeks.

My mind was in turmoil as I walked home to talk with Anna. If I took Professor Aust's suggestion, it would have all kinds of implications. I needed some time to think. I told Anna that for the first time I had a deep-seated confidence that I was on the right track. I explained the joy I had felt since my experience at Taliesin and later in the short design class in the department of landscape architecture. My interest in this subject was all consuming and far outweighed anything that I had ever felt before. I felt that this profession could combine everything that I was deeply interested in: painting, design, botany, and community action. Landscape architecture could encompass it all.

My concerns about going forward, however, were serious. If I went to Harvard immediately I would be leaving Anna alone in the first year of our marriage. Anna's reaction was generous and supportive. She said she had never seen me so happy. She, too, had read *Gardens in the Modern Landscape* and agreed with me that landscape architecture seemed just right for me. She wholeheartedly agreed that I should go. She looked forward to joining me at Harvard and said that as far as she was concerned the fact that it was a creative field of art was the dominant point. It would bring our two fields of study much closer together.

The next day, I went back to see Professor Aust. He told me that the Harvard scholarship was confirmed. I told him how grateful I was and I left him one of my paintings. Then I called Sydney and told him I was going to Harvard, which was also his alma mater. He was startled and bemused but very pleased for me.

Harvard

It was remarkable that Professor Aust managed to arrange a scholarship to Harvard University for me. In 1940 Harvard was the acknowledged leading design school in the country. Christopher Tunnard was teaching there and the architectural program had recently hired a number of internationally recognized professors from the German Bauhaus.

Professor Aust gave me a history lesson on the Bauhaus and explained that Hitler's regime had ousted many professors from the Bauhaus, among them Gropius, the architect who had founded the Bauhaus in 1919, Marcel Breuer, world-famous architect and furniture designer, and Laszlo Moholy-Nagy, painter and photographer. I learned that Paul Klee and Wassily Kandinsky, painters I greatly admired, had taught at the Bauhaus and that the philosophy was that fine arts and crafts should combine and be taught in an interdisciplinary setting. The Bauhaus curriculum had included classes in pottery, dance, graphic design, sculpture, photography, color theory, architecture, and interior design. Gropius, Breuer, and Moholy-Nagy had brought this philosophy with them and I was excited by the prospect of entering a world of such artistic creativity. I told Anna that some of the great modern dancers had also taught on the Bauhaus faculty and with Anna's support I took off for Cambridge and Harvard, arriving there in the winter of 1940. There, on campus, I felt myself thrown into a community where the interests and energy felt familiar to me. This joyful sense of belonging was similar to my youthful response to Jerusalem.

As in my Jerusalem adventure, fate intervened during my first days on the Harvard campus and someone suggested I room with Jack Warnecke at 49 Hammond Street. Jack was a Californian, had gone to Stanford University, and was studying architecture. His father was a well-known West Coast architect and it seemed Jack was born into the profession. This was fortunate for me because I knew nothing about architecture—Jack had to explain to me what a T square and a triangle were, and then he had to show me how to use them. It wasn't even clear to me that architecture and landscape architecture were two separate professions.

Of course there was a war going on and young men were being encouraged to join up. I was anxious to finish my studies and do my part so I was prepared to go at my program full throttle with the intention of moving through quickly. The first semester's approach therefore took me somewhat by surprise because the emphasis was not on solving real-life problems but on experiencing pure creativity in the arts. We were asked to produce abstract art and our professors pointed out that all architectural designs are based on abstract configurations. This concept was new to me but I found it extremely interesting and exciting.

Time passed quickly and soon Anna graduated and arrived from Wisconsin. She found work nearby in a settlement house with underprivileged children and at Windsor School in Boston for overprivileged children. Her income helped us to survive. She often gave dance performances on campus at the architectural school. I designed the stage sets for these performances and this was the beginning of our many future collaborations.

New insights came quickly in my first year: I found that much of the learning was done in creativity studios, not in lecture halls; that students worked on projects in teams; that professors gave criticisms (crits); that the work of great masters provides an important source of inspiration; and that talent is important. I soon learned that there was a student hierarchy that was vital to the learning process on various levels. Older students were involved in training the new students, who learned by helping the older ones with factual research, photography, drawing, and presentation assistance. In that way I got to know most of the older students; among them were Jack Warnecke, Philip Johnson, and I. M. Pei. Paul Rudolph came over frequently from Yale and many of the teaching assistants, such as Hugh Stubbins, were recent graduates. When it comes right down to it, the greatest influences on me at Harvard were my fellow students. I learned through their reactions in the studios and by interacting with them on design projects.

Harvard, of course, was bursting with energy. Not only was the faculty on the leading edge in the world of design, the student body was caught up in it as well. Philip Johnson, older, more experienced, and financially established, had already helped to assemble an influential show on the International Style of architecture for the Museum of Modern Art in New York and had coauthored a book that accompanied the show. On Friday evenings, at a house he had designed, he invited all his classmates into his world of sophisticated cocktail parties. It was a place where professors, professionals, and students would get together and share ideas. These parties provided important social linkages and seemed quite comfortable to me. Somehow my early training at Poly Prep with its subliminal Waspish elitism helped me to fit right into his world.

It seemed that almost every Friday night we were invited to Philip's house for cocktails and the light gossip that accompanied it. Philip had designed and built his house in an obvious Mies van der Rohe style, and Chris Tunnard helped him with the garden. The house and garden seemed as one. The house walls became high fences that extended out to the street and kept us all isolated in a courtyard. Those Friday night parties, at which there was lots of gossip, lots of drinking (which I was not accustomed to), and lots of confused dancing, provided some of my jolliest memories of my time at Harvard. Gradually, however, some discomfort began to seep into my consciousness. After Philip had sponsored the International Style exhibit, he had gone to Germany and there were rumors that he had somehow become involved with the higher echelons of the Nazi Party. None of us were quite clear about the particulars

Figure 17

Harvard parties were great fun. We put a lot
of energy into designing these costumes
for a special birthday celebration when
Walter Gropius turned sixty-five.
Image courtesy the Halprin family.

of this and Philip didn't talk about it, but it forever
formed a kind of cloud over our relationship.

The professors who set the philosophy of the
school at this time also made their mark on me by
the impressions I received from them in social and
informal settings (Figures 17, 18). A most treasured
memory is of the day Walter Gropius invited Anna
and me to lunch at his house in Lincoln. He talked
a lot with Anna about dance and the dancer Mary
Wigman, who was very important in the Bauhaus.
I had time to wander through the house and take
it all in. I was shocked at its simplicity. It was all
white, with a few paintings, a simple black fireplace,
and an outdoor trellis covered with wisteria. It
seemed to reflect his distant, iconic image. Breuer,
on the other hand, was much more approachable
and his house was more complex and much richer
in materials. One wall was all stone, and there were
several levels. His drafting table took over one
sunken level; it always seemed to be overflowing
with his work. Breuer once took our class on a trip
to Manhattan. As we walked around he described
the buildings to us and when we went to Radio
City Music Hall I was fascinated by the fact that he
spent most of his time and attention on the back-
stage area that he called "the real functioning part
of the building."

Despite the fact that Christopher Tunnard's
book had provided the initial inspiration that drew

me toward landscape architecture, I never did have
a studio with him. We did, however, talk together a
great deal and his was the only design crit that was
of any importance to me in the landscape school.
With his socialist point of view, he was, of course,
interested in my experiences in the kibbutz and it
brought us together on a political level. At about the
time I was finishing up at Harvard, he returned to
Canada and entered wartime service.

While I was at Harvard, most of my design
ideas were derived from the Bauhaus. The masters
we studied were Mies van der Rohe, Corbusier, and
Moholy-Nagy. We never mentioned Frank Lloyd
Wright, whose studio at Taliesin had captured my
imagination, and no one seemed at all interested
in his work. I presumed that we didn't pay him any
mind because he was essentially American while all
the other Harvard influences were European—and
represented the basic Bauhaus approach. Wright
was more flamboyant, an individual—kind of an
architectural cowboy—and his buildings were
designed to be complete environments carefully set
into their landscapes.

If it wasn't for another accident of fate, I
might have left Harvard without an introduction
to another American designer, one who arrived
from the West. In my last semester at Harvard I
had the very good fortune to meet the California
architect William Wurster and his wife, Catherine

Bauer Wurster. Bill Wurster had established a midsized office of talented young architects in San Francisco that was becoming very well known for its residential design work. His houses were built out of redwood, were carefully crafted, and were intimately connected to the land and gardens in which they were sited. Catherine Bauer was also well known as a planning consultant and had written a significant book exploring low-cost housing solutions throughout the world. She had acted as a

Figure 18
Gropius presented Anna with an award for best costume.
Image courtesy the Halprin family.

consultant to Eleanor Roosevelt, who was heavily involved in developing greenbelt towns.

I had learned of their work as a result of an inspirational exhibit of Tommy Church's gardens in the landscape architecture department. Most of the Church gardens were closely interwoven with Wurster's architecture, and for the first time I grasped the wonderful design possibilities that could result from a collaborative synergy between the two fields. Bill Wurster was switching from an emphasis on private residential work to wartime housing projects. He and Catherine had decided it was time to take an intellectual sabbatical at Harvard and study the latest planning theories. They had arrived without any fanfare and begun their studies before I realized who they were. I was anxious to meet them and asked Walter Gropius if he could arrange an introduction.

When we met I pointed out that all my studies in landscape architecture had been very theoretical and this was my first opportunity to ask about real-life projects. I told him how enthused I was by his collaborations with Tommy Church, which allowed house and garden to grow as an organic, living whole. My initial questions were simple: How did he and Tommy Church find clients who would allow them to work together as a team? And why aren't houses and gardens like this available in other parts of America?

Bill Wurster was very kind and generous with his time. We talked for quite a while and I told him about my background in botany and plant research and my time in Palestine where I had lived in a kibbutz and had been influenced by community activism and vision. I also explained that I was becoming increasingly interested in architecture and had many friends in the department. During our introduction he probably found out more about Anna and me than I found out about him. Eventually he suggested another meeting because he wanted Catherine to meet us. They were very outgoing and we shared many similar interests, and after just a few meetings we became good friends. Because of the wartime gas rationing, we often rode our bicycles together and took long architectural tours. One particularly long ride took us all the way to Martha's Vineyard. Their friendship was of great importance to us during our last months at Harvard. When they realized that we were leaving and that I intended to volunteer for the navy they urged us to keep in touch with them.

By the time I left Harvard in December 1943 with a bachelor's degree I was excited about my chosen profession and felt that the field of landscape architecture offered me the potential to express all my interests.

I felt it was high time to enlist in the war effort. This was a war that I believed in deeply—both as an American and as a Jew. I chose the navy because I understood that my architectural training would be helpful in navigation, and that they were taking young men into officers' training. At first they said I didn't qualify because of my feet. I learned I had a foot condition called hallicus phalanges. It sounded strange but simply meant that the angle my toes turned away from the rest of my foot was too extreme. I begged them to reconsider and to overlook the toes. I pointed out that I had done very well at sports, and I could do just as well fighting for my country. After some consultation and lots of discussion they let me into the officer-training program.

Within days I was on a train to Hollywood, Florida. Anna came with me so we could be together during the period before I sailed off to war. It was a difficult time and full of the odd contrasts that arise in a time of crisis. Those of us in the officer-training program were put up in the Hollywood Hotel, a pink building with elegant beach facilities. In the beginning we learned about the basic needs of shipboard life such as where to report for duty, where the cafeteria was located, the general layout of the ship. We also ran several miles a day on the beach and did a lot of exercises to get in better shape. The most enjoyable part was a daily game of volleyball, where our motivation was team competition. I was good at the physical side of training and even enjoyed it. Beneath all the training, however, there was a lot of anxiety, tension, and fear. Events in the Pacific theater were not going well and it seemed that was where I would be sent. It was a highly charged time. Anna's brother was slogging through mud in Europe, along with many of our friends. Sydney was already a major in the air force in Europe, and my good friend Butch Furman from Cornell had already lost his life. Despite the fact that Anna wasn't far away, it was quite a lonesome time.

Eventually, I was shifted to Combat Information Center (CIC) training, which involved learning about navigation, surface radar, and surface-to-air calculations. I was told that when I got on my ship I would probably be assigned to guide both surface ships and aircraft during battle. It seemed an overwhelming responsibility. On graduation night we put on our dress whites and after only ninety days of training I became an ensign in the U.S. Navy (Figure 19).

I soon learned that I would be assigned to a ship in the Pacific and would be meeting up with it in San Francisco. As Anna and I packed, I called Bill Wurster at Harvard. He offered to let us stay in their apartment on Telegraph Hill while I waited to ship out. Their apartment overlooked the entire bay and the Golden Gate Bridge. Even though the waiting was hard on our nerves, the view was calming.

6
World War II

Figure 19

Image courtesy the Halprin family.

Figure 20

Image courtesy the Halprin family.

After about ten days I received word to get ready and at 2:00 A.M. the next morning a bus came to pick me up. Anna was weeping and I was glad that I had to stow my gear quickly and take off so that our leave-taking could not drag on. The bus was full of other young men with their duffle bags and everyone was quiet. None of us knew where we were going next. The bus seemed to drive around and around in the dark and I wondered whether they were trying to confuse us for security reasons. When it finally stopped it was still dark. We got off the bus and climbed a ladder onto a ship. The tension finally let up a bit. I was in the navy even if I didn't know where I was going or what kind of ship I was boarding.

Once on board, we were assigned to bunks and told to sleep until morning. When daylight finally came I realized we were on a small aircraft carrier and already heading out to sea. For a long time we sailed all by ourselves. It turned out that we were on one of the smaller carriers headed toward New Guinea with a lot of personnel replacements for various ships in the Solomons. We were not told what ships we would board, nor what kind they would be. We would find that out soon enough.

Aboard ship the weather was beautiful, and all was quiet—as if we were on a pleasant cruise. After about ten days we arrived at Hollandia Harbor in New Guinea, a beautiful port with high hills looking down on the water. The harbor was chock full of all kinds of ships, from destroyer escorts to heavy cruisers. Small boats plied their way between the docks and the ships, and between ships and other ships, all displaying various kinds of camouflage. I felt like I was on a movie set (Figure 20).

When we got ashore we received our duty assignments. I was to be on the USS *Morris* DD 417, a destroyer that was moored close enough to the harbor that I could see her. I thought she was beautiful, a sleek, single-stack, elegant ship (Figure 21). I hitched a ride over, they whistled me aboard, and I climbed the ladder to the deck. This was a place where I was going to spend over a year, gathering experiences that I would never forget.

I was assigned to bunk with Herb Armentrout, the ship's doctor. He was kind enough to mentor me for the next few days until we got under way. I needed a lot of guidance in understanding life on the ship and all of the routines. I also met Captain Wheeler, commander USN, and the rest of the officers who had been fighting aboard the ship for many months. Soon I discovered that we also carried the squadron commander and several of his subordinates as staff and intelligence officers. We seldom saw them and they led a very separate existence on the ship. I joined the USS *Morris* with another ensign, George Jennings, and we soon became buddies. The difference between us was

Attack Transport
Hollandia Dec 6.
1944

World War II

Figure 21

Image courtesy the Halprin family.

that he had just graduated from Annapolis and he really *did* know his way around the navy. George's shipboard training was extensive. In my few months of training, I had learned how to salute and to track ships and aircrafts on the newfangled radar. As to the rest, I was completely ignorant. Perhaps the navy's intent was to throw us newcomers into the water and let us figure out how to swim. George could have resented my inexperience but, instead, he showed a great deal of empathy and helped me whenever he could.

Even though we all lived close together and ate together in our mess room it took quite a long while before I could feel at home. These officers had already been through combat together (Figure 22). They had sunk ships, rescued survivors off carriers, and lost friends. Even though the officers would sometimes talk about this, it was very different from sharing actual combat experience. That wasn't something you talked about in a chatty, conversational way. I felt very insulated from the rest of the people on board. The seamen all bunked and ate in a completely different part of the ship, and the only contact I had with them were with those I met and worked with during my watch.

After a few weeks we raised anchor and set a course for Guadalcanal. The feel of the *Morris* was much different from the carrier on which I had traveled from San Francisco. Once we left the bay at Hollandia I felt the swells of the Pacific, and the *Morris* began to heel over more and more. Eventually I got used to the movement underfoot and began to feel normal. The days were usually very quiet. We could hear the hum of the motors, but otherwise the only sound was the lapping of the water against the hull. Flying fish sometimes landed

Figure 22

Image courtesy the Halprin family.

onboard. At night under the full moon the horizon stretched on and on. The dappled reflection of the moon's light on the dark ocean was brilliant. I realized how seldom you could see the whole arc of the stars in the heavens come down around you when you're standing on land. The effect was especially stunning when I was on the stern, which was just a few feet above the water.

Gradually I became more and more accustomed to being at sea and the routine of everyday changing of the watch. As the weeks went by I learned the logistics of steering enough to take the controls myself. I enjoyed that because it broke up the inertia of just sailing and it was, in a way, more exciting to be up on the bridge rather than being down in CIC, where I would be stationed during combat. Mostly life was very serene, interrupted once by a closely passing torpedo from an enemy submarine.

From time to time, however, on the way to the Solomons, the *Morris* would drop anchor at an island. As the junior officer on our ship, I would be assigned the duty of taking a boatload of seamen ashore for a day of recreation and beer drinking. That was jolly enough, except on that initial excursion I had trouble rounding up the crew to return to our ship. The sailors had consumed lots of beer and had no intention of returning to the *Morris*. It all got very rowdy and noisy, and suddenly I found myself in charge of a drunken brawl. When I finally got them aboard the return boat, several sailors decided to throw me overboard. Even that wasn't too awful, and just seemed like a bit of childish fun. Then, all of a sudden, it turned serious. They forced me underwater and kept me there. Fortunately, the chief petty officer and George Jennings realized what was happening and dove in to pull me out. I was gasping and thrashing and as far as I was concerned they were just in time! When we arrived back on the ship in disarray, Captain Wheeler called me into his cabin and gave me a thorough verbal thrashing for allowing it to happen on my watch. All I could say was that I wouldn't let it happen again. As weeks went by, I became more and more a part of the ship's company and part of the whole unit. It never did happen again and I realized it was not really directed at me personally, but at me as a symbol of authority. They had been venting their growing frustration about life onboard ship and officers in general.

As we got closer to our destination the islands grew closer together. We had still not come under fire and all was calm when suddenly we received an urgent signal from one of the other destroyers in the convoy. The captain of our sister ship asked that we move closer and stand ready to take her under fire. He said that members of his crew were on the verge of a mutiny and he was losing control. Our captain did move closer in case we should have to respond but finally we heard that all was well, and that we could continue on as usual. I never did hear the details since we all had to continue north and get ready for combat. I was never ever quite sure what caused this potential mutiny but we on the *Morris* were certainly relieved.

We continued on without further excitement until we reached Leyte Gulf, where we joined a large assembly of other ships, including large landing craft. This was our first invasion of the Japanese-held Philippines and the *Morris*'s assignment was to cover the landings. I was in CIC directing gunnery fire and directing aircraft—my area of specialty. This was my first experience in combat and also the first time I felt that I was actually fighting a war (Figure 23). I was amazed to see that after months of relative inactivity, all the officers took their battle stations calmly, including me. My bunkmate, Herb Armentrout, set up the mess room as an emergency medical station. Our dining table would be used for any required surgery. Everyone acted with a kind of intense professional precision. I was shocked by the noise from the gunfire, bombs, and firing from the shore, but I remained calm enough to read the surface radar just as if it was a site plan and fed the information up to the bridge in the midst of all the chaos.

One very big surprise that took place in the middle of the first battle was when the captain decided it would be an opportune time to trade movies with some of the other ships that were close at hand. We had seen all our films over and over and we were absolutely bored with them. The captain sent signals to the other ships asking for information about a movie exchange and got several positive answers from neighboring ships. Then he asked for volunteers on our ship to take our skiff and sail across to the answering ships and exchange our films for theirs. He made it clear, of course, that there might be some danger in this film expedition, but just about everyone on board volunteered, including my buddy George Jennings. Off they all sailed with George as officer of the deck. I remained at my combat station and watched them carefully on the radar as they skirted through the rough sea and through the shells and bombs. They got the movies and returned with everyone in fine shape. The *Morris* piped them aboard amid a wild round of applause. Mission accomplished.

After the Battle of Leyte Gulf, the *Morris* returned to the humdrum life. We sailed south for days. It turned out that our destination was to be Australia and we were scheduled for several weeks of rest and recreation there. As soon as that information became obvious, pandemonium was loosed on the *417*. Australia had a remarkable reputation, particularly among the enlisted men. They reported that the girls in Australia were famous not only for their

Planes strafing & divebo
Jap position Hill 57

beauty but also their openness to share their physical charms. I immediately noticed an explosion of self-improvement. Haircuts became the order of the day. Dress whites were laundered. Special earrings were polished—even though the skipper had made them illegal on board. Among the officers there was an epidemic of shoe shining, ironing of dress shirts, and polishing of combat medals. It felt as if we were all getting ready to go to a party and great fun was to be had by all Then we got the message to "turn 180 degrees and sail north to Okinawa ASAP."

As we sailed north to Okinawa we were joined by many other ships until gradually we became an armada. I had put together some drawings and planned to post them to Anna from Australia but when I learned of several ships passing us heading east to the States, I saw an opportunity and decided to take a chance. I ran below to my bunk, grabbed the package, and rushed back up to the deck. As one of the ships passed close, I reared back and threw the package as far as I could. It landed safely on the passing destroyer's deck. We continued to sail on to Okinawa, while the package found its way to New York and to Anna. Many of the naval drawings in this book are from that pitched package.

As we sailed north I got to know Squadron Commander Solomon a little better because for the first time he joined us in CIC. He described where we were going, and told me how he anticipated

using our radar scanning. He even agreed to sit for a portrait in his cabin. Once I started drawing I realized how nervous I was about the finished product. If I didn't make it a good likeness, I wondered whether it would affect my fitness report. I was relieved when it turned out well and he said that he liked it (Figure 24).

Our squadron approached Okinawa at sunset. I focused intently on the radar, because there were hundreds of ships around us who depended on us to show them the way in since no one was allowed to use their running lights. Suddenly the radar went dead. I couldn't read anything. Radar was a completely new tool for all of us and we were, in fact, one of the first destroyers to have it on aboard. I had no training in the repair or maintenance of the navigational equipment nor, it turned out, did anyone else on the ship. "All right, Mr. Halprin," the captain said, "we are depending on you to avoid collisions in our part of the fleet. I will give you five minutes to have your radar fixed." And he went back up to the bridge.

When he left I turned to my petty officer in charge of electronics and asked if he could get the thing fixed in five minutes. All he could say was that he "didn't know what was wrong with the fucking thing," and until he figured that out he couldn't tell me how long it would take to fix it. I thought I'd better let him work in silence rather than keep badgering him—it was hard enough for him to even see

Figure 23

Image courtesy the Halprin family.

Figure 24

Image courtesy the Halprin family.

the working parts in the semidarkness. Within five minutes the captain was on the horn. "What the hell is going on, Mr. Halprin?" "Give me a few minutes more, captain," I said. The minutes dragged on and all of a sudden the radar went on, went off, and then came on and stayed. Everyone in CIC cheered and as far as I could see, we were still steering correctly and the squadron ships were still in the right positions.

Our first assignment in Okinawa was to provide cover for the landing ships as they approached the beaches (Figure 25). It turned out that there was no enemy fire to prevent the landings. Apparently the Japanese had withdrawn and were sucking our troops ashore and into the jungle where they figured it would be easier to trap them. After a while, the battleships that were positioned offshore behind us started firing inland. We could hear and feel the shells' whistles as they passed overhead. Our assignment soon changed to shelling in advance of our troops as they moved inland. We had some spotters onshore and they advised me how our shells were landing and whether our five-inch gun marksmanship was accurate. I got to know the spotters by name and the conversation became very chatty. I would ask them how everything was going, and they would respond with answers like "up ten percent" or "right thirty yards." This went on for a long time and then it stopped. No matter what I did I couldn't raise them. I was devastated and scared. I have never

known why they quit responding. I have always hoped that it wasn't because of our friendly fire and that hopefully they had been able to move farther inland and our shelling had been successful.

After a few more days things changed once again. Our ship was circling the end of the island on radar picket duty and at times we were standing inshore with some of the other destroyers when a new Japanese weapon appeared. We had heard reports of kamikaze attacks but they had so far been sporadic. Now at Okinawa the alerts increased until they became almost continuous with planes arriving in waves and hitting destroyer after destroyer. A destroyer would shoot down the first or second kamikaze plane but others would keep coming until the destroyer took a hit. Some ships were struck by as many as six planes. As the battle for Okinawa continued we followed the various kamikaze attacks over the radio. Some destroyers were sunk and many were terribly damaged.

Then we became a target. On April 6, at about noontime, we picked up a Japanese plane circling around and around about ten miles away, just outside the range of our guns. This went on for quite a while and we deduced that the pilot was either gathering his courage or trying to use up his fuel. Either way we knew he would soon come after us. While we waited, the skipper ordered everyone to eat some lunch. I watched our attacker on my aircraft radar

Figure 25

Image courtesy the Halprin family.

and continued plotting his position. All of a sudden the plot indicated that he was starting to come in. I informed the bridge, and told the five-inch guns to be ready. As the plane came within range, the whole ship started firing and didn't stop as the plane flew closer and closer. As soon as I lost him on radar I told the gunners to turn and pick him up going away. Then I felt the thud and explosion. We had been hit!

We were all okay down below in CIC. The plane had hit the ship at our waterline between the two forward guns and had blown everything away down to the keel, taking everything with it, including my cabin. The bridge was damaged, and the officers' mess hall had taken a hit. Herb was nowhere to be seen. Fires had started; it was chaos everywhere. An immediate concern was for the men who had been blown overboard—some were severely injured and all were in danger of being attacked by sharks. Without a question or an order, many of the guys dove into the water to rescue their injured mates. In retrospect, it was absolutely impossible to imagine beforehand that these men would be heroes. They just were.

The USS *Morris* was now dead in the water. Our sister ship saw what had happened and, at great danger to herself, quickly came alongside and tied us up to her. They sprayed us with water as best they could to put out our fires and that helped for a while.

Then we rigged a breeches buoy and sent as many of the injured as we could across to her for medical help. I did what I could by injecting the most injured men with morphine. Among the injured I found our doctor, Herb Armentrout, who against all odds had somehow managed to crawl out of the mess hall through one of its tiny portholes.

The bridge wasn't functioning and our skipper seemed to be in shock. We kept in touch with the admiral, whose orders were to attempt to get to the island of Kerama Retto before we sank. We were to anchor there, and await further orders. I was ordered to go amidships where there had been no damage and from there I manned the interim bridge where there was a rudimentary navigation and communication setup. On the way we did what we could to put out the many fires that were burning throughout the ship. On orders I destroyed all confidential documents to prevent them falling into Japanese hands should we not make it. By daylight the next morning, April 7, our sister ship had managed to pull us into Kerama Retto Harbor, a small island bay that the navy had set up as a makeshift shipyard for disabled vessels. It had taken seven hours to pull us twenty miles. The shipyard was already full of ships awaiting repair and we realized we would have to wait our turn (Figure 26).

In the midst of this carnage and destruction, came another devastating blow—we learned that our beloved President Roosevelt had died. Most of us had grown up with him as our president. He had brought us out of the Great Depression. Through his fireside chats he had established a personal relationship with each one of us. Now he was our commander in chief. None of us had realized the extent of his disability since the media had pretty much kept that a secret. In our minds FDR was a great leader—vigorous and energetic—and now he was gone. There was not a dry eye on the ship. It was an almost impossible concept to come to terms with.

While we were anchored in Kerama Retto we were sitting ducks. Every day Japanese planes flew over and dropped bombs while our guns were unable to fire back. That sense of helplessness was awful and for the first time I felt afraid. Then Tokyo Rose, one of several English-speaking announcers who made taunting propaganda broadcasts, got on

Figure 26

Image courtesy the Halprin family.

the air and singled us out. "Poor *417*," she would say over and over again, "we know that you've been hit. Never mind, we'll finish the job, just you wait." It was demoralizing.

One day the skipper sent for me. He asked me to go ashore to the cemetery where the men who had been killed were being buried. He wanted me to make sketches to send to their families. Sketching the cemetery and the graves was something of a closing ritual for me and it gave me a feeling that I was helping to preserve their memories (Figure 27).

As our crew worked valiantly to repair the *Morris* without blueprints or proper tools, we were subjected to a furious blast from nature. A tropical hurricane blew in and pounded the entire Fifth Fleet. There were gale-force winds that exceeded one hundred miles per hour and a deafening noise surrounded us for hours. It was like a boxing match in which our opponent kept on pummeling us over and over without letting up. The winds tore away our anchor and we began drifting out to sea. We sent out emergency signals, fearing that we were about to founder and sink. The admiral dispatched a repair officer to see what could be done. He determined we were beyond help and suggested we abandon ship. Our skipper would have none of that and we all remained aboard. The storm finally blew itself out leaving the bay and everything in it a complete shambles (Figure 28). But the *Morris* was still afloat, though barely.

The fleet's repair officer decided that the *Morris* was too badly crippled to fix in the Kerama Retto shipyard. He suggested that she be taken out to deep water and sunk but the officers and crew still didn't want to leave her. Despite the fact that we were shorthanded and lacking building materials, in two months we somehow managed to patch up the ship enough to make her seaworthy. The battle for Okinawa was over and those of us still aboard were allowed to take the *Morris* home. Then, we were given thirty-day survivor's leave stateside.

The war had come to an end in Europe but still continued with Japan. My naval career was essentially over. It took us nearly a month to cross the Pacific to San Francisco. From there I went to New York to join Anna and my family. We were exhausted, both physically and emotionally. There had been several weeks after the *Morris* was hit when Anna didn't know whether I was alive or dead. Sydney lent us his cabin in the Poconos to recover— we stayed there for a week and then headed to Manhattan. While I was overseas Anna had been dancing in a Broadway musical called *Sing Out Sweet Land* with Burl Ives. One night she suggested we go to a new musical called *Oklahoma*. In front of us an elderly gentleman sat with his arms around two very pretty, young women. His hair was completely white and he was wearing a cape. As we waited for the curtain to rise, Anna suddenly whispered, "I think

Figure 27

Image courtesy the Halprin family.

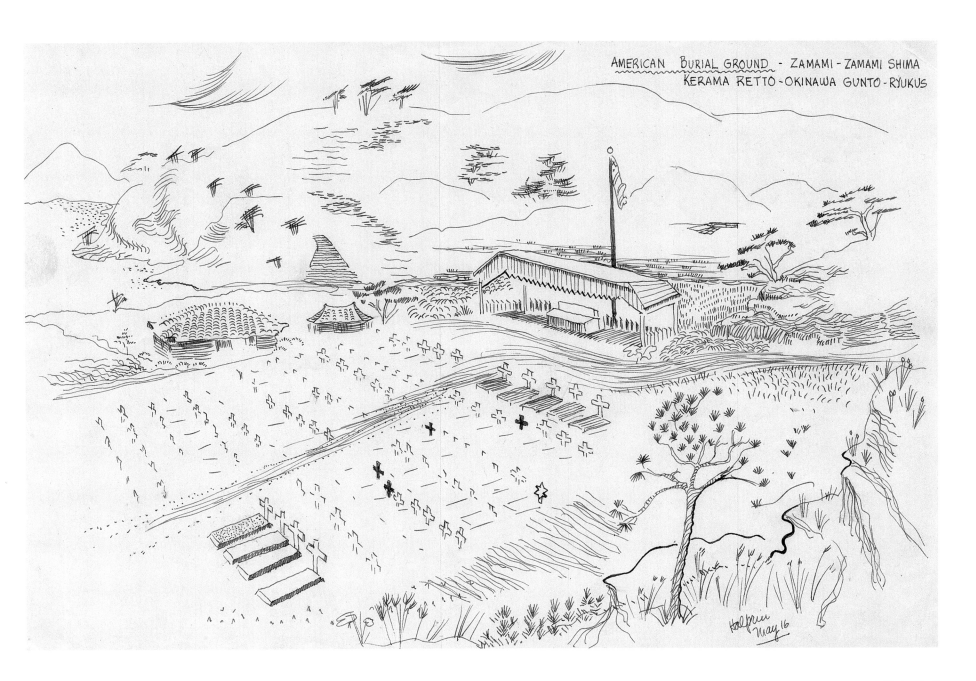

AMERICAN BURIAL GROUND - ZAMAMI - ZAMAMI SHIMA
KERAMA RETTO - OKINAWA GUNTO - RYUKUS

Figure 28
Image courtesy the Halprin family.

Figure 29
Image courtesy the Halprin family.

that's Frank Lloyd Wright sitting in front of us." During intermission I introduced myself and said, "Mr. Wright, I've been studying architecture at Harvard, and I just want to say how much I admire your work." He looked me up and down and said, "Young man, I thought you said you were an architect. What are you doing in that uniform?" I told him there was a war going on. "Young man," he said as he drew

himself up to his not very full height, "if you claim to be an architect you should know that the only war you have to fight is the war for architecture." And with that he stomped off!

After my survivor's leave, I was sent back to San Francisco to await the end of the war. I was assigned to Hunters Point Shipyard, where Anna and I stayed in a Quonset hut (Figure 29). At night I stood watch. As soon as I could I visited Bill Wurster's office in the city. Bill was on the East Coast, and so his partner Theodore Bernardi showed me around the office located in a three-story brick building on Jackson Street. Theodore finally got around to telling me that Bill Wurster had told him that when I turned up I should be offered a job. I was quite astounded but then Theodore went on to say that "Tommy Church said he would also like you to work for him and Bill feels that Tommy has dibbs on you."

I was dumbfounded! I left that building facing one of the most important decisions in my life. I had to decide whether I wanted to work for Bill Wurster as an architect, or stick with my intention of becoming a landscape architect and join Tommy Church's office. I went back to Hunters Point with my heart pounding and told Anna about my dilemma. The one thing I knew for certain was that I wanted to stay in San Francisco.

View from Hunters Point

Halprin
July 28
'45

PART II

I can still remember how difficult it was for me to decide which way to go, which offer to take. I understood that this decision would probably determine my professional future. It was fair enough to say that most of my time at Harvard had been spent among the architects and my biggest influences were Gropius, Breuer, and the teachings of the Bauhaus. On that level, I felt I could easily fit into Bill Wurster's office, especially since his partner, Theodore Bernardi, said he would mentor me. Still, my real feelings were with the land, community, and regional planning and my training in biology, ecology, and botany were well suited there.

For several days I walked the streets of San Francisco trying to make up my mind. On day three I walked up the hill to the Mark Hopkins Hotel, doubled back to North Beach, went up Telegraph Hill to Coit Tower, and came back down along Broadway. I ended up on Jackson Street, where both Bill Wurster and Tommy Church had their offices—Bill was on the third floor and Tommy was on the second. I walked up the stairs and knocked on Tommy's door.

In those early days after the war, Tommy's office was tiny. Only two people were working there—Tommy and June Meehan, who had been with him for many years. The feeling was casual and the space seemed more like an artist's studio. There were lots of Tommy's photos on the wall, several

drafting tables, and a coffee table used for lunch or meetings. Tommy and I hit it off well. I didn't have any professional work to show him but I had some of my war sketches with me. He offered me a job, I immediately accepted, and only then did we get around to my salary. Tommy said he was prepared to give me a good opening salary with the understanding that it would stay the same for a while. I would be paid seventy-five dollars per week. Although I hadn't much experience with that sort of thing, it seemed like quite a lot to me. I thought Anna and I could get along with that. So I stayed right there, we talked more about the office and I never did get up to Bill Wurster's third floor office that day. I had, however, truly started my professional career in the San Francisco Bay Area.

In 1945, there were only about 11 million people in the entire state, and about 700,000 in and around San Francisco. The city felt like a small but sophisticated town. Ever since the gold rush it had been the recipient of a continuous parade of newcomers—East Coasters, Italians, Irish, Chinese. Perhaps that is why we found it to be so extremely friendly. We felt warmly welcomed, and, no doubt as a result of Tommy's social status, we quickly received a dinner invitation from Jean Macaulay, an elderly aristocratic lady with a large house on Russian Hill. Jean had a strong, politically liberal point of view and her husband, whom we called

7

Beginning My Career

"Captain" Macaulay, had been captain of a luxury liner. His greatest achievement was that he had taken President Wilson across the Atlantic after the World War I armistice to work on building an enduring peace. After we were accepted by the Macaulays, Tommy's friends began including Anna and me in many social events and we were soon regular visitors at many homes in Pacific Heights. It all seemed very natural at the time. We didn't really understand that we were being introduced to the aristocratic power center of the city.

The answer to where we would live also came to us easily. Anna's uncle Jack and aunt Helen had left Chicago and settled in Marin County, across the bay from San Francisco. Like many Orthodox Jewish immigrant families, Jack's parents were distraught when he married a non-Jewish girl, a *shiksah*. They had ostracized him from the family and as a result he and his new bride moved as far west as they could. It was good fortune for us, however, to have a relative living in the parklike community across the Golden Gate Bridge. We visited him, fell in love with the area, and found a tiny house nearby on the edge of the bay, looking south to the skyline of San Francisco. There, from the comfort of our first house, I could feel that the war was truly over, the heaviness of the past years transformed into a great outpouring of energy and excitement. The world seemed full of opportunity. I was more

than ready to start my career and I felt a great surge of excitement and hope as if doors were opening all around me. I was ready to get on with life.

On the home front, Anna and I felt like newlyweds. We were both excited about living in Marin County. It seemed like the most beautiful place we had ever seen and life seemed wonderful with one exception—Anna's career. New York was the absolute center of dance in America. That was where all the energy and excitement was for her career. New York was the theater town, a hotbed of opportunity, and a magnet for all the most talented dancers— Martha Graham, Doris Humphrey, José Limón, and others were all there.

San Francisco, in contrast, was the middle of nowhere as far as dance was concerned. There was a ballet company, but that meant nothing to Anna. There were one or two other modern dancers in the Bay Area, but there was no great dance movement and no opportunity. That was going to be a problem. Anna said she knew she would have to work hard and find a way to express herself and develop her own form of creativity.

Our house was simple—a little nine-hundred-square-foot bungalow on a one-eighth acre lot (Figure 30). It cost six thousand dollars and that was something that we could afford if we took a small mortgage. It was surrounded by lots of open space and had a nice little backyard just waiting to be designed (Figures 31, 32). *Sunset* magazine gave me a small stipend to see how I would improve the garden and I could hardly wait to get started. We had no car at first, but the bus stopped at our street and dropped me off about twenty minutes later at Tommy's office. I loved the trip over the Golden Gate Bridge and all the transitions it represented. Eventually we found a used car that we could afford and that enabled us to explore the area even further.

My time with Tommy was happy and indispensable to my becoming a practicing landscape architect. Tommy's work focused on gardens, mostly estates, south of San Francisco in an area we simply called the Peninsula. In those days, gardens were built using relatively simple plans and extremely capable contractors and craftsmen. Clients were primarily well-to-do socialite types whose large gardens were designed as places to entertain out-of-doors. These clients reminded me of the families I'd met during my days at Poly Prep and perhaps that is why I was socially comfortable with the work even though it made me somewhat uneasy. Since my years at Poly Prep I had, after all,

Figure 30

The previous owners had done nothing to improve the front or back yards at our first home in Marin County; however, the location, the climate, and the price were right.

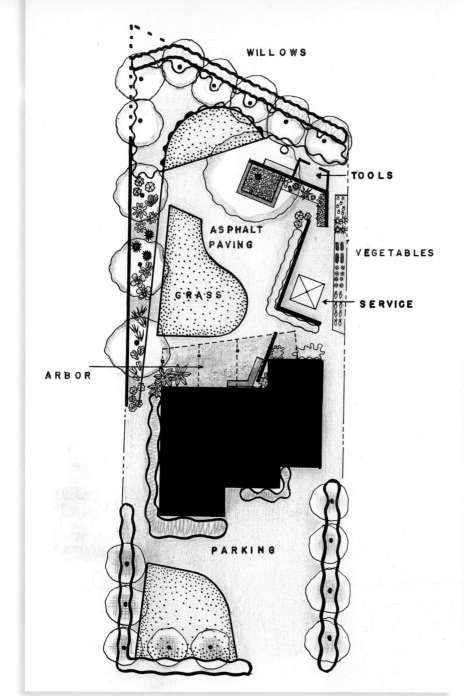

WILLOWS

TOOLS

ASPHALT
PAVING

GRASS

VEGETABLES

SERVICE

ARBOR

PARKING

Figure 31

Because of the small stipend that *Sunset* magazine offered, I was able to develop a simple, pleasant, and useful plan for our garden.

Figure 32

Anna, Daria, and I enjoyed spending time in our new garden. It expanded our lifestyle by giving us attractive and usable outdoor space.

identified myself with labor movements, Zionism, and efforts to change the political power structure in the world. Tommy, on the other hand, was apolitical and his gardens were terribly elitist.

Eventually, however, Tommy's projects became more complex. He took on a new hotel project in Panama that required more involved architectural working drawings and it was at that point that he hired George Rockrise, a young architect who had been working in New York. George showed us how to put together a good set of working drawings. Tommy, George, and I worked together on the Donnell Garden in Sonoma. It was more than a simple garden. Tommy chose a wonderful old oak tree as an orienting feature and paced off a curvilinear entry road through the wild Sonoma hillside. We laid out an organically shaped pool and I suggested adding a playful island sculpture. Tommy liked the idea and suggested his friend Adeline Kent as the perfect sculptor to design the island (Figure 33).

In most ways Tommy was an ideal mentor for me. He had traveled widely, studied the landscape movement in Scandinavia, and learned about the new urban communities there. His response to the land was intuitive and remarkably sensitive. His ability to site houses and roads at any scale was similar to that of a sculptor. He worked with the environment rather than forced it. Through

Tommy I learned about materials, what plants were appropriate to the West Coast, and how efficient constructability was as important as design. One of the most significant things I learned from Tommy, however, was about the importance of the relationship between client and designer. Tommy was a genius at that. All the way through the process he was able to maintain a creative and enjoyable relationship with his clients. They shared respect, social values, and friendships and even when there

Figure 33

Expansive views of Sonoma County were a major element in the design of the Donnell garden and pool.

were problems to face together I could see that they wanted to please Tommy.

In addition to everything else, Tommy had a remarkable ability to draw the best out of me. He encouraged my creativity and guided it to achieve solid results. He kept me motivated and focused and I felt that I was growing during all our years together. What I was lacking, though, was a true interest in designing for a socially elite client base. Because of my experiences in Israel, and specifically in the kibbutz, I wanted to expand my design potential into broader-scale community work. I wanted to break out of the "garden box" and work on large-scale projects. I wanted to expand the ideas of landscape design into new realms of social importance including architecture and art. That was why after four wonderful years with Tommy I decided to start off on my own. He understood and as a going-away present gave me a book on Chinese gardens. On the flyleaf he wrote, "To Larry, who loved me and left me."

I opened my own office in September 1949 and immediately felt a great sense of liberation and energy. I was only too aware that I had been lucky. Many of the men on my ship had not made it back. That seems to characterize how most young people felt in the years immediately after the war, the Holocaust, and Hiroshima. It was a time for us to let go of all the things that had been holding us back and face the excitement of a future that now seemed filled with endless possibilities. At the end of my apprenticeship with Tommy I suppose I felt an added drive because I was now free to make what I could of my professional life on my own terms.

I found an office space on Montgomery Street in San Francisco. It was between Gold and Jackson streets and was not far from Tommy and Bill. The elegant little brick building had character and was reputed to have been the first bank built in the city after the gold rush. I took the second floor along with Bob Marquis, a young architect friend, and a couple of avant-garde filmmakers named Frank Stauffacher and James Broughton. Bill Gilbert, a young engineer who had spent the war in the Pacific, asked if he could offer structural advice and surveying in lieu of rent. Bob and I both needed those skills so we agreed and he too came on board. Within weeks I realized that I couldn't handle all the work in the office myself so I hired Jean Walton, a truly great plant specialist who had just graduated from the University of California, Berkeley. Jean started with me as a girl Friday doing just about everything and she stayed in the office for twenty-seven years. It was a lovely, creative, and friendly group.

Soon after the opening of my office our first child, a daughter, was born on December 31, 1948.

We named her Daria (a name derived from the Hebrew word "Dar," which means "mother of pearl"). We then decided that our house was too small for our expanding family and decided to build a new one. It seems very odd now to think that at such a young age we thought we could afford to build a new house, but in those days Marin County was just being discovered and land was relatively inexpensive. The bank, however, wasn't interested in loaning money to such a young couple so Anna's father loaned us the money.

There were plenty of house sites from which to choose after the war but we had a very specific vision of what we wanted. We wanted to be close to Mount Tamalpais, a Marin icon that offered hiking trails, lakes, and redwood forests. We wanted privacy and a cul-de-sac or turnaround where our children could play safely. We also wanted a place where we might expand beyond the house and fulfill Anna's need for a dance studio on site. Finally, it would have to be something reasonably priced. It was not easy to find such a dream spot and we looked for a long time before we managed to find a place that met all of our requirements. It was a perfect four-acre site with a magnificent view of Mount Tamalpais and the bay for the very reasonable price of four thousand dollars (Figure 34). Our friend Bill Wurster agreed to be our architect and we built a barnlike house that we could add

on to as necessary (Figure 35). As work progressed on our new home, our second daughter was born and we named her Rana. In 1952 our family of four moved into our dream house and Anna and I have lived there ever since.

Anna by now had opened a dance studio on Union Street in San Francisco that she shared with Welland Lathrop, a Martha Graham dancer. As she began to teach and perform I collaborated with her, designing costumes and stage sets and contributing articles to her magazine, *Impulse* (Figures 36, 37).

As we designed and built our house we decided that it was important to move forward quickly with the development of the area where Anna could dance and perform. We did not want to put the expansion off indefinitely. The four-acre site we had found allowed us to design a place in the woods where Anna could meld her creative work with our family life. We thought that this would allow her to stay in constant touch with Daria and Rana while they were growing up.

Our site was steep and forested and its character has immeasurably affected the development of our personal and professional lives. The house was sited on an upper narrow bench with views south to the bay and west to Mount Tamalpais. I decided to choreograph the entire site as a walking sequence that meandered along an ancient logging trail through a redwood grove to a dance

Figure 34

Our hillside site in the community of Kentfield allowed us to accomplish everything on our wish list.

Figure 35

Bill Wurster and I sited the house so that it captured both bay and mountain views in almost every direction.

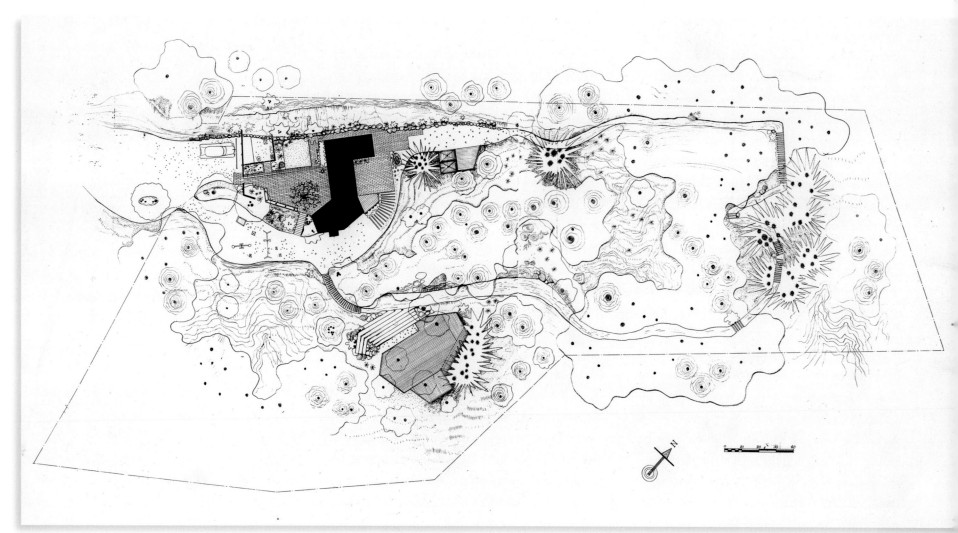

HALPRIN HOUSE

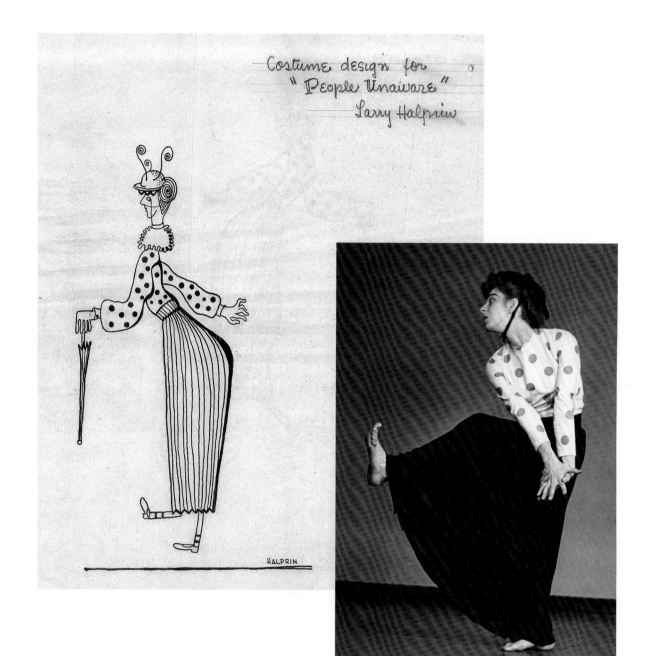

Figures 36 and 37

Anna and I collaborated a great deal during our courtship and the early days of our marriage. I made this sketch of a costume for her performance *People Unaware*. Images courtesy the Halprin family.

deck that would cantilever through the woods and float twenty-five feet above the sloping ground (Figure 38). We felt this linkage would symbolize our life—living and working, learning and growing together. The dance deck and rehearsal studio sited twenty feet below the house were designed to provide Anna with a personal creativity space that would be connected to the house by a set of stairs that climbed up to her office through an informal amphitheater of benches.

I had never before designed a stage for dance or theater, and so I invited Arch Lauterer to work with me as an adviser. Arch had worked with Martha Graham as a lighting designer and he was fortunately teaching at Mills College in Oakland. Together we designed a nonformal stage that moved around and through the existing redwoods, incorporating the great trees in the composition (Figure 39). We also included variations in the levels of the stage itself. Over the years this dance deck and the adjacent studio have induced remarkably creative and innovative dance, and with seating (that also serve as stairs up to the house) we are able to accommodate an audience of up to two hundred witnesses for performances.

When I left Tommy, my practice started in a manner that has always been somewhat typical in the architecture and landscape architecture professions. Anna's parents had come out from Chicago

to visit us when Daria was born. At first they intended to stay for only a short while and rented a house for the summer. As the months passed, however, they fell in love with the Bay Area and decided to stay and build a house of their own. This turned out to be my first major project including both site planning and architecture.

The client, my father-in-law, insisted that although they enjoyed being close to our family they wanted to live far enough away so that "we wouldn't continually be visiting each other." I, therefore, began my search for a site on the Peninsula, about an hour's drive south of San Francisco and two hours from our home in Kentfield. To me this part of the Bay Area felt somewhat like the Winnetka area north of Chicago where they had lived, and in the small town of Woodside we found just the right place. The four-acre meadow lot was not far from Stanford University and it was shaded by some magnificent old California live oaks. For my father-in-law, it had the added advantage of being close to an eighteen-hole golf course.

This site offered me a perfect opportunity to explore an idea that had been growing in my awareness. I had lived in California long enough by now to understand that the California coast was ecologically a semidesert with less than twenty inches of rain a year. Six or seven months of the year there was no rain at all, and water was, there-

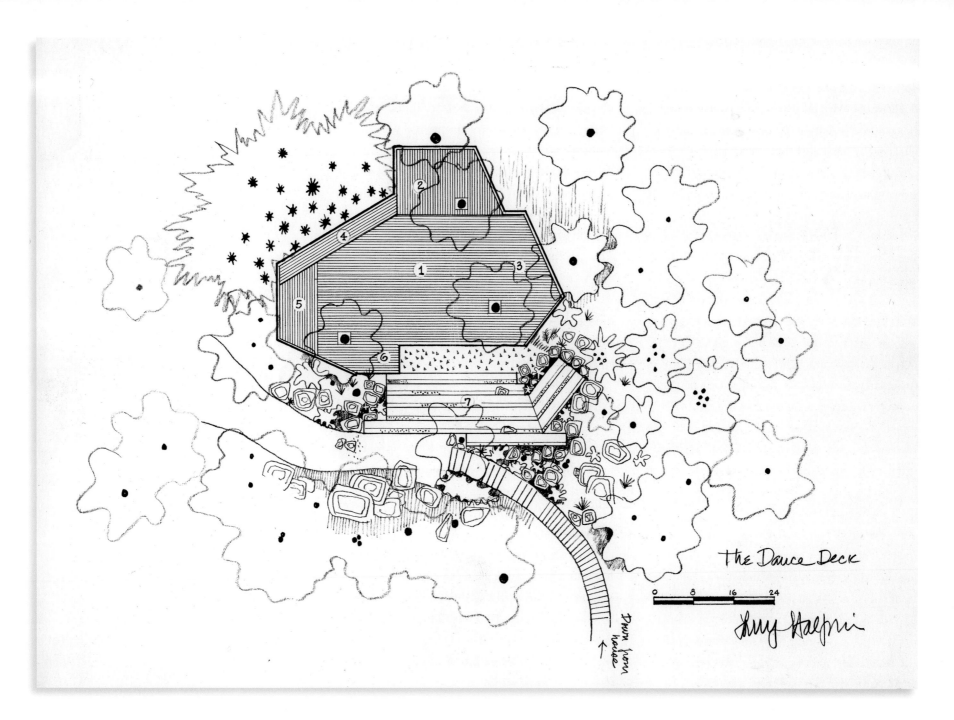

THe Dance Deck

0   8   16   24

Larry Halprin

fore, a precious commodity. Tommy's typical clients had covered their land with gardens that demanded irrigation for plantings and vast areas of lawn. Here at the Schumans' house I felt we could make a major ecological shift with a design that would accept the surrounding wild oat meadows and use them as the major enveloping theme of the design (Figure 40). I left more than half of the site in this natural state—green during the winter months and a beautiful golden tan during the dry part of the year (Figure 41). Within the great meadow we established special locations for a modest swim-

Figures 38 and 39

By building a dance deck in the redwoods below our house, we set the tone for an unusual and creative life together.

Images courtesy the Halprin family.

ming pool, a putting green, a kitchen garden, and a tan bark play area under the shade of the great oaks. Each of these intense use areas was linked by long curvilinear walkways of brown decomposed granite (Figure 42). I admittedly designed the visual shape of this choreography under the influence of the painter Miro. It was, after all, fashioned much more after the gardens of the Mediterranean than those of England. The entire extended family enjoyed the garden immensely for many years and my father-in-law especially appreciated the low maintenance it required (Figure 43).

While the Schuman house and garden were being built I grew busy designing small backyard gardens in and around San Francisco. The Bay Area climate allowed a wonderful amount of outdoor living, and there was a great demand for new houses after the years of the war. Many of the homes were designed by young architects just starting out and I was delighted to be working at that scale. The projects turned around very quickly and I was able to watch as the designs were built in short order. I often think back to those days of quick results and I think I was studying for larger designs and projects that would come later.

There were very few landscape architects in Northern California in the early fifties. Besides Tommy Church, I only recall Doug Baylis, Garrett Eckbo, and Bob Royston. This was part of the

Figure 40 *(facing page)*
This plan for the Schuman Garden was my biggest project to date and the scale and complexity gave me the desire to produce a painterly plan in the style of Miro.

Figures 41, 42, and 43
By the time I developed this plan I had already become as enamored with the golden tan summer landscape as I was with the lush meadows we enjoyed during the rainy season.

The Schumans' swimming pool was modest and it was carefully integrated into the natural terrain of the site.

Anna, the girls, and I spent many wonderful weekends and holidays with Anna's parents. The girls loved it there.

excitement of the time. We represented a new and burgeoning field and it was exhilarating to help define it as we struggled to meet the enormous pent-up demand. There was not only a need for private gardens but also for larger-scale projects such as the University of California campus in Berkeley and an enlargement of a small agricultural University of California campus in Davis. There were new hospitals for the United Mine Workers Union in Appalachia, and a large low-cost housing project in an old abandoned quarry in Richmond, California. I was also asked to work on a new type of project outside of Chicago. The concept was to pull the shopping experience out of the downtown and install it in the suburbs. The project was called Old Orchard; it was one of the first shopping centers in the country.

Suddenly, my professional world expanded well beyond my experience at Harvard and at Tommy's office. Although this is what I hoped I would be able to do, it was all happening far faster and sooner than I expected. These opportunities forced me to break new ground in areas where I had little formal experience. I was excited, delighted, and concerned because I was facing problems for which I had no ready solutions. The more I became involved in design at this large scale the more the intricacies became obvious. Campus and shopping center design, for example, required more than an ability to site new buildings. There were requirements that I had never thought of—designs for street furniture, signage, night lighting, automobile and bicycle circulation, and parking. I had to think of paving for various scales and uses, space-control elements like bollards, and mini-architecture such as bus shelters, kiosks, and restrooms. I found I needed orienting devices to show visitors how to

Figure 44

Memories from our early family tour and my first solo trip at the age of sixteen drew me back to Paris and the wonderful quality of walking by the Seine. As a young landscape artist, I studied the elements that had so greatly impressed me in my youth.

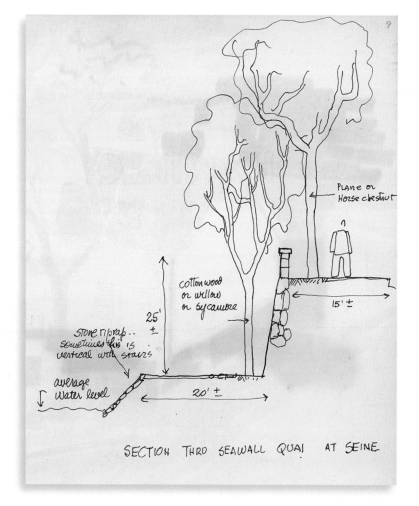

get around and sometimes sculptures or other forms of artwork to enlarge the experience. I was well aware how little I knew, but my small staff, all recent graduates, knew even less than I did.

As I thought about it I realized how little of this kind of design I had learned at Harvard. I also recognized for the first time that most American cities were extremely limited in these intricacies and memories of my trips through Europe and the Middle East came flooding back to me. The grand tour with my parents snapped into focus. I remem-bered the variety of streets and churches I had seen. I remembered the great pedestrian plazas in Italy, the Trevi Fountain, the Spanish Steps, the way the Seine was treated not just as a river but as a long beautiful walking experience through Paris (Figure 44). I realized that the great cities of Europe were role models for joyful, large-scale environmental design (Figures 45, 46, 47). They enlarged people's lives and offered far more to one's living experi-ence than did the office buildings and streets in the American cities where I had lived. I also thought

Figure 45

Broad walkways, sidewalk cafes, lively plazas, the comfort of water, open markets, and a sense of regional lifestyle and history all flooded back to me as I tried to decipher what I found so exciting and attractive during my early visits abroad.

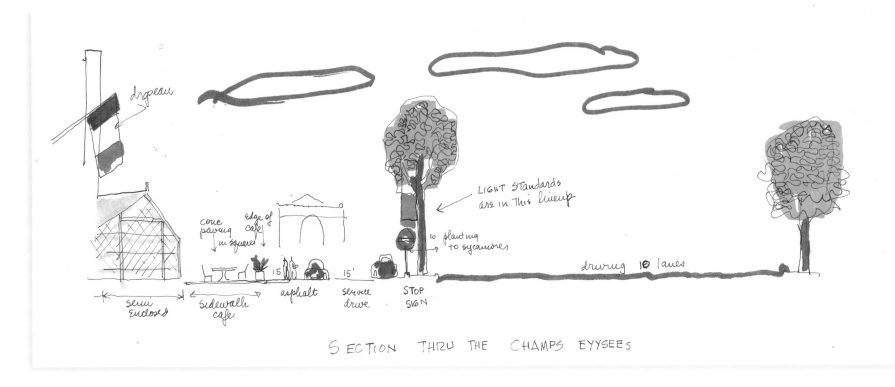

SECTION THRU THE CHAMPS EYYSEES

Figure 46

Venice
Saturday noon July 15
Grand Canal from St. George Isle.

Venice is urban & urbane & completely man-made — the LIDO area shows how
this quality can fall apart by gardens & bastardized camouflaged copies but largely
the spaces between buildings grows too big fills with green & suburbia creeps in. Venice
solved many of the problems posed by Jerusalem. it is clean there is no sense of poverty
poorness mebbe (but not poverty) & the public spaces including the great one at San Marco give
a sense of measure & tempo & place. and of course NO AUTOMOBILES. The sound is great!

Figure 47

The lights hanging from the center of the arches on the outside are apparently an afterthought -- they are crackled like Sam Hurst suggested for College of the desert & have a hole in the middle -- they look extremely well! the lights down the center do not give enuf light. The sense of movement in the square is enormous & exciting !!

Piazza San Marco - Venezia.
Friday July 14.

Figures 48 and 49

back to my time in Jerusalem and my walks in the Old City with my friend Yigael Yadin. I remembered that whenever the two of us could, we would spend our time walking through the ancient marketplace. The streets there were bustling with activity. The entire walled city of Jerusalem was like a wonderful piece of theater—a mixture of all kinds of people, all kinds of uses. It was a pedestrian city devoted to the daily lives of its people—churches, synagogues, schools, small-scale manufacturing, and shop after colorful shop. There was a cacophony of life all around (Figures 48, 49).

These memories provided a significant breakthrough for me. I suddenly saw that the solutions for these larger-scale projects was to think about and approach design in a whole new way—a way that could include a combination of many art forms, multidimensional movement through space, sound, texture, and all forms of human activity. In this new approach, elements such as street furniture or circulation patterns simply became one of many tools that I could use to develop designs that expanded daily life. I wanted to offer options and greater diversity such as I had experienced in other parts of the world. I was excited and challenged by this new awareness because now I had a vision.

On the surface my life was moving beyond my wildest expectations. Anna and I were loving partners and my small office provided remarkably interesting and challenging commissions. I realized, however, that I was constantly filled with angst. My relationship to Israel had never been resolved and I was emotionally charged with feelings of guilt. My contact with Kibbutz En Hashofeth had taken on a kind of dreamlike quality. The utopian ideals that had so intrigued me in my youth continued to haunt me. Israel had become a state in 1948 but it was still in the throes of consolidating its security and here I was in America, not really helping in a process to which I still felt committed.

On the other hand, I was American and loved my country. My roots were here, my education was here, and my attitudes were completely American. By now I had accepted the advantages of my life here. Anna lacked any deep connection to Israel so I decided that I needed to somehow maintain a relationship with Israel through my profession. In that way I hoped, I could contribute, in a vital way, to the building of the utopian state.

In the meantime, an Israeli friend had been assigned the incredibly important job of preparing a master plan for the entire physical development of the new state: land use, transportation, and community development. He had come to the United States to study development here, and spent time with me in my little office discussing planning issues. We talked at length but when he eventually returned to Israel, I felt left out. It was especially frustrating for me because I was beginning work on a series of American projects that were particularly relevant to the situation in Israel. One of these was the Easter Hill Village, a development for low-income families in Richmond, California. It was a uniquely challenging project at the time. The reason the land had become available was due to the fact that it was an old, abandoned rock quarry. The improbably difficult condition of the site and the great outcroppings of leftover granite had made it appear useless. I decided to view the site differently. Instead of trying to remove the enormous rocks, which the contractor pointed out would be excessively costly, I decided to keep them on site and use them as great sculptural elements (Figures 50, 51). I knew that this type of site difficulty was constantly cropping up in Israel (particularly in the Negev and Sinai) as they tried to locate appropriate places for the founding of kibbutzim.

The architect for the Easter Hill project was Vernon DeMars. Vernon lived in the Bay Area and was one of my heroes from the days of the Southwest Farm Security Administration projects. I had known of him back at Harvard, where we had studied his work as an example of architecture

8

The Israel Thread

that performed social functions and solved social problems. Vernon and I soon formed a lifelong friendship. Our connection was helped along by the fact that he had learned Native American dancing while in the Southwest, and he and Anna also developed a wonderful dance relationship. Vernon loved my idea about the boulders, and we talked further about ways to create communities that would be better than run-of-the-mill housing projects. Vernon had recently traveled to Scandinavia, where he had seen new communities bring a sense of joyfulness into play through the use of simple devices like porches, bright colors, open spaces, and street design.

Another project that would have been relevant for Israel was the site planning for five United Mine Workers hospitals in Appalachia. The architect, Moreland Smith, his staff, and I worked with the miners' social service worker to develop the idea that the hospitals could be perceived as community centers, and that the landscape solution for their open spaces and gardens could serve social purposes badly needed in those communities. I envisioned gardens where patients, families, and friends could meet and relax away from the crowded hospital rooms. I believed that they could act as parks for the larger community as well. The union work supported my hope that my practice would always have social relevance as well as aesthetic meaning.

Landscape architecture has always meant both to me but this emphasis was particularly important at the beginning of my professional career. It reinforced my political point of view at a time when I was forming my career ideology and encouraged me to believe that I could make a difference.

I truly enjoyed my trips to Appalachia and the discoveries I encountered there. This was a remarkable part of the country and one that I barely knew existed. On one level it was very isolated and backward but on the other hand the isolation had preserved folkways that went back to the eighteenth century and carried through into their language, songs, and dances. These cultural relics enriched the lives of the people in remarkable ways. It confirmed for me the importance of traditions and folk arts, as active ties to our cultural pasts. These ties were rapidly getting lost in American society and I realized that I had appreciated these same core values in the community life in Israel.

In 1955 a wonderful project arrived in my office. The Weizmann Institute invited me to come to Israel and develop a master plan for its scientific university campus in Rechovoth, which was a small town in the center of the country. The institute named after Chaim Weizmann, a scientist and the first president of Israel, was already the center for scientific research in Israel. This was my first trip back since the formation of the state and I was overjoyed

Figure 50

Vernon DeMars and I saw opportunity in the desolation of an old abandoned rock quarry.

Figure 51

Leaving stone outcroppings in place was cost effective and gave Easter Hill Village a unique character. It was a very solid reminder of the site's history.

Figure 52

Arab mosques and their towers dotted the hillsides and the call to prayer was a constant audio reminder of place.

with the invitation. The trip would help allay my personal anxiety over Israel and give me an opportunity to introduce Anna to a place that was dear to me. Anna had already made connections with the dance community in Tel Aviv, and she was excited about the adventure.

One of the lovely congruencies that came about during this trip was the opportunity to renew our friendship with Malkah and Alex Keynan and their children. The Keynans lived in Rechovoth, but we had met them in the San Francisco Bay Area. Malkah had been in charge of a visit that the Martha Graham Dancers made to the West Coast. We had attended the Mills College performance so that Anna could renew her acquaintance with Martha. During the intermission I heard a couple speaking in Hebrew, introduced myself, and began a lifelong friendship. On this trip we were able to visit them in Rechovoth, where Alex was in charge of a small biological institute not far from the Weizmann Institute.

University campus planning is complex and it seemed especially so for the Weizmann Institute. I found it almost impossible to balance the science requirements, the day-to-day human needs of the faculty, students, and employees, the difficulties of housing, car parking, open-space planning, and funding limitations. It was a tense and intense project and challenged me both professionally and

as a negotiator. I had to grasp the program requirements and design implications quickly and defend my intentions in Hebrew and English. I had to argue for a greenbelt area of terraces, parks, and groves around the institute.

Despite all of the adventures encountered on this trip, the memory that is most vivid after all these years was our initial landing at the Ben Gurion Airport. I had not been back to Israel for twenty years and the arrival was very emotional for me. During the flight many of the Orthodox Jews crowded the aisles, put on their *talis*, and prayed in the aisles. When we landed most of them knelt and kissed the ground. This was their ritual of return to the Holy Land. I once again felt the depth of my early utopian feelings and I was surprised by my own internal reaction. In those days, the airport terminal was an enormous open-shed-like building, and as we entered we were met by huge flocks of birds darting overhead and singing. It was a magical reception and I shed a few joyful tears.

While I was involved with my campus meetings and planning sessions, Anna took the opportunity to take the bus to Tel Aviv and meet with colleagues in the fields of dance and movement such as Moshe Feldenkris and Sarah Levy. Together they developed several workshop sessions, and I was delighted to see her start to integrate herself into Israel's creative dance and movement society.

At long last, I was also able to contact my friends at Kibbutz En Hashofeth. Having established a permanent home on the south slopes of the Emek Yisrael, they were now part of the great agricultural valley that stretched from the city of Haifa to Lake Kinnerett. This lake was well known as the headwaters of the Jordan River, which flowed south to the Dead Sea. My old friends were now very busy in their kibbutz—harvesting crops, planting trees, and establishing their buildings around an eating hall. Sarah and Shimon had married and had several young children. They were more than delighted to see me and I slipped back into the life of the kibbutz for a couple of days to visit with all of my old friends. The years dropped away and I felt like a teenager again.

Later, we discussed what had happened since I'd last seen them in 1935, and I found that my friends in the kibbutz had gone through a series of hellish experiences. Shimon had been air dropped behind the German lines during the war to help the Jews isolated in the Polish ghettos. Even more recently, during Israel's War of Independence, he had served as a general in the Israeli Army's Southern Brigade. It was he who had accepted the sword of surrender from the Egyptian general Nasser in the Battle of the Sinai. During those difficult times, the kibbutz had to defend itself, and they showed me the concrete underground defense tunnels where the children were sent to sleep at night.

During this trip I traveled up to Jerusalem for a few days. In my memory, I could picture the choreography of the route and remembered that it had the most inspiring arrival sequence of any city I had ever seen. In 1955 it was still much as I recalled—the road swirled around the flanks of the Judean hills along the old route that the British had improved. Vista after vista opened up as the car climbed slowly up to the Jerusalem plateau at a two-thousand-foot elevation. Along the way, we passed villages dating back to biblical times, mixed here and there with recent Israeli agricultural communities and kibbutzim. The hills were rounded and had been terraced since ancient days by stone walls supporting vineyards and olive groves. Arab village mosques punctured the skyline with muezzin towers (Figure 52). Along the way, the British had also built their military outposts. The experience unfolded slowly until suddenly the city of Jerusalem appeared like a mirage with its ancient walled silhouette unchanged since biblical times (Figures 53, 54). This trip, from Babel Wad to the summit, used to take about an hour and was great environmental theater—gripping not only for its beauty but also for the ineffable overtones of centuries of human history. Unfortunately much has changed since 1955. The road has been leveled and widened so that now cars speed up to Jerusalem in half the time. Traffic has increased so dramatically

Figure 53

I always had an emotional response to my first glimpse of the walls of the Old City of Jerusalem after I had been away.

march 30- 1979

looking down on - כֹּתֶל מַעֲרָבִי
the wailing wall May 30 1979

Figure 54

On my earliest visits to the Wailing Wall
in the Old City of Jerusalem, the men and
women prayed separately.

that instead of a slow, gently paced trip focused on wonderful views, the driving experience has become intensely focused on speed and the traffic that threatens on all sides.

Once in Jerusalem I had a few days to visit with old friends—particularly with Yigael Yadin. He, too, had gone through some incredible experiences. During the Israeli War of Independence he was the first commander in chief of the Israeli Army. Their resistance against the invading armies of Egypt, Jordan, Syria, and Lebanon was miraculously successful despite the fact that the Israelis were poorly equipped. After that, Yigael and his father, Eleazer Sukenik, acquired a number of the Dead Sea Scrolls, perhaps the most amazing archaeological find of our time, for the Israel National Museum.

Yigael was by now a professor at the Hebrew University and was busily at work deciphering the scrolls and documenting his discoveries. My teenage hiking buddy had become a historic figure. Our reunion was happy and exciting—I walked into the house I remembered from the old days, we gave each other a quick embrace, and then began enthusiastically slapping one another on the back.

Finally, we started to talk about what we'd been doing. Yigael told me all about the Qumran caves where the scrolls had been found and I filled him in on my days in the navy and my new projects. Together we walked into the Arab quarter to our favorite old restaurant for lunch and we sat there for hours talking over all that happened to both of us.

Coming back home to the Bay Area was a cultural shock. After the experience at the airport in Israel, the Los Angeles airport seemed crass and ugly when we stopped there to go through customs. San Francisco's airport was a bit better but I felt unsettled as we drove down to Woodside to retrieve the girls from their grandparents and then drove across the Golden Gate Bridge to our Marin County home. In Israel the sense of history, the pace of time, the linguistic cues had so quickly felt familiar. It was strange that the return home should feel jarring. The next day, at my office, I was relieved to find plenty of work to help me get grounded. In spite of having a wonderful support team of young people in the office, there was a good deal of decision making that only I could handle—it included some unhappy clients, unpaid bills, and design questions awaiting answers. I also started my report on the Weizman Institute plans.

In those early days there never seemed to be any time to catch a breath. Soon my projects grew in number and it was obvious that our space was too small. We moved the office to a larger place where Pete Walker, Don Carter, and Rich Haag joined the staff. All of us were trained as landscape architects and for a time we were able to keep our heads above water workwise. Gradually, however, the projects became more complex and included several University of California college campuses

as well as a new hospital site in Marin County. The work in Israel had also expanded to include the new Hebrew University and the Hadassah Medical Center (Figure 55). At that point Richard Vignolo joined us; he had graduated from UC Berkeley and gone on to the Harvard School of Design. Satoru Nishita also came aboard and we became a group of seven. This group carried the work for several more years, until we became eight with the addition of graphic designer Tak Yamamoto.

Around that time, I ran into serious problems on the Old Orchard shopping center project. First of all, we were behind schedule. But, what bothered me most was I did not have the expertise to arrange for contractors in Chicago to carry out the work. In addition I had begun to realize that a new project of this scale required trees of a major size in order to sustain the aesthetic character when it opened. I realized that I was in way over my head. Fortunately the architect Jerry Loebl (whose firm was already established in Chicago) became a sort of "how-to-do-it" mentor for me. He agreed to introduce me to the best landscape contractor in the Chicago area, who in turn took me to the best large-scale nursery in the region. I was relieved but at the same time aware that two other difficult issues remained. One was that to make our schedule I had to leave San Francisco and spend time in Chicago and the second was financial.

9
Growing Pains

This was my first major financial challenge. Largely through lack of experience, I had signed a contract that was laughably low for the work we had to do in the office. If we continued the way we were going, we could soon be bankrupt. The project was important and needed all the attention we could give. I felt terrible and was unable to sleep at night. I didn't know what to do. Finally, I called Phil Klutznick, my Chicago client, asked for a meeting, and made my flight arrangements.

Preparing for that meeting was one of the more difficult experiences in my professional life. On the plane, I rehearsed what I was going to say. When the time came I knocked on Phil's door and walked in. I must have looked pale, because he asked me to sit down and startled me by saying, "You're having financial troubles, aren't you Larry." I gasped and burst out with the truth, telling him that my fee was too low and I had already used it up. He was very amiable and soft-spoken when he said, "I rather

Figure 55

I was pleased with this design for the main entrance to Hadassah Hospital.

thought that your fee was too low, but you are doing a really great job, and I want to help. How much do you need to make you whole?" I was thunderstruck. I thought for a moment and then said that twenty-five thousand dollars would help a lot. Phil said, "Okay, that will be fine, keep doing a good job and enjoy your stay in Chicago." I was speechless. That was the remarkable way we solved the Old Orchard financial problem and Phil Klutznik became a friend as well as a client from then on.

The Old Orchard money, however, didn't resolve all of my problems. I still had too much work, and while my staff was wonderfully able on a creative level, they were completely lacking in administrative or managerial skills (Figure 56). In those areas, everything fell on my rather inadequate shoulders. Looking back to Tommy's office for management solutions did no good at all since his practice was very personal. It seems to me that his garden contracts were essentially based on a

Figure 56

From left, Don Carter, Jean Walton, Lawrence Halprin, Richard Vignola, and Rich Haag at work in 1959.

Figure 57

This sketch reflects how I felt on entering the hospital in August 1955.

handshake. So I was in a boat without a paddle, as we used to say. From the business management perspective, things continued to get worse. The University of California at Berkeley asked me to start a master plan for their expanding campus. Clark Kerr was the new president and he was a forward-looking visionary and a wonderful client. I wanted to extend myself in every way for his project and I wondered how I would deal with all the pressure that was building in the office.

I think this was when I began to have an emotional breakdown. In the middle of the night I would wake up shaking, unable to control my tremors. I was short tempered with the girls. Driving home in the car became a trial every evening because my nerves were shot. Ever since the war I had suffered from bad dreams and perhaps nowadays they would call my condition posttraumatic stress syndrome or an anxiety attack (Figure 57). In those days, however, most people had no experience with psychological problems. I was scared by all of this and while Anna was supportive she didn't know what to do except to talk to our family doctor, Marty Griffin. Marty recommended a psychologist; the visit was completely useless. He gave me a Rorschach test and I had no idea what that was supposed to prove. I remained worried and unimproved.

Meanwhile, of course, I had to keep the office afloat and moving ahead creatively on our many wonderful projects. We were continually breaking new ground in everything that we were doing and I knew that none of us had adequate background. Still when I was in the office everything was okay; it was when I had to go out for meetings or conferences with clients that I became anxious and unnerved. Marty Griffin finally convinced me to take some time off and put me in the hospital for a week on some type of tranquilizer. After that Anna and I went off to the Big Sur for a rest. I was in the throes of what they called a nervous breakdown in those days, and I thought that the only person who could help me was going to be myself.

Not long after our Big Sur trip, however, Anna realized that one of her friends and a member of her dance group was married to a well-known Jungian psychoanalyst named Joseph Henderson. I was introduced to Dr. Henderson and in a friendly way he asked if I'd ever been up to the Sierra Nevada, a mountain range in eastern California. When I explained I had passed through but not spent much time there he suggested I join the Sierra Club. He told me that the Sierra Club led group camping trips, and that image appealed to me right away. At the time Daria was seven years old and I thought it might be great if she and I could go up to the Sierra together. If it worked out well I thought Rana would be able to join us in a few years when she turned seven. That is how I was introduced to one of my most life-changing experiences.

My very first trip up to the high Sierra was extremely rewarding. Daria and I took off for three weeks. The four-hour drive across the constantly shifting landscape of the state provided time for decompression and transition as we drove through ever-smaller cities and towns. I would get caught up in the pastoral views of the great San Joaquin Valley and then the terrain would dramatically change to rolling foothills with wonderful stands of oak and rock outcroppings. Finally we climbed to the entrance of Yosemite National Park and met up with the Sierra Club group in Yosemite Valley. By the time I'd spent my first night in a sleeping bag I was already feeling much better.

Psychologically, that trip and many that followed helped me enormously. I was able to put aside my daily worries in a stress-free environment and use up nervous energy hiking and climbing. The Sierra Club group community shared cooking and child-care duties that allowed me to have enjoyable time with the girls as well as free time to myself. The Sierra experiences, however, provided much more than an emotional refuge. The powerful yet refined order of nature opened up a vast aesthetic territory that transformed my basic approach to design. Up in the high Sierra, above the timberline, I climbed mountains over ten thousand feet

high and scrambled across naked granite domes unlike anything I'd ever imagined. I witnessed the natural elements at work and made sketches of the lessons they presented in order to internalize them. In those magnificent surroundings I felt open and vulnerable (Figure 58). I became sensitized to nature on a very deep level and carried this new appreciation back to Marin County and on to other natural areas I visited. Daria and Rana made new friends with the children they met on these

Figure 58

The remarkable quality of the high Sierra experience took my mind off of my problems and gave me a new sense of freedom.

Figure 59

Sitting on a boulder above the timberline, I felt a true connection to the earth and took my time capturing my feelings in sketch form.

trips; we hiked, climbed, and swam together and sometimes we'd rest quietly for hours on the edges of lakes so deep and blue they seemed bottomless. I shared a long series of summer trips with the girls and the privilege of spending a month in the mountains with them each summer was priceless. I treasure those memories (Figure 59).

An added benefit of our summer trips was that Anna was pleased with them as well. She liked the idea that I would spend focused time with the girls. And after spending a major portion of her days with the kids in a dance cooperative, she found she needed time to stretch professionally. She was becoming increasingly involved with teaching intensive sessions where participants would spend long days and continue into the evenings searching and experimenting with new ideas about dance. Anna already had students contacting her from around the world and she wanted to invite them for month-long sessions. Using the Bauhaus vernacular, she called these month-long intensives "workshops." Over the years these workshops evolved into a major creative force, not only in the field of dance but in my profession as well for they led me into developing the RSVP Cycles.

I also found that the administrative needs and the pressure of finances which had seemed so overwhelming and stifling in the office seemed much less so when I returned from the mountains. By seeping into my deepest consciousness the power of natural processes began affecting my approach to everything. I slowed down and began to actively analyze my life situations and restore some balance in myself. Eventually the high country experiences and lessons on how things evolve teamed up with the RSVP Cycles and led me to form new

Bishop Pass
from chocolate peak
aug '62

ways to be both more creative and organizationally effective.

During this whole period Joe Henderson's presence continued to help me a great deal. I appreciated his deep understanding of my commitment to my art. Perhaps more important, I realized that Joe had a unique knowledge of the artistic process and its psychological relationship to deeper human needs. Gradually we came to the conclusion that I would come to him once a week as an advisor. I felt that we had shifted our relationship from doctor/patient to colleague/consultant, but as the years passed, I came to understand that Joe was a truly great Jungian psychotherapist and that I was, in fact, in psychotherapy. Mostly, we worked with dreams and dream analysis. Joe taught me to wake up and record my dreams. I would write them down or make drawings and later, as we discussed the content of each dream, I saw how much I used them to vent my feelings and solve specific problems—both personal and professional. Perhaps the most important insights I gained under Joe's tutelage have been those that link our modern lives to the experiences of people in primitive times. This is an understanding he derived from his own work with Carl Jung. It involves modern psychology and anthropology and results in the recognition of the importance of archetypal images, which have no antecedents and emerge from the unconscious. I believe this recognition of our shared needs and symbols has brought an underlying universal quality to my designs.

Although I may never be completely over some sense of anxiety, after time in the Sierra, I was always prepared to get back to work and take on new projects. I was especially pleased to receive important new commissions in Israel. The projects there were always unique and reinforced my physical connection since I needed to travel there often. My next Israeli project was Givat Ram, the new campus for the Hebrew University in Jerusalem. When I arrived there in 1957 I found that the city was moving its cultural center westward away from its historic core. This was largely because the Jordanians had occupied the eastern slopes since the Israeli War of Independence.

The campus was already under construction, and there was a division of opinion within the Israeli planning team as to how the central core of the campus was to be designed. My assignment was to resolve the division of opinion and then with the architects and planners create a design that would carry it out. The initial question was whether the entrance plaza should stand alone, and not relate to the rest of the campus, or should be linked to the university library, which stood by itself in an important axial relationship. I felt there was no question that the two central parts of the campus should be linked together. A broad, low set of steps could easily accomplish this by differentiating the entrance plaza and providing a generous entry experience to the entire campus. I imagined a distinguished fountain feature and perhaps a biblical sculpture. This would be easy to design as well as to construct. During the initial design meeting I made a simple diagram to explain the solution and left our session feeling I had made my point. I went off to reconnect with friends feelings I had made a good beginning with my colleagues and sank into the warm, comfortable feeling of my reunion.

The next day I found that my solution for the entry plaza had not been well received. The project manager pointed out that the campus architects were all opposed to my suggestion. Their idea was that there should be one great paved plaza and they had started to design it with no difference between the parts. I argued that this would result in a vast paved public space as big as an American football field. Although it would be big enough for events for thousands of people, it would be barren, without any shade, and would feel inhuman when it wasn't occupied by a large group. I also pointed out that there would be no inherent relationship to its context in the ancient city of Jerusalem. I realized that the architects had been mightily influenced by the cubism of the Bauhaus and that the library building design was derived from modern archi-

tectural examples. The plaza idea itself was derived from the new University of Mexico plan. I, on the other hand, was trying to create a design more in scale with the site and with the probable needs of a smaller student body. I wanted a plaza that would express the quality of being rooted in Jerusalem—not somewhere else in the world.

In retrospect, I realize that this was just an example of a particular landscape design conflict I kept encountering at the beginning of my career. How could I fulfill the modern sense of aesthetics in art and also remain expressive of each place—its people, culture, and the character of its surroundings? I did not necessarily want to introduce naturalism but I needed to evoke the sense of what would feel appropriate. This is a struggle I have wrestled with all my life. Somehow at the Givat Ram campus I was successful. I convinced the architects of my point of view and the campus was built on that philosophy. It was an important success for me and I have always enjoyed revisiting that campus (Figure 60).

Although by now the office had spread its wings to my primary interest of larger public works, I had continued to accept a series of private gardens. With the constant pressures of running a growing office I found them increasingly difficult. Relationships are extremely personal with garden clients and they are fraught with psychological overtones and hidden agendas. Everyone has extremely intense feelings about their own home and garden because they reflect not only who people are but also who they want to become. All garden clients wanted my personal attention, at all times—never mind that I had other projects. Private-garden projects inevitably revealed any basic dichotomies between husbands and wives and these often became more and more obvious as the design moved forward. Sometimes the conflicts led to compromise and more closeness, but often they led to stalemate and divorce. I was growing weary of such encounters.

Figure 60

At the Hebrew University I was able to break up the entrance plaza with a stone paving pattern, a reflecting pool, and a flight of steps to a second, less formal level.

Figure 61

The long runnel at the McIntyre garden was purposely hidden by a low wall. The sound of the water was what drew visitors toward this surprising niche.

I remember one strange experience in particular because it surfaced early. One day a woman called and explained how much she had admired my gardens. She described her house and said that it lacked adequate out-of-door space—would I please come over soon to take a look at the site and discuss how to proceed? We made an appointment for me to come by her house the next week. I arrived, knocked on the front door, and a man, obviously her husband, answered the door. "Good morning," I said, "I'm Larry Halprin, a landscape architect. Your wife asked me to stop by to discuss your garden." At this point I stuck out my hand. He pushed my hand aside and began to shout, "You can get the hell out of here right now you son of a bitch. I don't need any goddamn landscape architect." And then he slammed the door in my face. I was stunned and made a quick retreat. It made a strong impression—one does not ever want to get caught in the cross fire between husband and wife.

Despite all of this, part of me still enjoyed the small-scale gardens. I was already learning that large public projects could go on for years and it was a real pleasure to work on a project that could finish quickly. I also knew that gardens were a wonderful testing ground for details and a great learning experience for how things are constructed. When gardens were successful they provided great personal joy and led me to some interesting discoveries and remarkable friendships.

During this period there was one major garden commission that really shifted my point of view, the McIntyre Garden. The McIntyres had hired Joe Esherick as their architect and selected me to do the garden. They immediately stated that they loved Spain and Spanish gardens and hoped that I did as well. They said they loved the hard geometric forms and the use of water as a major element. The McIntyre site was unusual. It was in effect a rectangle formed by linear plantings of seventy- to eighty-foot-tall eucalyptus trees on both of the long sides of the rectangle. Within the rectangle was a long tilted plane of meadow grass. It provided an existing frame as if for an abstract painting. I decided to strengthen this quality and fill the frame with simple rectangular shapes and a long thin runnel of water splashing down into a square pond. This was all to be enhanced by a seven-foot-tall retaining wall along the back of the meadow. All of these abstract levels were made of concrete. I choreographed the space by developing a low wall that hid the water runnel, which you could hear but not see, until you walked around and into the space. It didn't look like a Spanish garden, but it felt like one in its manipulation of the spaces. I enhanced the feel with a few plants in the gray range—olive trees, lavender, and rosemary. They were all Mediterranean in shape, color, and smell. The garden as a whole felt like a four-dimensional piece of sculpture. In its own way the McIntyre garden expressed a regional California character. It was oasis-like and was very low maintenance as it had no lawns and required no irrigation. Joe and I worked closely with the clients, and they loved the result. This garden broke new design ground and pointed me into new directions for future public spaces (Figure 61).

Meanwhile the office continued to grow and changed somewhat in character. At long last I had found in Jerry Rubin a person who I felt provided all the competencies that our design group lacked. His background was landscape construction and that included business experience and know-how. He moved right in and began straightening us out administratively and financially. Not only was Jerry an organizer, he was also a "peacenik." He knew Igal Roodenko, my old college roommate from Cornell. All of this gave me great confidence in Jerry and enabled me to trust him right off the bat. I felt a great sense of relief.

Another weakness that had tormented me for a long time was our inexperience in structural construction drawings. As our projects expanded, my staff's inability to work with architects on an equal basis was even more worrisome to me. Though I was not trained as an architect, my experiences at Harvard with both classmates and faculty gave me a very strong grounding in architectural design and I spoke the language. My employees, however, were

Figure 62

Over the years, Ian McHarg provided my office with numerous well-trained students. We both enjoyed the symbiotic relationship.

Figure 63

Jacques Overhoff's art wall provided privacy for the apartment units as well as a backdrop for my fountain.

not as prepared; they were more traditionally trained landscape architects and lacked a strong grounding in engineering and construction. I believed our profession had great potential and we needed to expand our training and be prepared for entering a greater arena of planning and design.

In casting around for a solution, I found that Ian McHarg, a new professor at the University of Pennsylvania, had initiated courses in ecological theory and practice. These were brand new at the time, and in order to fill these classes with interesting students he had thrown out a wider net than most landscape programs. Ian was a Scotsman, and his best contacts were in England, where he offered scholarships to graduates of the architectural schools. Then Ian overlaid their previous training with his new approaches to landscape architecture. This was just what I was looking for so we set up sort of an interactive partnership. Ian asked me to come give some lectures at Penn and I stayed there for several weeks. I wanted employees with more architectural background and he wanted to find jobs for his best students. For many years Ian filled my office with young architects with training in landscape architecture. As a result of all this Ian and I became close professional allies and good friends (Figure 62).

I found I was beginning to enjoy myself more and more. Most of my anxieties and psychological stresses were fading away as our growing office became more capable and varied. A number of important staff members joined during this period. An Israeli, Aryeh Dvir, joined us to help with the work in Israel. Sue Yung Li came on board from Harvard. She had traveled a great deal, had an expansive interest in the arts, and brought us a wider view of the world beyond landscape architecture. And finally we hired an authentic secretary, Leslie Shenk, who released us all from some daily administration tasks. There were now thirteen people with an interesting mix of backgrounds, talents, and abilities.

In 1957, when I became a member of Seattle's World's Fairground Commission, I found myself on a team with Paul Thiry, Perry Johansson, Charles Eames, Minori Yamasaki, and Eero Saarinen. We were also doing some early urban housing in Sacramento with architects Edward Larrabee Barnes and Bill Wurster. I was now working closely with some world-class architects and I was getting a great deal of experience. I designed my first urban plaza at the center of the Sacramento project, and brought in the sculptor Jacques Overhoff to work on an enclosing cast concrete wall. I was developing street details for these larger commissions and I was learning about graphics from the great graphic designer Saul Bass, who was collaborating on some of these projects (Figure 63).

At this point, Anna's dance group was also expanding and becoming multidisciplinary

through collaborations with poets (James Broughton, Richard Brautigan, Michael McClure) sculptors (Charles Ross, Bob Morris), and musicians (Luciano Berio, Terry Riley, Lamonte Young, and Morton Subotnick). Members of my office would participate at times as well so architectural design was also represented in the collaborations. These artists produced a series of profoundly interesting and innovative events. They were exploring a new and vital art form. It was at this point that Anna changed the name of her studio to San Francisco Dancers' Workshop. We used the dance deck that I had built for her as a major venue for experimentation. It was all very wonderful and exciting. I guess we were subconsciously getting prepared for the sixties.

During this period the office was full of high energy, boundless enthusiasm, high spirits, and an eager search for new ways of doing things! It was wonderful to bring new talents together to solve the unique problems we were tackling and evolve innovative designs for our clients. We worked symbiotically, synergistically, and felt ourselves stretching with every new project that came in the door. I had a sound creative team behind me.

Then in 1959, Jack Warnecke, my old housemate from Harvard, asked me to join with him on an unusual project. The Navajo Nation needed a master plan for their headquarters in Window

Rock. They wanted a plan that would help guide their growth and development, not only in the central community of Window Rock but for the outlying areas as well. For us this project presented a new cultural challenge and a typical city plan would not be appropriate. I was excited about the idea not only because it opened up a new design challenge for me but also because Anna was beside herself with excitement. As a teenager she had traveled through the Southwest with her parents, and had been captivated by the Native American culture—the way they integrate dance, costume, music, art, and architecture into the very fabric of their lives. This creative combination of art forms in all aspects of life was what we intended for our lives as well.

Our first day in Window Rock was remarkable because we were immediately taken to a pow-wow that seemed to include everyone in the tribe. I had never experienced anything like it. Here in the middle of the twentieth century it seemed the tribe remained much as it had for hundreds of years. Their traditional dress, dancing, and drumming were intact. They largely spoke Navajo to one another and I was told that many of the outlying people didn't speak English. While pickup trucks were the main mode of transportation, horses were still ridden. What was most difficult for me as I tried to gather information was that, except for the tribal chief and his assistants, no one wanted to talk to us. The only other place we could interact at all with members of the tribe was at the tiny roadside museum shop.

I was drawn to this exotic culture and colorful landscape. Everything about it was new and fascinating yet on some level it reminded me of my experiences with the Bedouins in the Sinai. I felt very comfortable in this tribal atmosphere in the desert but I quickly realized that it was going to take a very long time to understand their way of life. Their decision making was particularly confusing to me because it seemed so very different from any other form I'd ever experienced. In the Navajo meetings, for example, everyone very carefully spoke in turn. They did not interrupt one another. It was very difficult to discern whether any conclusions were being reached. They simply quietly discussed issues for a very long time and then stopped. I sensed that I had a lot to learn from them.

Jack and I visited many sites in and around Window Rock where we thought there were possibilities for the proposed tribal center. I also traveled throughout the reservation as much as I could, studying the superb land formations and the native plant species. By the time my work was finished I knew I would return.

Exciting as life and work was at this point, I soon began to gnaw on a very different kind of problem. It had to do with the nature of my personal design process and my role in the office. I am deeply enmeshed in design—it is after all my primary concern and the ultimate reason I am a landscape architect. I always believed in the value of teams, enjoyed the camaraderie of working closely with members of my staff, and sometimes enjoyed mentoring, but when it gets right down to it I always ultimately want our projects to reflect my design and my way of doing things. I have always wanted to deal with every aspect of the design process, from nuts and bolts to large-scale issues, from planning through construction.

In the early days of the office, my way of doing things had always been clear to the staff, most of whom had started out with me as soon as they left UC Berkeley. The newer folks, however, coming in from Harvard and the University of Pennsylvania, had often worked in other offices and they did not arrive with this assumption. The problem was growing, as the projects got larger and more complex—particularly when I was away on more and longer trips. In addition, we were beginning to collaborate with large architectural offices. Their procedures further undermined my established pattern. Although I would start out working with the principal, as a project moved on they would delegate ever more day-to-day responsibilities to project managers, and my staff would get used to working directly with their staff. I did not want to relinquish any design decisions and I tried a number of ways of confronting this issue but for the most part I was just trying to handle it by keeping a close eye on every design and challenging changes. It required working longer hours and stretching out the time I spent in the office.

Finally I realized that I just didn't have enough time and would need to control the projects by focusing more of my energies on working intently with the client and primary design architect on each project even if it meant some shake-ups and hurt feelings in my office when I had work redone. It was, however, much more easily said than done because I could not walk by a drafting board without wanting to review every line that was being drawn.

As the country entered the sixties a new energy and outlook emerged, and it gained strength as the sons and daughters of my generation came into their own. The San Francisco Bay Area was often at the center of that energetic upsurge, and it was sometimes expressed by sit-ins, marches, and demonstrations. The shift was strongly reflective of what was happening in the country and Anna and I both felt its impact in our lives (Figure 64). We were stretching beyond the classical images of our professions and were trying to become more holistically involved as we reached out to include multiple art forms in our lives and careers. In all of our efforts and experiments with design, dance, film, and movement in the landscape we were constantly reaching out to young people and new experiences (Figure 65).

I had all but stopped working on private gardens. I wanted to focus on community life and ways of incorporating democratic social living patterns into the design of housing and large public spaces where people came together. In addition to the emotional demands of garden clients I had also begun to feel that they often represented a form of social egotism. My image of the kibbutz as an organic result of communal living kept gnawing at me. In 1960, architect Bob Marquis and I worked together on a housing project for the International Longshoremen's Union in San Francisco. The master plan involved an innovative move for a U.S. housing project. We turned the housing inward, away from parking and the street, so that community life could be quiet and available for families and children. This approach was very different from what was being done at that time. The union community also developed a cooperative way of managing the housing. The project, called St. Francis Square, followed a European model more than anything. It worked extremely well and I felt good about this as a new direction.

In 1961, a trip to Israel gave me even more fuel for my shifting interests. Daria was now twelve years old, and Anna and I thought it would be good for all of us if I could take Daria with me to Israel. In response to the important memories I carried of my own youthful trip, I decided to model it after my grand tour with stops in Paris, Rome, Venice, and Greece. I hoped it would give Daria an appreciation for other cultures and their great cities. I looked forward to having this time with my daughter and felt it would give her some insight into her father and his career. It would also, of course, give her an opportunity to visit Jerusalem. In my mind I envisioned a trip that would lay a foundation for years of discussion.

The trip was not at all what I expected. I had been imagining that it would be similar to our easygoing outdoor adventures in the Sierra where

10
The Rebellious Sixties

Figure 64

In the sixties, San Francisco was at the forefront of fashion. Boots, beads, beards, afros, bell-bottoms, and bright colors were all part of the look.

Image courtesy the Halprin family.

other Sierra Club adults helped to keep an eye on the kids. I had also envisioned my own early impressions of exotic city life in Europe as well as the utopian idealism I had personally experienced on the kibbutz. I expected this trip with Daria to mirror those experiences but I soon found I was traveling with a young woman coming into her own, and filled with her own ideas. In the cities of Europe I found myself keeping a parentally concerned eye on Daria and we had a few angry eruptions. During one such event in Venice Daria threw our room keys off the balcony and into the canal. I began to realize that this trip would not be a rerun of any others.

When we finally arrived in Jerusalem Daria and I spent a few wonderful days in the Old City together retracing my favorite walks. One day we entered the Jaffa Gate and strolled along David Street and down through the marketplaces and shops to the Wailing Wall and the plaza near the Mosque of Omar. Another day we started at the Lion Gate and climbed the stairs to the walkways that followed the top of the city wall. As we walked I explained the history of the ancient wall and recounted how many times it had been destroyed and rebuilt since King Solomon's time. I told her about the Crusader period and Richard the Lionhearted. I have never tired of walking through the Old City and recapturing the upwelling of emo-

tion I've always felt there. When it came time for me to buckle down to work on my professional projects, I called my old friend Sarah at Kibbutz En Hashofeth. She was excited to hear that we were in Israel and invited Daria to stay there. We arrived on Shabath and after lots of hugs and catch-up conversation, Sarah told us Daria could stay in the children's village with kids her own age. We all agreed that Daria would stay a week and I went back to Jerusalem relieved that Daria was in such good hands.

When I returned the following week I found that Daria's experience and reactions were much different than mine and I turned to my friend Yona Yanai, head of the kibbutz school system, to help me answer all her questions. He was delighted with the challenge and I sat in with them, making entries in my notebook as the interview unfolded. Daria questioned everything from the women's lack of makeup and the treatment of domestic animals to the uneasy feelings she sensed between the members of the kibbutz and the Arabs who lived and worked in the nearby village. Daria's questions were remarkably to the point and she did not readily accept Yona's answers. The experience caused me to think a great deal not only about my own experience in the kibbutz but also about Israel in general. It punctured a bit of my romanticism from years before when I had been a vulnerable teenager, overflowing with a youthful infatuation for the kibbutz life. I was reminded of a time when my mother and others in the Zionist movement had supported a two-nation state for Israel. At that time they felt it could overcome the issue of the Palestinian Arabs wanting their own country and the tension this created in parts of the Arab world. Despite these concerns, my overall support of Israel as a state for the Jews, a haven for Holocaust survivors and oppressed Jews, remained strong; so too, however, did my dream of a utopian democratic community that included a state for the Palestinians. I carried all of these thoughts back home with me but as we landed at the Los Angeles airport I was once again pulled from my philosophical reveries by a blast of culture shock. That ugly airport once again reminded me of the problems I had to tackle at home.

The Sea Ranch

Soon after I got back to the office I received a call from Al Boeke, a project manager from Oceanic Properties, regarding a ranch site on the California coast about a hundred miles north of San Francisco. The Del Mar Ranch turned out to be not far from a cabin where my family often spent summer weekends with Professor Punk Vaughan, chairman of the department of landscape architecture at UC Berkeley. We all knew and loved this wild coast where we had camped, climbed rocks, and gone fishing. I was delighted to find myself driving about twenty miles farther north with Al Boeke to see what eventually turned out to be one of the most exciting sites and projects of my professional career.

At first blush, Oceanic's idea seemed simple enough. Boeke explained that they were thinking about the possibility of a second-home development. I thought of it as a north coast version of the Big Sur. The Del Mar Ranch was ten miles long and quite narrow, stretching from the Pacific Ocean to the Gualala River, which flows along the San Andreas Fault. The ranch was not much more than a mile wide on average. At the north end the river swung westward to the ocean and on the other side was the small town of Gualala. There were many fishermen living in the area as well as loggers, who harvested the pines and redwoods on the heavily timbered hillsides. The ranch belonged to the Ohlsen family, who grazed cattle and sheep. Earlier farmers had grown artichokes, which thrived in the foggy climate. To control the northwest winds early settlers had planted hedgerows of Monterey cypress that had grown fifty to sixty feet high.

Al Boeke and I drove up that Highway 1 coastline many times. We would turn onto the ranch, park, and get out to discuss whatever it was we were going to try to achieve on that particular trip. These discussions would last only a few minutes

Figure 65

The high-energy film *Bullitt* was shot in San Francisco. My office became a set location and I was told it would take one day. Although I enjoyed meeting the ultra-cool Steve McQueen, my office was disrupted for at least a week.

The Rebellious Sixties

before we would be seriously distracted by the fierce winds from the northwest. Out in the vast meadows we were unprotected and soon learned to hide behind our cars or more effectively to park in the lee of one of the long cypress hedgerows. The hedgerows helped a great deal and I quickly determined their importance for any community we might build here. We would have to set the houses in relationship to the existing hedgerows and plant new ones to protect future development.

The more we studied the site the more we realized that its stunning location, perched for ten miles along the cliffs, also implied great difficulties (Figure 66). My early experiences on the site forced me to face the need to start the planning with a wide range of studies. Beyond the wind patterns we also needed weather patterns, soil types, precipitation amounts. Fortunately, Dick Reynolds, a young geographer from UC Berkeley, had recently joined our staff to fill just such a niche and I was able to introduce him to Boeke at the beginning of our process. It was unusual at that time to request such specific studies, and the term ecology was not yet part of a developer's vernacular. The usual planning process called for civil engineers, not ecologists.

Our Sea Ranch project signaled the beginning of a very new way to plan a community. When Boeke agreed to this novel approach I became even more excited about the adventure we were embarking upon and presented a series of new ideas. Taking a cue from my experiences on the kibbutz, I felt that we should design this community for people of like minds in terms of living values as well as aesthetics. I felt we could design with a poetic attitude about the environment and cluster buildings together, not scatter them around separately on the site. The idea was to develop overall units of design, not just individual houses. It was a tough decision to ask a client to make because it might be difficult

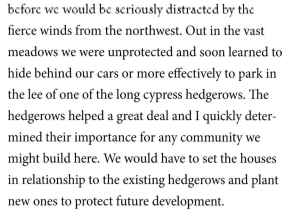

Figure 66

Looking south from the town of Gualala on my first flyover, I could see large open rooms formed by cypress hedgerows.

to sell this unusual new housing concept. Al Boeke, however, exemplified a principle I have witnessed throughout my professional life—that making incredible places required creativity on the part of the client as well as on the part of the designer.

As Boeke and I moved forward with these ideas we realized that we were developing a new type of community that linked this unique environment with a new point of view and a new architectural aesthetic. I realized that we would need very special architects to work on the planning of this community. They would have to be innovative and excited about developing new forms to relate the buildings to this dramatic site and a new form of living lightly on the land. Perhaps most important, they would have to be willing to cluster individual houses. Strong clusters were regionally appropriate in this landscape where indigenous architecture, historic Fort Ross, and rustic farm compounds had already left their mark (Figures 67, 68). As I thought about these requirements several names kept cropping up in my mind. The first name was Joe Esherick because he had greatly impressed me when I worked on the garden for his house in Kent Woodlands and later on when we worked together on the house and garden for the McIntyres. The other name was Charles Moore. When sitting on a jury for *Sunset* magazine I had fought for recognition of a unique little cabin he had designed adja-

Figure 67

Traditional Pomo roundhouses are built from the local materials and feel as if they've grown from the land.

Figure 68

On my first drive along the length of the Sea Ranch, it was obvious that the Knipp-Stengel Barn was a prominent local feature.

Clustering is not a way to get more buildings on the land & thus build up density (altho' some people want to use it that way).

It is a way to take a given amount of land and KEEP most of it open by concentrating the buildings on it in one area. Farmers have used this idea for years to KEEP as much of their land in productive agriculture.... as they could.....

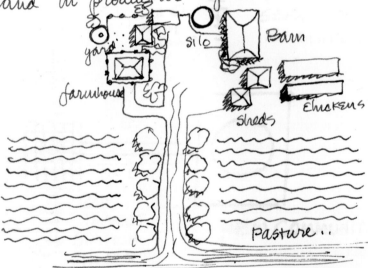

Typical American Farmhouse Cluster.

Figure 69

cent to an amazing redwood tree in the Santa Cruz Mountains. Although I had not yet met the man, I had heard he was working on innovative projects in the San Francisco Bay Area with a group of young partners. They were called Moore, Lyndon, Turnbull & Whitaker (MLTW). Al Boeke agreed to interview Esherick and MLTW as the primary architects for our new community.

I then began to focus more seriously on the basic master plan for the community. In order to really understand the atmosphere and geography of the landscape, I decided it was important to know the site intimately, so I began hiking up and down the eleven miles between the old stagecoach stop at Stewart's Point and the town of Gualala. I was able to explore all the various coves, beaches, drainage swales, and hedgerows along the way. For me this was the only way I could really envision what the community should be like when we built it. The cypress hedgerows added a unique rhythm and quality to the hikes (Figure 69). They broke the long spaces into a series of great rooms and the more I walked the more it became clear that these outdoor rooms could become neighborhood commons around which houses would share unbroken views of great beauty looking north and south along the cliffs. It also became clear that we could develop a variety of cluster types that would each be protected from the relentless wind in their own way while allowing spectacular, uninterrupted views (Figures 70, 71).

This idea for a community of clusters around commons immediately established the basic form of the Sea Ranch. The master plan unfolded as a long, thin spine starting from Stewart's Point just south of our site to the small town of Gualala (Figure 72). The plan emphasized clusters of buildings located in the lee of the hedgerows to protect them from the severe winds of the Northwest. Fences connecting the individual buildings reinforced the strength of the clusters and provided additional wind protection. The concept was in fact quite simple—based on functional protection, preservation of views, and the inherent idea of a pedestrian path along the coast passing through the great outdoor rooms of the commons (Figure 73). The idea of commons was perhaps the most unusual part of the plan and it was central to it. Commons created open space that would remain untouched and inviolate. Commons allowed all houses to preserve their view corridors. Commons provided direct access to the coves and the pedestrian corridor along the cliffs' edges for the whole length of the community (Figure 74).

In the meantime, Al Boeke had interviewed the architects I recommended and was delighted with all of them. As soon as the team was signed up they became enamored with the novel approach evident

Sea Ranch
looking South down the
coastline - aug 9-69

Figure 70

My response to hikes through the rugged
beauty of the Sea Ranch was similar to
what I felt in the high Sierra, and sketches
captured and enhanced my feelings for the
unique quality of this wild place.

Figure 71

Figure 72

The concept plan for the Sea Ranch
attempted to protect the wild, open quality
of this remote stretch of northern California
coast by keeping development out of sight
yet allowing views for all.

Sea Ranch - big beach
Aug 20 -

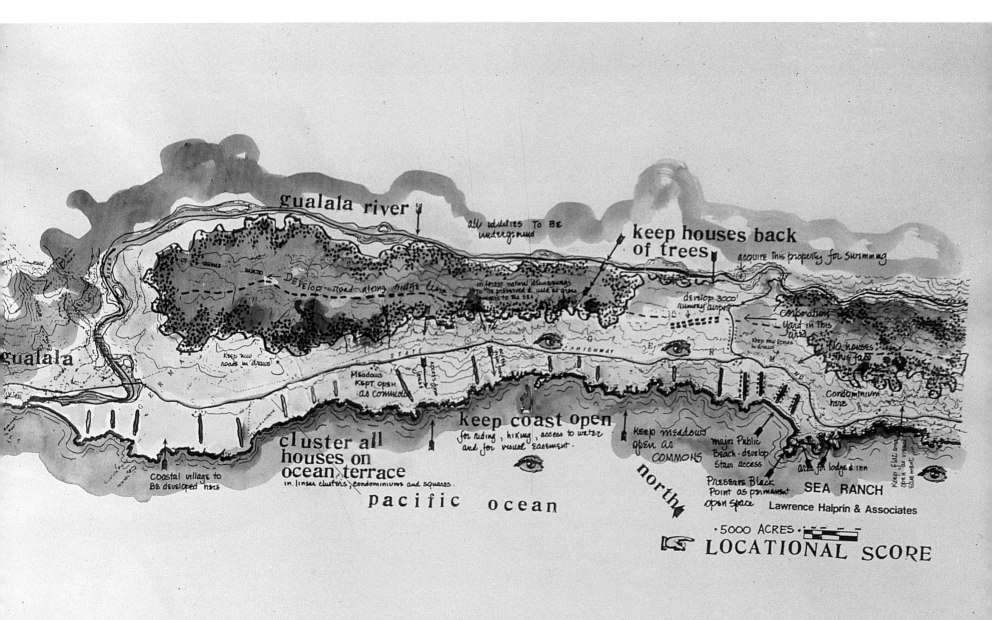

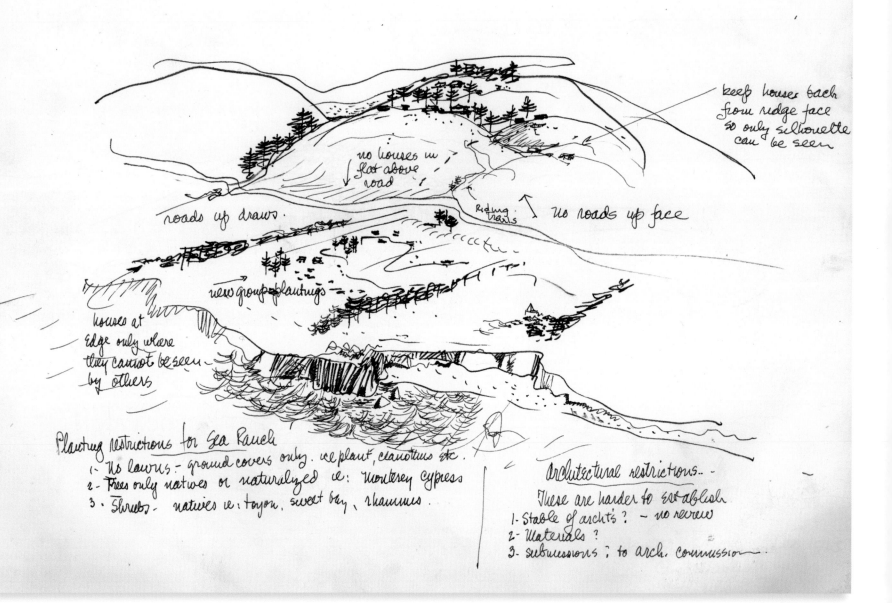

SEA RANCH   Dec. 1963

keep houses back
from ridge face
so only silhouette
can be seen

no houses in
flat above
road

roads up draws.

Riding trails   no roads up face

new group plantings

houses at
Edge only where
they cannot be seen
by others

Planting restrictions for Sea Ranch
1. No lawns - ground covers only. ice plant, ceanothus etc.
2. Trees only natives or naturalized ie: Monterey Cypress
3. Shrubs - natives ie: toyon, sweet bay, rhamnus.

Architectural restrictions -
These are harder to establish
1. Stable of archt's? - no review
2. Materials?
3. submissions; to arch. commission

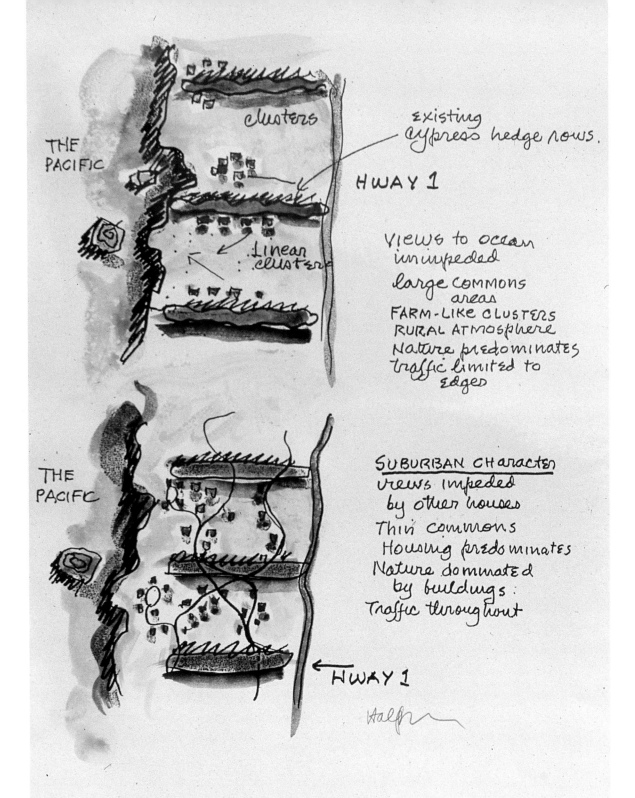

THE PACIFIC

clusters

existing
cypress hedge rows.

HWAY 1

Linear
clusters

VIEWS to ocean
unimpeded
large commons
areas
FARM-LIKE CLUSTERS
RURAL ATMOSPHERE
Nature predominates
traffic limited to
edges

THE PACIFC

SUBURBAN character
views impeded
by other houses
Thin commons
Housing predominates
Nature dominated
by buildings:
Traffic throughout

← HWAY 1

Halp

Figure 73 *(facing page)*

The essence of the basic premise was to live lightly on the land.

Figure 74

These comments from my notebook explained how I hoped to use the hedgerows and clusters to protect the views.

Figure 75

Joe Esherick wanted a private location at the westernmost end of a hedgerow.

Figure 76

Charles Moore was outgoing and gregarious and enjoyed sharing the courtyard at his condominium.

in the master plan and almost immediately we all decided to buy into this incredible place. Perhaps it was this level of commitment that helped us to establish the creative group dynamic that remained with us all throughout our careers. Each one of us selected a living arrangement that reflected our lifestyle at that time and the selections gave a clear emotional image of what home meant to us. Joe selected a small house that was part of the first model grouping at the end of the cypress hedgerow near Blackpoint. Joe was a very private person and his selection was a statement of his desire for privacy and aloneness in his own house (Figure 75). Charles Moore's selection was just the reverse. MLTW designed the ten-unit condominiums and Charles selected one of the condominium units for himself. Emotionally, this would place him close to others in his living arrangement because the condo had a common laundry, common garages, and a central garden overlooking the ocean. All of these elements brought people together in a communal social form (Figure 76).

My selection didn't take long. I remembered a place near the southern end of the site where I often stopped on my hikes. I thought it contained opportunities that fit all of my family's dreams. The cove was accessible down a series of natural rock steps and I could imagine us fishing among the rocks below. On the cliff's edge we could easily locate a cabin that would make us feel as if we were riding the waves on the bow of a ship. There was plenty of space for an art studio for me, an outdoor dance space for Anna, and lots of room for the kids and their friends. Our site has provided all of this and more for us during these last forty-plus years (Figure 77).

The initial design for our cabin started enjoyably and with great enthusiasm. One spectacular weekend Charles Moore, Bill Turnbull, and I sat down at a drafting board at the Sea Ranch. We were full of an almost musical energy for what we were going to design, and we were not working with T squares, triangles, or other architectural tools. We were working with our Berol #314 drafting pencils and drawing everything freehand. Our remarkable Sea Ranch contractor, Matti Sylvia, was totally comfortable with this approach and we drew and designed fast as if we were playing a symphony. The process was great fun and easygoing. We placed the cabin running eastwest among a grove of Bishop pines at the entrance to the cove and on the edge of the western cliff.

Matti was ready to start building the forms for the foundation on Monday morning, and when we arrived with the plans we realized with a shock, that although the cabin was wonderful, it was in the wrong place. In our enthusiasm, we had forgotten to consider where we would park cars and how

The Esherick Clusters @ SeaRanch

65

SeaRanch

section

mound to obscure Hwy 1
parking

condominium Courtyard
9/26/97

that place would relate to the cabin. We admitted nothing, just told Matti that the plans weren't ready and we needed a few more days. The three of us sharpened our pencils and in the next two days moved the cabin farther south on the site. The final design stepped down the site enough to give us a feeling of being intimately involved in the environment. The house sits in the lee of a shell midden, a place where the Pomo Indians have camped and eaten shellfish long enough to leave a substantial mound to provide wind protection. The proximity of the cliff's edge allowed us easy access to a fishing cove where rockfish, abalone, and sea urchins were still plentiful. It was also possible to for me to visualize a trail leading to another building site where I hoped I would someday have my own studio. This was where the cabin really belonged.

Matti took the corrected plans and as if by magic the cabin was erected within several months. Our new retreat was at once small and yet expansive, opening as it did onto a magnificent ocean view and the five acres surrounding the cabin. We quickly moved into a structure that was part home for our family and part school for our students. During construction we improved the natural stepped access down to the cove and soon performances were possible on the rock islets while witnesses sat on the cliffs surrounding the cove. Anna and I quickly developed other ideas for a variety of venues we could use. To the south, above the seal cove was a flat area that we set aside as a place to be used by the Pomo shaman, Essie, and a place to dance with our Pomo friends. Just to the north of our cabin, against the side of the shell mound, we built a small amphitheater around a barbecue pit and a short walking trail beyond that led to the quiet spot where I hoped I could someday build a studio. Over the years all of these areas have been used for innumerable events.

My involvement in Anna's dance groups and our joint creativity workshops became increasingly intense during our early days at Sea Ranch. The more I focused my attention on the issue of choreographing movement through space, the more I was frustrated by the lack of an appropriate system by which I could plan, design, and even describe movement through the environment in any detail (Figure 78). There was one system called labanotation, but it was very limited in its application to dancers in motion and their use of various parts of their bodies. My landscape practice was now being hired for larger planning and transportation issues and I needed tools for exploring and explaining the challenges of expansive design problems. During the sixties I began to work in earnest on developing such tools.

The first of these tools I called my motation system. I wanted the system to encompass the idea of motion and action, and it had to be flexible enough to be used in manifold ways. Much of its development was based on my travel experiences with visits to various dynamic cities and communities such as kibbutzim, communes, and Native American communities. The cities and communities that had most impressed me had been incredibly lively and involved constant social movement, interactive community life, dance, art, and music. I wanted my system to take all of these elements into account as

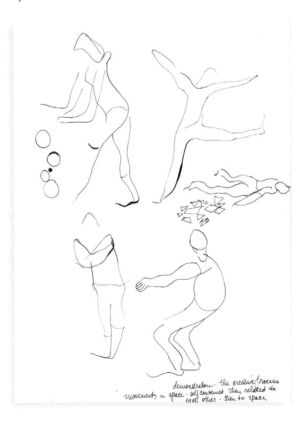

Figure 77

My daughters, Daria and Rana, enjoyed climbing on the cliffs despite our attempts to limit their adventures.

Figure 78

I often made sketches of Anna's workshops with students. Exercises often began with individual movements and then progressed to interactions.

well as the dynamics of personal interrelationships and variations of speed.

In fact, I started working with variations of speed as the base of my system—child crawling speed, pedestrian walking speed, bike-pedaling speed, slow car speed, heavy traffic speed, etc. I needed to delineate all kinds of speed on a plan and show how each would move through an environment. I also needed to indicate the effect the speed would have on the environment and how it would affect other occupants using the environment. Motation allowed me to show how speed would affect an environment and how the design or shape of the environment (park, plaza, road, or freeway) could also affect the speed. This whole issue of the interactive effect of speed on environment and vice versa impacted me immediately as I started to develop the motation system graphically.

As my excitement grew over the graphic revelations of the motation system, I discussed my ideas with Anna. I realized then, and even more so now, the vital impact that graphic notations can have on physical results. It was relatively easy to imagine the music that springs from the graphic notations of a musical score but I was seeing that movement scores could have similar results for actions. I could compose scores where the notes or symbols denoted both sound and action. Anna could use the system for choreographing her performances and happenings, and I could use it to develop scores for designing spaces and environments.

Late in the summer of 1965 Anna was asked to travel to Stockholm to perform a piece she called *Parades and Changes*. We discussed how she could possibly take enough of her dancers to perform such a program and I suggested that we make it a trip for the whole family. In that way, we would have our two girls as well as several of their friends who had been Anna's students for many years. In my mind it would be like a summer camp. I proposed that before the performance, we fly to Bergen and drive across Scandinavia. I thought I could study Scandinavia's advanced new towns and visit Tivoli Gardens, Carl Milbe's garden, and the great Forest Cemetery designed by Gunner Asplund, as well as get a look at Alvar Aalto's architecture and furniture designs.

Anna was delighted with this idea as long as I "could handle all those kids" on my own. It turned out that she wanted to fly directly to Stockholm so that she could find and train some local dancers for the performance. I readily pointed out that I'd had a great deal of success with these same kids on high Sierra trips so I didn't think it would be a problem. Do we all think so optimistically when we're young?

The kids and I began our great adventure with a visit to Tivoli Gardens in Denmark. We all agreed it put Disneyland to shame. Then we took a car ferry to Bergen on the west coast of Norway, and rented a van. In the van we worked our way through some pretty wild country from Lillehammer to the Swedish border on our way to the Stockholm Contemporary Music Festival.

This ten-day trip with a van full of teenagers was one of the most wonderful experiences of my life, but it wasn't all that easy. Everyone started out fine—full of joyfulness and enthusiasm. Gradually, however, decision making became an issue. Should we stop at the next restaurant or go on to the next town? Should we stop and follow the reindeer trail? How late could we drive and still expect to find a hostel that could take all of us? At every turn we found places that seemed wonderful and worthy of more exploration but we could never arrive at consensus. The backseat arguments finally got to me. As a way to avoid the chaos I proposed that we appoint a travel leader for each day and his or her decisions would be absolute, for that day. The idea worked surprisingly well and we continued on dispute free to Stockholm. There we found Anna and her artistic crew. Charles Ross, a sculptor, was already well along in setting up the stage set. Patric Hickey was arranging the lighting design. Morton Subotnic, her composer, was concentrating on the performance.

Parades and Changes is a wonderfully theatrical piece. It has quite a complex choreography of events and involves many dancers. Anna's plan was to include local actors and dancers to fill out the dance troupe and she had, in fact, found them at the local ballet company. They just needed to be trained in Anna's choreography so that they could be integrated into our group. Since our van had arrived several days late, rehearsal time was short and there was a language problem. Anna was having difficulty communicating what she wanted and after some frustrating attempts we decided that I should design and write a score for the new dancers (Figure 79). We hoped that would make it easier for them to absorb the direction. In addition to a general overall score that lacked specificity, I added scores for each performer. The scores worked and the rehearsals proceeded to successful performances. This had been a dramatic, multilingual test for scoring, and it had effectively communicated movement, stage sets, music, attitude, and timing (Figure 80). It was an exciting adventure fueled by youthful energy and creative collaboration. It undoubtedly gave my developing design theories a positive jolt and expanded my vision.

In retrospect, the social and cultural upheavals that shook the United States during the sixties are more clearly understood. No matter where you lived, eventually everyone in the country felt the effects of the Berkeley Free Speech Movement, the Democratic National Convention in Chicago,

Figure 79

I made sketches of the rehearsals for *Parades and Changes* and Anna and I talked about how to speed up and improve communication.

Figure 80

I drew up a scoring system for the dancers that included all of the elements required for the choreography.

student unrest, the Vietnam War protests, Haight-Ashbury flower power, the sexual revolution, and psychedelic-drug experimentation. In my professional life I was especially aware of attitudinal shifts in the areas of art, creativity, design, and community involvement. I was also feeling a shift in the way my office functioned. Although I was frustrated by the old-fashioned role I played and felt that it, too, needed to change, I was not prepared for a serious uprising among my office staff. Revolutionary energy was everywhere, however, and it did not wait on anyone's timing.

In some ways Anna was way ahead of the curve because she had already gone a long way toward changing the way she was working and choreographing. She had already broken away from the classical forms of modern dance used by Graham and Humphrey and was trying a new, innovative approach where life and art had profound similarities. Anna's approach was reminiscent of what we had both learned from the Bauhaus. She brought together diverse teams of artists and used their multiple forms of creativity to expand the group potential. This interactive form of creativity somehow allowed participants to reach an innovative consensus. I enjoyed working with her groups. They helped me see things in new ways in my own field and I found myself thinking of the possibilities for using these same

techniques to solve the unrest I was feeling among my office staff.

The unique dance environment we had created on the Kentfield dance deck triggered much of Anna's innovation. On the deck in the redwoods she brought together groups surrounded by nature rather than interior man-made theatrical spaces. The sight and sound of birds and animals, the changing sky, and the shifting wind became part of their everyday creative processes, in much the same way the high Sierra had radically influenced me for years. Both of our art forms were influenced by and arose from natural processes and Anna and I recognized that the Sea Ranch provided another powerful place for such studies. That was how we decided to conduct a series of workshops called "Experiments in Environment." The basic approach was to bring together a group of graduate students with a wide variety of talents starting with architects, dancers, landscape architects, sculptors, painters, then later photographers, musicians, and psychologists. With this widely varied group of young people we hoped we could examine the basics of creativity and explore how to harness it collectively. We wanted to examine how creativity merged and emerged within different fields of interests and within the disparate points of view of our students.

In 1966 we issued invitations for this new group dynamics to design schools throughout the coun-

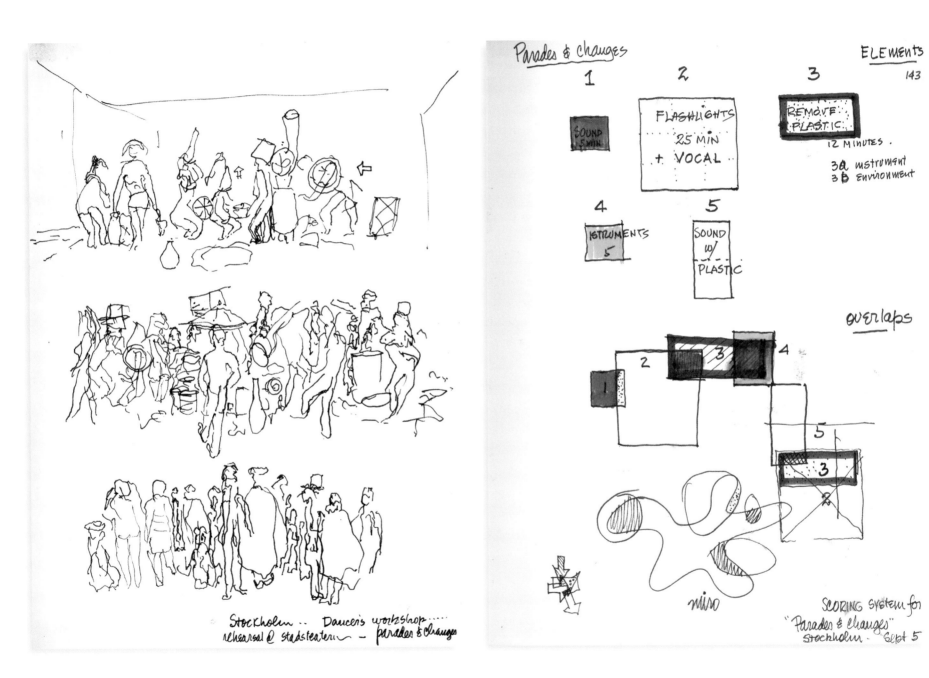

Stockholm .. Dancer's workshop .....
rehearsal @ stadsteatern - parades & changes

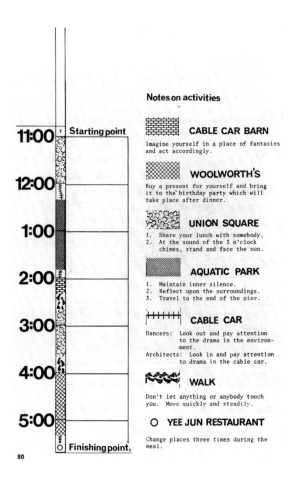

11:00	Starting point	
12:00		
1:00		
2:00		
3:00		
4:00		
5:00		
	Finishing point	

80

Notes on activities

CABLE CAR BARN
Imagine yourself in a place of fantasies and act accordingly.

WOOLWORTH'S
Buy a present for yourself and bring it to the birthday party which will take place after dinner.

UNION SQUARE
1. Share your lunch with somebody.
2. At the sound of the 3 o'clock chimes, stand and face the sun.

AQUATIC PARK
1. Maintain inner silence.
2. Reflect upon the surroundings.
3. Travel to the end of the pier.

CABLE CAR
Dancers: Look out and pay attention to the drama in the environment.
Architects: Look in and pay attention to drama in the cable car.

WALK
Don't let anything or anybody touch you. Move quickly and steadily.

O **YEE JUN RESTAURANT**
Change places three times during the meal.

Figure 81

There was a master score for day one of the "Experiments in Environment" workshop, but participants were only given their own part in the choreography. At the end of the day they saw the whole score.

lry—Harvard, Yale, Rhode Island School of Design, Berkeley, Michigan, etc. We made it clear that the goal of the summer program would be to take the architects and landscape architects off their drafting boards. We wanted to put them in the real world and induce them to deal directly with structures in space and to experience the relationships of body movement as a major force in design. This was quite different from the usual visual importance they had been concentrating on in their architectural classes. Our intentions for the dancers and other artists were the reverse. We wanted them to experience the impact that the design of structures had on their movement during events and happenings of different types. As a result of the invitation, forty young people joined our summer program and spent one month with a diverse group of artists and professionals in a variety of environments along one hundred miles of California coast—from San Francisco to the Sea Ranch.

I've often been asked about the motivation behind my particular interest in exploring new approaches to creativity. I think that what drove me was a desire to inspire my own office and expand our creativity in order to meet the ever-growing demand for innovation that the country needed. I was frustrated by the roadblocks I encountered in the office whenever I presented new and different approaches to thinking and designing. I even ran into this resistance with associates who were young chronologically but had already bought into the old ways. That is why I needed to look outside the box of my own office organization. I sought out college students who were fresh and open to the adventure of new ideas. I wanted to reach beyond the limitations of my own profession and explore our art form with musicians, dancers, sculptors, theater designers, psychologists, and others. This month-long workshop was the vehicle for doing just that.

The "Experiments in Environment" workshop began in downtown San Francisco in the summer of 1966. We designed the first day as a prolonged introduction and developed a score that would heighten students' awareness of the urban environment, human activities within that environment, the individuals they were there to meet, and, finally, themselves. The "City Map" we prepared indicated the overall score for the members. It signified location, general attitudes, and times, as well as notes on the actual activities. Each student was given their own personal track to follow for the day's activities. The initial score moved each participant along their own path to Union Square, a major plaza in downtown San Francisco. There, at precisely 3 P.M., all forty of them rose to the sound of chimes, faced the sun, and for the first time met their fellow explorers (Figure 81).

In July 1968 we held a second month-long "Experiments in Environment" workshop but shifted the focus to the concept of communities. We asked psychologist Paul Baum to join us and he was intrigued by the prospect. Once again the participants worked experientially and traveled from urban San Francisco to the wooded slopes of Mount Tamalpais and the driftwood-strewn beaches at Sea Ranch. They worked intuitively and followed scores that had them do and feel rather than think and discuss. During this intense time together the workshop participants developed a shared vocabulary of experiences. At times they were blindfolded or told to work in silence. During one day-long score on the beach, the group was told to work in silence and build a community. With no verbal communication they moved out on the beach collecting driftwood, seaweed, shells, and pebbles, and constructed an archetypal community with entrance gateway, main plaza, central tower, and individual houses. Those who participated in these seminal workshops were profoundly affected by the insights, intensity, joy, and creativity that resulted.

The more I worked with scores and expanded the information I included in them, the more I realized both their potential and their limitations. Scores were wonderful tools but the variety and scale of projects I was working on demanded some-thing even more complex. I was well aware that a great deal of information gathering and decision making went into the design of a successful score. I understood there was a vast creative expanse between scores and their performance (between the process and the result). I knew that feedback and redirection were often necessary as a score evolved. I struggled with my need to explain and describe how all of these things were part of a process that allowed creativity to flourish and evolve.

That is when I realized that I was developing or defining a new creative process that was essentially made up of four parts: Resources, Scores, Valuaction (a word I coined to describe feedback and action), and Performance. Because creativity is not linear, one can start at any point in the cycle and go in either direction. Scores (a musical score for example) are the crucial point of the cycle because they generate the communication that triggers participation. This was the foundation for the RSVP Cycles. The symbol I immediately drew to describe the cycles had two levels, for I realized that the inner circle was self-oriented but there was also an outer, community-oriented circle (Figure 82).

The book I wrote to explain this process was published in 1969, titled *The RSVP CYCLES: Creative Processes in the Human Environment*. Over the years this approach to design became second nature for Anna and me and for anyone who spent

Figure 82

I found that the graphic representation
of the RSVP Cycles helped students
understand the process.

Figures 83 and 84

I found I could use scores in many ways.
These two pages from my notebook
represent a score for a fountain design.

any time working with us. Between Anna and myself I am sure we've introduced the process to thousands of students, collaborators, associates, employees, workshop participants, and clients. I believe it has become part of the general consciousness of our professions. I constantly hear from a variety of professionals who have used the process for business, therapy, science, and various types of problem solving beyond those we encounter in design. It has given me a direction for approaching nearly every imaginable problem (Figures 83, 84).

I developed scores for creativity workshops, planning projects, books, and my design work. Still later scores became the engines that drove workshops when I wanted to involve citizens to participate in the design process. I had long felt that citizen involvement was vitally important for public projects because in a democracy we all need to have a sense of ownership in our communities. The RSVP Cycles allowed me to design workshops that empowered citizens. Over time I learned a great deal about how to listen actively, diffuse potential logjams, and summarize the input generated at our public workshops. Although at the time it was considered avant-garde, input from local citizens was to eventually become a requirement for all public projects.

During this same time frame, Anna received a call from James Wood, the director of Studio Watts.

He said he had recently seen a dance performance she had choreographed for an arts council in San Francisco and the audience participation aspect of the performance intrigued him.

Studio Watts was an art center that served the residents of Watts, and in those days Watts was infamous as the location of a devastating six-day race riot that had erupted in August 1965. The Watts riot was notorious because of the number of people killed, injured, and arrested as well as for the destruction wrought on the neighborhood itself. James explained that he wanted to commission Anna to choreograph an original piece for her dancers to perform at the Mark Taper Theater.

Anna was surprised by the call but it seemed serendipitous. Despite the wonderful sense of community and exploration that was developed in our creativity workshops, Anna had been feeling that something was missing. Our groups were very homogeneous and Anna was feeling the need to expand and explore creative energy with a more diverse group. She wanted to push the envelope. Despite the positive discussion she had with James and her own piqued interest, her immediate response was no. She instinctively knew that it wouldn't be right to create a piece and simply take it to Los Angeles. After thinking about it Anna contacted James and proposed developing a company of performers in Watts. Then, she said

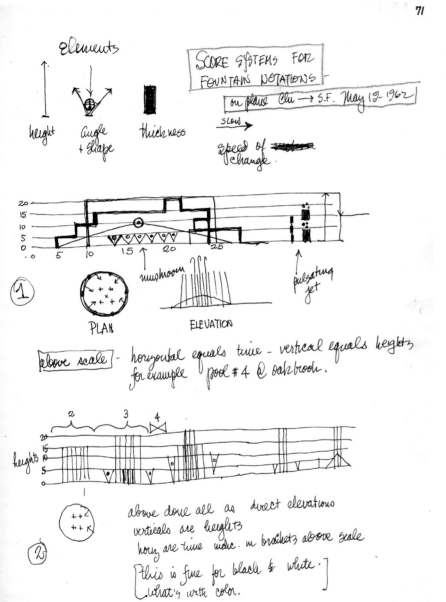

Elements

height | angle + shape | thickness | speed of change.

SCORE SYSTEMS FOR FOUNTAIN NOTATIONS —
on plane Chi → S.F. May 12 1962

slow →

① PLAN   mushroom   ELEVATION   pulsating jet

above scale — horizontal equals time - vertical equals heights
for example pool #4 @ oakbrook.

②

heights

above done all as direct elevations
verticals are heights
horiz are time indic. in brackets above scale
[this is fine for black & white.]
[what's with color.]

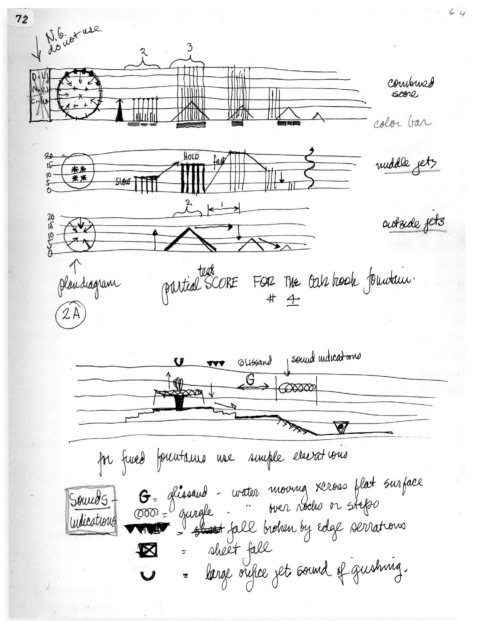

N.G. do not use

combined score
color bar

middle jets   HOLD fast   SLOW

outside jets

plan diagram   partial test SCORE FOR THE Oak brook fountain.
4

②A

glissand   sound indications
G

for fixed fountains use simple elevations

Sounds indications

G = glissand - water moving across flat surface
⟨⟨⟨ = gurgle " over rocks or steps
= fall broken by edge serrations
= sheet fall
U = large orifice jet sound of gushing.

she wanted to introduce them to her San Francisco company and, by bringing them together, explore the emotional territory that the interaction produced. Anna felt that by developing the two groups separately they would find their own strengths and she could then use the workshop process to meld them and develop their commonalities. It was a demanding new challenge for our workshops and she hoped it would engender freedom, involvement, and equal participation by all.

In accordance with Anna's score, the two groups worked separately for five months. She flew to Los Angeles every Saturday and spent the day working with the Watts performers. Then she would return to San Francisco and use the same scores with her San Francisco group. At the end of the five-month period the Watts performers came up to San Francisco and worked with the San Francisco group for ten intense days.

There were conflicts, of course, and differences that were very difficult to unravel. The scores made the creative process visible and Anna put enormous energy into her effort to insure that all participants were heard equally. She felt that she could work through their issues with a shared language of movement. Throughout this process Anna was the link and the negotiator. She wanted these two groups of strangers to become a creative community and work together.

When it was time for the performance, members of the Watts community were bused downtown to the Mark Taper Theater so that they could witness the joint performance and mingle with the more affluent audience. Many of the Watts participants have stayed in touch over the years and have told us that the experience was life transforming. During that time of working together they experienced intense feelings and in a short period of time confronted and began to explore ways of dealing with decades of assumptions, stereotypes, and biases. I feel that to a lesser extent the performance began an exploratory process for the audience members as well. James Woods saw the theater as a symbol and the members of the Watts community were asking to be "let in." The whole concept was a call for social change.

Although Anna and I expended a great deal of time and energy on our exploratory work in the sixties, a huge variety of public work flowed into my office. For the most part, my steadfast associates and the boundless energy of the young people on staff matched the challenge. We received major commissions in San Francisco, Minneapolis, Dallas, and Portland. We were asked to prepare master plans for the Anacostia River in Washington, D.C., and for the Virgin Islands. In Fort Worth, Texas, we planned the downtown, and for the first time ever I based the plan on input gathered from citizens involved in community workshops.

While I was working on the Anacostia River plan in Washington, D.C., I was appointed as a panelist to the first White House Conference on Natural Beauty, under the aegis of the First Lady, Lady Bird Johnson. We struck up a close, friendly, and collegial relationship that led to my involvement in a project of great personal importance to her — the development of low-cost housing and improvements in the east Washington area. I was astounded by the First Lady's interests and energy and particularly by her wide-ranging concern for civil rights. She became very involved in the plan for the Anacostia River, which divides Washington into two housing areas (north and south).

I particularly remember a day when I was going out to the river with Stewart Udall, the secretary of the interior. Lady Bird asked if she and her press secretary could come along. I was delighted. As we looked across the river I told them of my idea to develop an existing island and dam up the river to create a naturalistic swimming area. I thought it would be much more interesting than a swimming pool and could serve people who lived on both sides of the river. Both Lady Bird and Stewart thought this was a great idea. The press secretary, however, objected on the grounds that it would become a place where blacks and whites would swim together and "that" she said "would be unacceptable." "Libby," Lady Bird said, "that is exactly why we should do it."

Although our projects now encompassed a whole range of large-scale work and public commissions, one that really captured my imagination was the San Francisco Bay Area Rapid Transit system (BART). Bill Wurster's office (Wurster, Bernardi, & Emmons) was commissioned to plan the architecture and station locations. They asked me to work on the site planning while they developed the architecture. Don Emmons and I were both excited by the possibilities. I was particularly interested because my motation studies gave me a unique tool to design area-wide plans for the train system. I was sure BART could take a big load off an already overloaded freeway system and thought that with stations located in the outlying suburban areas we would have a fine opportunity to incorporate modest central shopping centers around them. I thought those centers could replace or at least offer alternatives to the already ubiquitous shopping malls that I felt were destroying the landscape. Don Emmons and I had long been friends as well as professional colleagues. I had worked on his house in Marin County and he had worked on my in-laws' house in Woodside. We worked very well together and enjoyed the process. In the days before fax machines and computers, it was extremely helpful that our two offices were located in a building that we owned together at 1620 Montgomery Street (Figures 85, 86). In this case, we also resigned together when the BART board refused to consider the criteria

Figure 85

I bought this building at 1620 Mongtomery Street with the architect partners at WB&E. The building sat at the foot of Telegraph Hill—just a few blocks from San Francisco Bay.

we recommended for softening the transit system's impact on the communities it touched. The BART board (made up primarily of engineers) argued that they were in the business of transportation—not community planning.

During this same time frame, the San Francisco Board of Supervisors was also faced with the development of a new series of freeways. The purpose of the freeways was to connect east bay counties to those to the north and south. In order to accomplish this, traffic had to go over the Bay Bridge and through the city. The freeways came within the purview of the California State Transportation System (CAltrans) and the supervisors were very concerned about the potential citywide damage these freeways could wreck on San Francisco. In an effort to prevent such damage, the supervisors arranged for CAltrans to hire my office to develop a report regarding the design of the freeways. I was both excited and concerned by this assignment. The freeway's purpose could not be realized without passing through San Francisco neighborhoods and the neighborhoods had to be protected. The motation system allowed me to study choreographed movement through space and it proved to be an excellent design tool. I employed it to visualize the effect of the automobiles in terms of *all* their impacts—speed, noise, time, on the environment, on neighborhoods, on architecture, and the interactions of all the above. I was, therefore, able to envision the cumulative effects of these elements before committing to design concepts. The motation system also provided a tool to communicate my design intent to a wide range of stakeholders whose lives would ultimately be affected by such a freeway. Unfortunately, widespread and incorrect media attention implied that the freeway would cut through Golden Gate Park and the plan was rejected before it received a fair review. I began to understand that early involve-

68

Telegraph Hill
March 1, 1962

Figure 86

Many hours were spent on the roof deck at
1620 Montgomery, where we enjoyed this
view of Coit Tower on Telegraph Hill. The
hill blocked wind and fog and we enjoyed a
wonderful microclimate.

ment with the media and the community could have prevented this disappointing loss of an important opportunity. I vowed to consider how to communicate better in the future.

Although my involvement in both BART and the San Francisco Freeway Plan were cut short, it was clear to me that they represented design problems that needed to be studied and expressed in layers of time, space, sound, architecture, physical impact, and community involvement. Although subway trains and cars performed in an expansive public theater, their choreography intersected in a most interesting way with the scores I drew for Anna. It was at this point that I began to think in

terms of "environmental designs" that were oriented to a holistic audience. With this new perspective in mind, I took a critical look at my office organization and decided to divide the office into teams whose approaches to design would be new and visionary as well as technically competent. I began to train the office in this new approach to design.

In retrospect, I suppose my personal difficulties in the fifties helped prepare me for the tests and turmoil of the sixties. Dr. Joe Henderson had by now become a friend and I looked forward to our sessions. I continued to record my dreams in a notebook I kept by my bed, as he had suggested, capturing the essence of them and solidifying the

Figure 87

My dreams and reveries are peopled by landscapes: rocks, fissures, platforms and outcroppings—through which people in solemn processions move. They encounter each other in theatrical settings in a slow and carefully articulated choreography.

ephemeral images while they were still fresh in my mind (Figure 87). Then Joe and I would discuss them in a novelistic way as though they were stories I had written. Joe would interpret what they meant in Jungian terms and place them in an archetypal and historical context.

Through Joe I learned that I could use my dreams for all kinds of problem solving. Eventually the dreams pushed me toward a return to the high Sierra, where I became even more deeply involved with natural forces and explored ways to include them in my design process. In those studies and sketches I relinquished any romantic notions of nature in favor of a firm belief in its process of growth and change—the evolution of natural form making, the movement of water. I did not want to copy nature but I wanted to design an experiential equivalent that would be appropriate for each situation. This desire has kept me focused on the value of the RSVP Cycles as my basic approach to creativity. I will be forever grateful for Joe's early lessons and the realization that psychology provided important resources for design as well as life (Figure 88–93).

In 1966, President Lyndon Johnson appointed me to the first National Endowment for the Arts (NEA) Council (Figure 94). Until this time America lacked any federal vehicle to financially support the arts. That first year we gave away almost three million dollars. This money was used to support organizations (museums, theaters, and symphonies) as well as individuals with outstanding abilities. Although the grant amounts have always been relatively small, the national focus on the arts helped to stimulate much needed attention to American arts and culture. I was honored to be on the NEA Council as it signified to the world that at last art was recognized as a major facet of our national identity. It could now be thought of as a profession instead of a hobby or a game for amateurs and the country could now acknowledge and financially support the arts for their contribution to American culture and values. I was equally pleased by my appointment because I felt that it indicated that my profession, landscape architecture, was finally recognized as an authentic art form. I thoroughly enjoyed every moment on the NEA. It gave me an opportunity to meet with some of the great artists of the time. We did not always agree, though, and I recall several verbal jousting matches with Charlton Heston, whose views were less liberal than mine. Such exchanges were always carried out in good spirits (Figure 95). At the council meetings I felt like I was in a museum of talent garnered from every artistic field. Later, in September 1967, I received a second presidential appointment, to the first Advisory Council on Historic Preservation.

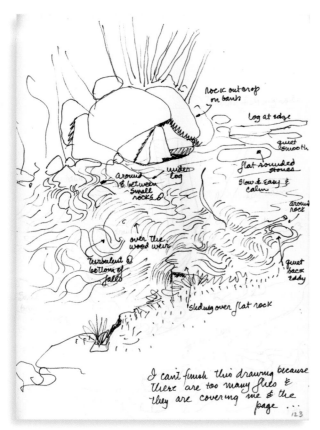

Figure 88

On all of my trips into mountains I sketched as a way to study the primary design forces of nature.

.

Figure 89

Figure 90

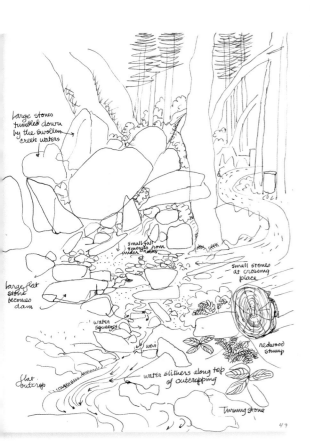

Figure 91

Figure 92

Figure 93

Figure 94

During the sixties I often visited the White House in my role as a member of the NEA.

It was during these heady times that my office received an interesting call from South America. Carlos Guinand Baldo, governor of the province of Caracas, invited me to Venezuela. Mayor Baldo was himself an architect and was extremely sensitive to the problems facing his city. We began our discussions with his concerns regarding the urban population of poor. As people flooded into the city from the countryside, slum areas, called barrios, were creeping up the hillside. Although

they had existed for thirty or forty years, there had recently been a big explosion in the numbers. The barrios grew without any infrastructure—no power, water, or arrangement for sewage. We talked a great deal about minimum physical requirements, programs that were under way, and how they could be improved. Schools, churches, and community centers were needed once the basics were established. Then our focus turned to the environmental future of the greater city and what

it might become. Mayor Baldo was a very forward thinker and hungry for creative input on how to prepare for growth and ensure that the city would remain healthy, attractive, and livable. Eventually we agreed that I would provide urban design studies of the downtown core. By the time these studies were completed they included open-space areas, pedestrian walkways, boulevards, transportation systems, plazas, open-air markets, local parks, and even a new zoo.

I had leapt at this Caracas commission because I saw that it encompassed all aspects of landscape architecture as well as searing social problems that we could tackle through design and planning. Fortunately, I was able to involve Professor Fran Violich from Berkeley, who was an expert on South America and whose wife was from Caracas. They, in turn, recommended I speak to their close friend Dr. Tomas Sanabria, a leading architect in Caracas and a potential colleague. He was, in fact, a perfect fit for our team. I was fortunate to work with Tomas and we became friends as well as colleagues. We were all excited by the prospect of our joint efforts.

Initially we began our studies by traveling throughout Venezuela for several weeks. Tomas was anxious to show us what he considered the "real" Venezuela. This involved exciting jeep trips through the wild countryside to see the local animal and plant species. He also suggested that I join him on one of his regular weekend flights with a group of flying buddies for an "overview." After what I had experienced in my navy training, I wasn't anxious to attempt this adventure in a small private plane but I saw no way I could graciously refuse and we had a day-long journey with six small planes in our flying group. The dense jungles and heart-stopping takeoffs and landings on primitive landing strips were an exotic contrast to my usual site visits at home or on my frequent visits to Israel.

The work in Caracas was eye opening in regard to the extraordinary opportunity it gave our team to explore the possibilities for planning in an atmosphere where strict lines did not define professional limits. In Caracas we all worked together companionably on all the reports that responded to the governor's concerns. Our client was very appreciative of our proposed solutions and the reports were published. It was a very great disappointment to all of us when this visionary governor was not reelected and our proposals were set aside.

While such exciting, innovative projects stretched us all creatively, the staff continued to expand (Figure 96). New additions to the office were all very much part of the sixties culture and they brought their outlook, frustrations, and insistence for change into the office environment. I think much of the tension in the air at that time was triggered by antagonism to the Vietnam War.

Figure 95

When I was on the National Endowment of the Arts Council, Charlton Heston and I often disagreed on grant proposals. He presented me with this sketch to acknowledge that there were no hard feelings.

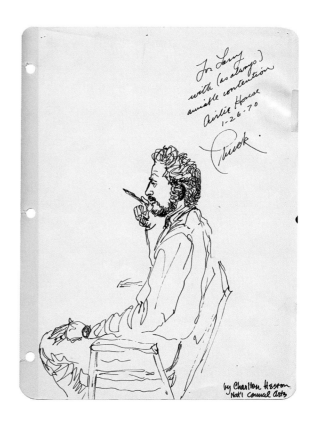

The Rebellious Sixties

I remember that rather than urge young friends to join the military as I had, I suggested they find ways to opt out and avoid going to Vietnam. I was, nevertheless, the symbol of power in the office and I was over thirty. The office dissenters wanted change. At the time I thought it had very little to do with issues of design, planning, or the professional approach we followed but was instead a desire to rearrange what they considered to be a hierarchical organization in which I controlled everything in the office. So, in the middle of all the exciting work and provocative social energy, I faced the difficult process of an intense reevaluation and restructuring of my office. I found I was quite sympathetic with the need for change. I was however, opposed to a move toward chaos. I wanted an orderly evolution toward a form that would resolve both their needs and mine.

It was at this point that I turned to a communication psychologist, Jim Creighton, to help us in our search. I asked Jim to act as our facilitator and to lead weekly meetings and workshops as well as retreats at the Sea Ranch cabin. We continued these dialogues month after month, exploring the various points of view in order to arrive at some form of consensus that would respond to our differing desires. The internal workshop process was harrowing. Much of it revolved around generational differences—the original staff members (who were now associates) versus the new younger folks. In this dichotomy I thought I was quite neutral. I stated that my point of view was to keep the office creative and innovative and to keep myself deeply involved in the design and quality of the work we produced. In retrospect I realize that my desires were not neutral at all and were perhaps the most

Figures 96 and 97

These two staff photos disclose the type of change that was taking place in the dynamics of LH&A in the late sixties.

difficult ones to accomplish. I wanted to understand and respect their needs as long as they didn't interfere with any of my design projects.

The process we were going through was incredibly tough primarily because it was a constant juggling act. We could not carve out time to focus single-mindedly. We had to keep our professional noses to the ground and remain immersed in our work while we searched for solutions to our office puzzle. I was beside myself much of the time trying to keep the office afloat financially and keeping our national and international clients happy and unaware of our internal conflict. This tension impacted us on a daily level through 1969–70. Jim Creighton was an enormous help to me during this period because he seemed to ride this great emotional wave on an amiable surfboard. From my perspective he always appeared calm and in control—that appearance helped me as much as anything because I was so personally involved. Eventually, perhaps inevitably, this process led to what has been called my "deck speech" where I exploded and fired everyone after receiving a list of ultimatums. As dramatic and shocking as the speech was, no one left and the emotional process continued on through a number of iterations. Finally, in March 1970, I held individual meetings with all staff members and twenty out of fifty decided it was time to move on. The office felt exhausted but also relieved and hopeful. We had

passed through a highly charged crisis and emerged on the other side (Figure 97). I quickly retreated to my main love—design—but I was beginning to realize that there were some qualities in myself that would require me to set some new limits.

Although I had by now encountered the revolutionary spirit of the sixties in politics, in the

Figure 98

I had experienced sit-ins, happenings, and demonstrations in San Francisco, but I was not expecting my dignified neighbors in Kentfield to engage in a head-on encounter with the police.

arts, and in my office I was still surprised to see it rise up in my own quiet neighborhood in Marin County. In this case, the fight was triggered by the Army Corps of Engineers. They wanted to convert a lovely, tree-lined, spring-fed creek, into a concrete-lined monstrosity. The newspapers called our local fight a "Ditch War" and it felt like a real war to those of us in the community who desperately wanted to save this vital part of our natural surroundings (Figure 98). I tried to stop the ditch by offering a more naturalistic design edged with

boulders and plant material, but it was deemed too costly and, from the corps's perspective, required too much delicacy and sensitivity to accomplish easily. On April 28, 1969, a story in the *San Francisco Examiner* picked up our fight and reported, "About 40 conservationists were arrested today for bodily attempting to block the army's conversion of tree-lined Tamalpais Creek into a concrete drainage ditch."

The sheriff and deputies who arrested us were polite and we were well treated although many of the women were in tears at the booking desk. The bail was set at $625 but most of us were released on our own recognizance. Our environmental protest failed, and the army engineers built their concrete ditch. I always felt this was a useful confrontation, however, and I was glad that my girls and I had been arrested for an important cause. The neighbors who went through that experience together became friends and formed bonds. We learned a lot during the Ditch War.

By this point my work in Israel was allowing me to visit on a much more frequent schedule. When the state of Israel was formed in 1948, my mother, in her role at Hadassah, worked closely with its first prime minister, David Ben Gurion, and his young assistant Teddy Kollek (Figure 99). I had known Teddy for a number of years and our long friendship made for an ease of communica-

Save the Creek Sit-In—40 Arrested

Dawn Attack in Ditch 'War'

CONSERVATIONISTS TRY TO HOLD BACK THE SHOVEL
Mary Kent Jones and Lawrence Halprin's attempt is in vain

A SHERIFF'S DEPUTY REMOVES A CHILD FROM SCENE
Other officers assist in escorting demonstrators out of the creek

40 Nabbed In Marin Ditch War

"I WANT TO DEFEND MY CREEK"
Mrs. Mary Kent Jones weeps after being arrested

tion. During all my years of involvement in Jerusalem, Teddy and I often talked about the opportunities and planning problems facing Jerusalem. In 1969, Mayor Kollek formed the Jerusalem Committee—a group that would help him plan the "new" Jerusalem. His idea was unique for the time. Instead of convening a group of Israeli architects and planners, he decided to select from an international stable of professionals. He invited talented specialists and experts of all sorts from many countries, the only criteria being that they love Jerusalem and not bring any biases. Despite the fact that there were no fees offered for our involvement, about thirty of us answered the call. The group included, among others, Buckminster Fuller, Louis Kahn, Moshe Safdie, and Bruno Zevi. We met three or four times a year and were all honored to be part of the committee. The concept was so successful that I recommended it to many planning groups over the years.

At the end of the sixties I was spending more and more time in Jerusalem on ever more interesting projects. Mayor Teddy Kollek and I were both concerned about the quality and character of modern development in Jerusalem, especially in the downtown core. A quality of Manhattanization was already insinuating itself into the downtown core and it was beginning to have an effect. If it continued we feared Jerusalem would begin to take on the modern character of Tel Aviv. An example of this was a proposal for the end of Ben Yehuda Street (a popular shopping area), where foreign developers were proposing high-rise structures. The street itself was already jammed like a parking lot for taxis and the experience was becoming more like a modern shopping mall. I felt that this modern direction was anathema for the city of Jerusalem.

Teddy and I talked over these concerns and somehow he managed to stop the process long enough for me to propose a plan to convert Ben Yehuda Street into a pedestrian promenade that would convey some of the character and charm of the ancient Old City. It was not really a difficult task. In addition to adding a few pedestrian amenities, we would simply limit cars, high-rise buildings, and modern signage. Teddy was supportive of the transformation but as a politician he was worried about the powerful taxicab lobby. The lobby was violently opposed to the concept because tourists required taxis to access the stores along Ben Yehuda Street and these drivers did not want to limit their access to this lucrative source of income. The issue went before the city planning commissioners, who supported the taxicabs. The back-and-forth arguments were loud and vehement and went on for quite a while. When I proposed any idea that favored business and the economy everyone was behind "Lawrence Halprin's ideas."

Figure 99

My mother, Rose, and Teddy Kollek became friends during her days as president of Hadassah when Teddy was an assistant of David Ben Gurion.

The Rebellious Sixties

When I proposed something perceived as a threat to the business interests on Ben Yehuda Street, I became "that foreigner."

I turned to Teddy and explained how I felt the pedestrian promenade concept could improve the ambience and bring in more income for the shops and restaurants. I was sure that without cars and cabs the quiet street would be reminiscent of the *sook* in the Old City of Jerusalem. I was certain it would be more attractive and enjoyable for everyone, locals and tourists alike. Once Teddy was convinced, the battle was won because when Teddy favored something it usually got done. All of this took years to work through but I was finally released to prepare my scheme, remove the noisy cars and cabs, and return quiet to the street. Fortunately, the project was a huge success and people of all kinds were drawn to this quiet refuge with its sense of old world charm.

As we entered the seventies, the San Francisco office grew to about sixty people (Figure 100). We had worked hard to understand and use the creative wave from the sixties, which had been a great adventure and a tumultuous ride. It had not been easy but we had accomplished a great deal professionally and had expanded personally. Some of our numbers had no doubt left in frustration and anger but there were also many interesting spin-offs. Several of my colleagues had gone out on their own to focus on community workshops. Anna's Dancers' Workshop became interested in the application of scoring to

real community sociopolitical issues. Some of our office alumni had gone off to start the ANTFARM, an experiment with new art forms.

Challenges in Cities

Despite all of the exploration and experimentation we encountered and produced in the sixties, my office had steadfastly gained a respectable reputation for our solid work in the postwar redevelopment of cities. In San Francisco we had been involved in the early restoration and reuse of Ghirardelli Square, a nineteenth-century chocolate factory on the edge of the bay; the redesign of Market Street, the city's main east-west thoroughfare; and the development of Embarcadero Plaza and Fountain, a four-acre gathering place at the foot of Market Street where it met the waterfront. We pioneered an early conversion of a downtown street to a transit mall in Minneapolis, Minnesota, in an effort to keep businesses and customers downtown; and introduced a major open-space network of plazas, fountains, and parks in downtown Portland, Oregon. I had by this time written a book called *Cities* that explored my memo-

Figure 100

In 1970, the staff at Lawrence Halprin & Associates included landscape architects, architects, geographers, photographers, graphic designers, and illustrators.

11

A Time for Introspection

ries of what made European cities fun. I had also written a 119-page study for the city of New York, and it gave me a fantastic high when the *New York Times* architecture critic Ada Louise Huxtable said, "the report should be read by everyone and taped to the forehead of city officials." I received invitations and commissions to work in many cities during the seventies. I will mention just four.

In my book *Freeways*, published in 1966, I had considered the idea that freeways could become a new art form, if they were thoughtfully designed. I noted that when they failed to live up to their form-building potential it was because their designers ignored the inherent possibilities. I was determined to show that it was feasible to handle freeways in such an elegant manner that they could improve, rather than destroy, the cities they served. In 1970 the Seattle Park Commission decided to let me try. They approached me to help resolve the problems they faced with Interstate 5, a freeway that had divided their city (Figure 101). They invited me to build an urban park on a site adjoining the free-way. I had experienced the beautiful parkways that Robert Moses had built in New York and I was

Figure 101

Seattle Freeway Park did a great deal to heal the damage done by Interstate 5 when it divided the city.

ready to take on the challenge. After beginning my studies, however, I thought that it would be even more productive and healing if we could expand the park by using the air rights over the interstate. This proposal reconnected the city and enlarged the park site. I was then able to suggest utilizing the rooftop of a proposed parking garage and a strip of unused right-of-way alongside an exit ramp (Figure 102). The park contained dramatic, joyful water-falls that masked the traffic noises and, in one case, allowed visitors to view cars passing on the other side of the water (Figure 103). We planted large trees in gigantic planter boxes and the park quickly

Figure 102

These giant planter boxes over the freeway break up the concrete chasm cutting through the city and the trees provide park users some protection from the channeled wind.

Figure 103

In order to attract young people, I felt it was important for Seattle Freeway Park to provide a fun and adventurous atmosphere. The water fountains and waterfalls cascading down over the freeway chasm brought this youthful energy to the park.

A Time for Introspection

Figure 104

Denver's Skyline Park was three blocks
long and one hundred feet wide. The
three-dimensional treatment of each block
created opportunities for people to use the
park in a variety of ways.

Figure 105

A handsome clock tower provided a unique,
historic orienting feature.

took on the feel of an exciting nature park and not a highway right-of-way. Throughout the process I felt that the trick was to perceive the old freeway as part of the cityscape and tame it, rather than complain about it.

The Seattle Freeway Park proposal was innovative and complex. Building a bridge across a canyon and using its elevation changes to provide stairs and platforms would have been normal in a park but they were novel for work in a city. I needed a skilled and experienced team to explain the concept and work with the city, the traffic engineers, and the myriad consultants required to carry it out. I had been building my office for over twenty years at this point and we were ready. Freeway Park was completed in 1976 and received many awards and a great deal of attention. I believe that it influenced many cities and designers to look for hidden opportunities in unexpected places in their own backyards.

In virtually the same time frame, the city of Denver contacted me about a three-block-long centerpiece for their 113-acre redevelopment program. They were coping with a problem that many cities were experiencing: Large areas in their downtown core had fallen into disrepair after the war when large numbers of the urban population moved to the suburbs. The challenge was to bring these downtown areas back to life. Once again I focused on ways to bring a liveliness and excitement to the area. In Denver, there was a framework of architecturally handsome buildings and a wonderful tower. We felt that the three-block series of small parks and plazas, which became known as Skyline Park, would provide desirable open space, and I designed a series of fountains based on the regional red rock terrain. The blocks stepped down away from the streets and provided an urban open space where Denver residents could step away from the traffic and begin to return, enjoy, and appreciate their mile-high city (Figures 104–6).

Figure 106

I particularly enjoyed designing this fountain sculpture based on the local red rock area just outside of Denver. It gave the park a joyful and lively attraction.

Rochester, New York, and Everett, Washington, were going through similar problems and each needed a solution appropriate to their locale and ambiance. In Everett, a federal grant financed a planning report to guide future growth for the entire region. I insisted that the report involve the entire community and we held several two-day workshops with citizens. I wanted to elicit their visions for a regional and citywide future that would be appropriate for the sudden socioeconomic changes that were dramatically shifting patterns in the Northwest. The report provided them with short- and long-term conceptual plans for the future, and I hoped their involvement in the analysis and development would help them to understand that they had choices (Figure 107). In Rochester, Manhattan Square Park, a five-acre expansion of the downtown, offered a more immediate opportunity to rejuvenate the city. The new facility offered plazas and fountains as well as venues for concerts and plays and introduced an enormous space frame that added a new dimension (Figure 108). This was before the Americans with Disabilities Act and we were able to invite the public to climb up and enjoy views from this high vantage point. During performances in the plaza, the space frame also held the sound and lighting equipment. In addition, an underground tunnel was part of the plan and it provided a link to downtown that separated pedestrians from the cars.

Figure 107 *(facing page)*
In Everett, Washington, a comprehensive city plan emerged after a two-year study based primarily on community participation and ecological protection.

Figure 108
Manhattan Square Park in Rochester, New York, was designed as a multipurpose facility that would encourage user participation. The four-dimensional space frame I designed for Manhattan Square Park was the most innovative structure I had ever built.

A Time for Introspection

The two Doxiadis conferences I attended gave me time to consider how my RSVP workshops could be used in a larger context. They also provided an opportunity to meet and share my ideas with a brilliant group whose talents triggered wide-ranging discussions.

Figure 109

Doxiadis

In 1971, as the office churned with such projects, the Greek architect and planner Constantinos (Dinos) Doxiadis invited me to participate in a conference in Athens. In the fifties and sixties, Doxiadis had designed and built new towns throughout the world: in Ghana, Iraq, Lebanon, and Pakistan as well as the United States. He had developed a visionary and scientific planning system he called *Ekistics* and described his approach and explorations in a maga-

Figure 110

zine of the same name. For ten years, Doxiadis held conferences on a yacht sailing through the Greek islands, and each year he invited a multidisciplinary group of experts to join him for dialogues about the state of the world, particularly as related to issues of human settlements. This was the ninth conference and, through discussions, Doxiadis was attempting to arrive at a consensus of how to best design all communities. In my mind, the conference contained elements of the Jerusalem Committee, NEA meetings, and our own creativity workshop explorations.

Although the process and intentions of the conference seemed somewhat familiar to me, they were quite exotic and unique. Doxiadis's conferences traveled—the whole group corralled together on a ship as we meandered through the Greek islands. Doxiadis invited participants from a worldwide list of recognized intellectuals—Buckminster Fuller, Margaret Mead, Marshall McLuhan, Erik Erikson, Lady Jackson (Barbara Ward), Jonas Salk, and others (Figures 109–13). Each day Doxiadis, as chairman of the conference, would make a statement

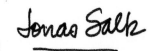

speaks of the idea of "voluntarism"

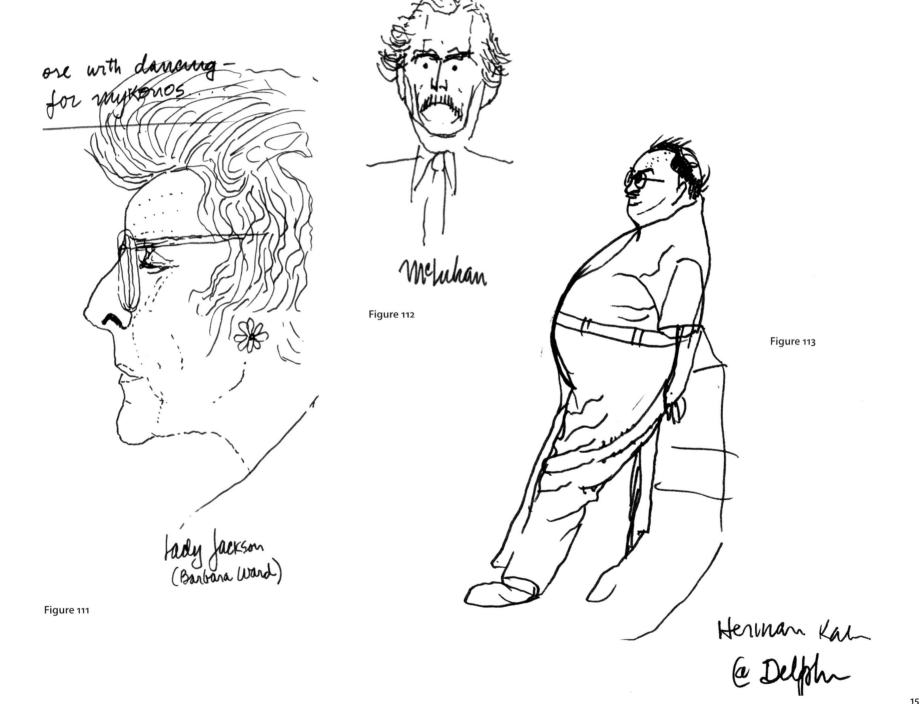

ore with dancing—
for mykonos

McLuhan

Figure 112

Figure 113

Lady Jackson
(Barbara Ward)

Figure 111

Herman Kahn
@ Delphi

159

that established the theme for the day. There was a great deal of order and formality in his meetings and participants were given an opportunity to make a presentation on their own points of view.

On the first day of cruise number nine, Doxiadis opened the discussion by saying that the theme would be "Architectural Crimes: Confessions of a Criminal." He drew a diagram to show how a primitive culture approached building a community and a second that represented a modern technological approach. Immediately, the anthropologist Ned Hall rose to respond with a series of his own illustrations that he referred to as the idea of the "human bubble." He described how buildings related to human settlements and how they must therefore allow for the possibility of interactions. "High-rise buildings don't work in this way," Ned said, "They interfere with communication." The conference was off and running.

Doxiadis's morning dialogues were followed by visits to the various islands in the afternoons, and festivities were celebrated in the evenings with local townspeople. Throughout it all, we continued our ardent intellectual dialogues. My notebook is full of quotes I captured, comments I recorded, and dreams that surfaced during the adventure. The dreams ran the gamut from practical to mystical to fantastic. I made notes of our exchanges, recorded ideas to follow up on later, and filled pages with sketches of the environments we experienced and my traveling companions.

In retrospect perhaps the most significant difference between the Greek conferences and those in Jerusalem and Washington related to conclusions. This intellectual conference was immensely exciting, very social, enjoyable, and informative. It was wonderful to have an opportunity to hear what these remarkable people had to say about their own work and to hear how it might relate to the rest of the world. It was wonderful to have them as new friends I could call upon and visit in the future. But as someone who wants to produce a physical result for my efforts, I felt the lack of conclusions. We never actually resolved anything nor had we even tried to come to any consensus.

My own presentation was made to the group on day five. I remember feeling that it was important for me to emphasize participation as a vital part of group creativity. I began by talking about my favorite subjects—creativity and scoring. I explained about choreography and my motation system and why it became necessary to develop the notion of "open" versus "closed" scores. I explained that scoring was not goal oriented but objective oriented. I described how all the art fields were working in this mode—John Cage in music, environmental happenings with Allen Kaprow, the concrete poets, etc. I felt that what was emerging in the art world was an inclusive rather than an exclusive attitude. This led me to describe participatory events in the environment—in regard to fountains and plazas and other places where people were invited into the experience on a multisensory, not just a visual, level. I worked my way through group dynamics and the interactive possibilities of group creativity. I talked about the mechanism of active listening as opposed to exposition of points of view and then moved into a description of the RSVP Cycles. At each stage I noted that scoring was at the core of the process. The last paragraph of my presentation follows:

> In recent years I have been deeply involved in the application of open scoring techniques and involvement and participation in city planning. We use the RSVP Cycles as a base of operations holding judgment to its proper place in the process and thereby encouraging input. In regard to scoring, first we develop awareness from which common language arises. Then there is interaction from which motivations and recycled scores emerge as a way of developing and observing alternatives with maximum participation. I have worked with groups of various sizes in various cities. . . . The results have been very rewarding to us and to the people with whom we have worked. The work is still experimental on a large sustained

scale so I cannot yet relate to you how significant it is on a physical design level in terms of communities. I can assure you, however, that the sense of creative involvement is enormous and the process releases energy at a very high level in all kinds of people and at all ages. It has aroused a great surge of interest in planning and counters the sense of alienation.

The Greek conference made me acutely aware that our RSVP workshops presented a way to reach consensus. The process required a lot of interaction between participants and daily attempts to tell one another not only what we believed but also how we felt. Eventually, almost organically, we reached a consensus. After my time at the Doxiadis Conference in 1971, I concluded that this was one of the differences between art and intellectuality. The more a group can get out of their heads and into a creative art form for communication, the faster they can reach consensus. In my experience, this concept has proven itself again and again and whenever I've allowed a workshop to veer into extended dialogue and debate we have lost our forward motion toward consensus.

In 1972 I was pleased to be invited back to conference number ten, the final Doxiadis yacht conference. The conference started in Athens and we traveled southeast past Ios and Mikonos to Thira

Figure 114

and Santorini. The next day we made our way to Nafplia and then went on to Rhodes, off the coast of Turkey. Memories of this trip remain extremely strong. I recall for example—Herman Kahn standing at Delphi expounding on the future of mankind (Figure 114); Margaret Mead, feisty and impetuous; Jonas Salk, serious and inspiring; Marshall McLuhan, tall and saturnine, commenting on his book *The Medium Is the Message*; Bucky Fuller professing his utopian vision of architecture; Arnold Toynbee sitting on the steps of the Acropolis talking about the past and the future; and the wise psychologist Erik Erikson, making the most of the Mediterranean culture. I was overwhelmed by the incredibly brilliant group Doxiadis had assembled.

It seemed to me that throughout the Doxiadis conferences Dinos was desperately seeking scientific facts and analysis that would allow for a humane and reasonable planning equation (Figure 115). Although I was fascinated by the dialogues and intrigued by the guests, I found many of the financial, political, and philosophical discussions long-winded and ephemeral. I was anxious for concrete ideas I could put to use in solving the problems I was dealing with daily.

Several of the participants, Ned Hall, Peter Shepheard, and Jonas Salk, would surface later in my professional life and others, like Bucky Fuller, remained an inspiration. I found myself fretting over some of the presentations and continuing to feel that the RSVP process I was employing could offer any citizen a voice in the regional requirements for design in their own communities. It was not a universal equation but I was sure that such a voice would empower them and encourage a sense of ownership and care for the places they built (Figure 116).

Conference ten concluded in Delphi at the end of Lions Promenade with a final talk by Jonas and Françoise Salk. Afterward Doxiadis asked how many of us he could count on for future help resolving human-settlement issues and everyone raised their hands joyfully. The two conferences provided great personal memories. I was inspired by all the remarkable people I met there. They enlarged my world and my views and in that way they have been forever burned into my consciousness (Figures 117, 118).

Back home in 1973, I learned that the Ditch War, which we had fought and lost over our neighborhood creek, had not been forgotten. The adjacent wetlands had enjoyed a five-year respite during which time they continued to be enjoyed as a riparian corridor for wildlife and a breathing space for humans. Developers, however, had their eye on the marshland and they now proposed filling the area and building condominiums. We were more prepared this time around and a group of local

citizens, which included Supervisor (now Senator) Barbara Boxer, asked me to lead a workshop to review the proposal. The workshop firmed their resolve to fight and they mounted enough public pressure to convince the county board of supervisors to buy the site and maintain it as a natural park. I felt the earlier loss had laid the groundwork for this win by raising the public's awareness of our wonderful local resources and the need for public advocacy.

In the early seventies I was feeling exhilarated by the success of the office and the pride I felt in so many of our projects, when in March 1974, I received an extremely exciting invitation to submit a design concept for the Franklin Delano Roosevelt Memorial in Washington, D.C. Only seven landscape architect and architecture offices were asked to participate. I already knew that a congressional resolution for such a memorial had been introduced in 1946, right after the end of World War II, and that there had been a number of failed attempts to select a design. I had, in fact, resigned from a team during one such competition in the sixties. My life had been intertwined with the influences of FDR, and now I might have an opportunity to build a national monument to honor a man who had inspired me my whole life. I poured a great deal of energy into my submittal and was overjoyed when I heard that I had won. I realized,

Figure 115

Figure 116

Figure 117

Larry Halprin
ned Hall
Las Vegas - Sept 16-77

Figure 118

Toynbee

A Time for Introspection

of course, that the process would be complicated because of the importance of the commission, the high-profile site on the Mall, and the Washington protocol, but I had no idea how long it would actually take to accomplish.

The following year I worked on a basic design concept that was approved by the FDR Memorial Commission, the Federal Commission of Fine Arts, and the National Capitol Planning Commission in 1975. During that period I felt very focused on what I was doing but it was becoming ever more clear to me that the office was out of balance. In hindsight the office energy was still somewhat raw and unresolved after our in-house problems and, as I look back, I realize that some of the new young staffers were dabbling in drugs and experimenting in new-age living patterns and relationships. I found myself caught in the middle of lifestyle issues. Divorcing couples, employees found camping out in the basement, and emotional breakdowns were all brought to my attention because of the impacts they were having on the office. All of this echoed what was going on in the world at large and in San Francisco in particular but the strain of it all pulled my energy away from the design projects. Here again were the uneasy feelings I experienced after our in-house workshops. At that time I had known I was going to have to set some limits for myself. Finally I was acknowledging the depth of my feelings

and the extent of the limits I wanted to set. I wanted to design without all the responsibilities and distractions of a large office. In 1976 I decided to disband Lawrence Halprin & Associates.

RoundHouse

Having made such a major professional decision, I needed to decide how to get on with my creative work without wasting more energy in the dissolution process. I invited one of my LH&A associates, Sue Yung Li Ikeda, to join me, we rented space in an old railroad roundhouse around the corner from the LH&A office, and hired a girl Friday. That is where the tiny, personalized think tank called RoundHouse was born. Its intention was to explore modes of collective creativity and search for innovative solutions to significant issues through workshops, films, and design. It was a vehicle for creative exploration and in retrospect, a stepping-stone away from the large office culture.

Dalí Film

One of our first RoundHouse adventures was a trip to Spain to visit Salvador Dalí. This came about because I had been asked to consider designing a museum in Cleveland, Ohio, to house one of the world's most comprehensive collections of Dalí paintings. The collection had been compiled by a prominent local couple, Reynolds and Eleanor

Morse. As I began conceptualizing I realized how important it was to experience the quality and ambience of the places that inspired Dalí's work. In other words, I needed to visit Dalí's home and studio in Cadaques, north of Barcelona. I discussed the importance of such a visit with Herb Strawbridge, one of our major Cleveland contacts, and he agreed to sponsor the trip.

In the short time before we left for Spain I happened to talk with Chloe Aaron, an old friend from my days on the NEA. She asked how I intended to record my impressions of the visit and I showed her my notebooks. She was pleased to see how well I collected my thoughts, but she felt we were missing a great opportunity. She thought the visit should be filmed. I loved the idea—my father had been greatly attached to his primitive movie camera in the 1920s and had recorded our trip to Europe and Palestine in 1929. At Chloe's insistence RoundHouse presented a proposal to the NEA. It was approved and just in the nick of time we were able to arrange an intense week-long training session in filmmaking at MIT. We contacted Paul Ryan, a photographer friend, and started planning in earnest.

Meanwhile, Herb was becoming concerned about our trip and was very insistent in urging that we get a contract with Dalí in place. He noted that there were innumerable groups of filmmakers who were anxious for an opportunity to film Dalí. He was afraid that we would arrive in Spain to find that Dalí had changed his mind and been seduced by another group. He was absolutely right. Although we talked with Dalí endlessly, until he agreed and signed a contract, once he was back in Spain, he refused to comply and insisted on a large fee. Luckily Herb had brought the contract along, "just in case."

Experiencing Spain through the process of filming Dalí was tremendously exciting. I couldn't believe that I had access to the home and studio of this remarkable surreal icon (Figure 119). We spent about a week and a half in Cadaques—in the house, by the swimming pool, on the beach, and throughout the small town. The most amazing thing was how accurately Dalí's paintings represented the scenes and activities that surrounded him (Figure 120). The local people and environment appear constantly in his paintings. I recall a moment on the beach when a one-legged man emerged from the ocean and limped toward us using a crutch—hadn't I just seen this very image in a Dalí painting?

Despite all of this access to his surroundings, Dalí remained somewhat elusive. Perhaps he was a bit perturbed by our contract, the lack of an appropriate fee for such personal access, or the invasion of his privacy. At any rate, we rarely had a moment to catch him on film. Then, Sue Yung had an idea—if we set up an interesting situation and generated a lot of energy (but did *not* ask him to participate) he

Figure 119

Visiting Spain with Salvador Dalí gave me a new appreciation for surrealism and how it could be incorporated into architecture and design. Dalí's life—his environment and his dress—was as surreal as his art.

would undoubtedly show himself. And so he did and in some remarkable improvisational moments in the film, Dalí succumbed to the bait and entered the space, a surreal room dominated by a couch in the shape of a pair of large, red lips.

During our stay we were informed that there were plans for a fiesta in Figueras, Dalí's hometown. Dalí had opened a museum there in the ruins of an old theater bombed during the Spanish Civil War and the town wanted to celebrate the first anniversary of the Teatro Museo Dalí. When we arrived, Dalí gave us a personal tour of the museum and we were told it was a museum in process—more like an artist's studio (Figure 121). Workers and associates were anxious for Dalí to review the various projects and comment on their progress and I saw his intense interest in every detail—from the costume for a mock-up for a four-dimensional statue called a polytope to the color of the water that was to issue forth from the mouth and hands of one of four new fountains representing monsters (Figure 122). The party was a small-town extravaganza with local circus performers building pyramids and a bullfight in honor of Dalí and his wife, Gala (Figures 123, 124).

Figure 120

Dalí's house and garden were a theatrical set for his unique life.

Figure 121

Dalí gave Reynolds and Eleanor Morse a detailed tour of the Teatro Museo Dalí—a work in progress.

Figure 122

Dalí's assistant explained that Dalí wanted milk-white water to flow from the gargoyle's mouth.

Figure 123

A human pyramid was built under Dalí's balcony and the youngster on top was ultimately lifted up to join Dalí there.

Figure 124

At a bullfight in their honor, Dalí and his wife, Gala, were treated as royalty.

Before leaving Spain, I asked Dalí about the source of his creativity so that we could refer to it in our film. "Well," he said in his broken English, "when I get up in the morning I start by eating a pink grapefruit. After I finish I go and make le peepee, and then I paint." As a result, we somewhat flippantly named the film *Le Pink Grapefruit.* The film almost immediately received a special jury award from the San Francisco Film Festival but we never did arrange for a good distribution mechanism. Perhaps that oversight plus the title that we had so casually chosen kept it below the radar these past thirty years. The Dalí Museum for Cleveland was never realized but was in fact built in Saint Petersburg, Florida, in 1982.

Berkeley Workshop

In the fall of 1977, RoundHouse found some grant money and we approached the University of California, Berkeley, with the idea of doing an extended workshop for the College of Environmental Design (CED). We thought this would be a fine opportunity to further explore the essence of the human/environment relationship. Instead of telling students what to think in a lecture we would engage them in an advanced workshop that was in effect a continuation of the "Experiments in Environment" series. The basic theme was to be the relationships of people and nature, both personally and in communities. All primitive people are comfortable in this arena and they have sorted out and passed on their wisdom regarding these relationships for millennia. They have rituals that usually have something to do with religion or spirituality and it all relates back to their shared myths. It seemed vital to me to reestablish this basic awareness in modern times. The overwhelming growth of our societies and the increasing development of high tech separate us from our roots and our basic needs.

The CED workshop was titled "TAKING PART in the Environment" to indicate that it would be experiential and participatory. We held the number of participants down to thirty because in our previous creativity workshops we had found that to be an ideal number. In addition, fliers announced that the workshop would follow an RSVP Cycles format, the score would run October 14–22, and the primary venue would be Sea Ranch. We felt it was important to arrange for the students to be released from their other college commitments for this period and, in my estimation, the nine-day workshop was a great success. We introduced two new scores that proved to be especially interesting. The first explored our relationship to life and death, and the second explored the differences between male and female energy in the environment.

On day four of the workshop my RoundHouse partner, Sue Yung, presented the life/death score.

She talked about the use of inner rhythms as a way to perceive the environment and began the exercise by asking everyone to close their eyes for five minutes. During that time she suggested they breath deeply, slowly expel each breath, and clear their minds until there was nothing left but a white blazing light. Then they were to open their eyes, traverse the large coastal site, and find their life spot and their death spot. Then they were asked to draw or diagram the cosmic forces on the site and locate their life/death spots within their designs (Figure 125).

The objective of this score was to have the participants get in touch with universal rhythms and life processes that are always present and let them experience how they can begin to understand their surroundings on that primal level. These basic rhythms are involved in our life/death relationships to nature. Such cosmic forces impact us at all times. In the Chinese concept of the universe, people can either impede or improve upon the forces. This is the ancient art of geomancy or Feng Sui.

The choosing of these life/death sites proved to be demanding for the young participants—particularly the death spot. They spent much more time, attention, and concern deciding on their death spot. A few chose the same spot for both but most of the group chose settings that were greatly contrasting. When the selections and drawings were complete,

all returned to a circle to share with the entire group. It was a quietly moving experience. Two recurrent forms appeared throughout the presentations. Convex forms, open and outward-looking, seemed to relate to life. Enclosed forms seemed to refer to death. In general, participants chose low places (down in a drainage, among trees, closed, warm, protected) for death places. There was often an expressed desire for mystical and magical settings.

Later that same day, we moved to another powerful site extending out into the ocean for the male/female score. I divided the group into males and females and gave each group the same score. They were given two hours to 1) explore the environment, and 2) collectively prepare a silent presentation of the site to the other group. Each group was then given a half hour to present the site to the other audience. The results of the score were remarkably different for the two groups.

When the women entered the site they immediately spread out to investigate and experience the qualities of the site individually. They got involved intimately, experiencing the site by smelling the flowers, gathering stones, picking some interesting grasses. As they came back together they reassembled in a sheltered hollow near the center of the site. They talked about their discoveries and how they thought each item could become part of the presentation. The women encouraged one another. They

Figure 125

After finding a place that symbolized life, each workshop participant made a presentation explaining their choice.

A Time for Introspection

chatted and laughed and even danced around a bit. There was a strong feeling of camaraderie and enjoyment in their working together (Figure 126).

As the men explored the same site they moved down the point as a group. They developed a tribal feeling of cohesion. Eventually, they climbed to the highest point and various men started expressing their ideas about how to present the site. Each expression was passed over and, in effect, rejected by the others as they put forward their own ideas. The men expressed annoyance at the women's chatting and laughing and their frustration began to grow. Even from a distance, it was obvious that there were disagreements about what approach to take (Figure 127). Their body language revealed sparks of anger. They reminded me of the kids in the van on my trip to Stockholm. I moved farther away to let them figure out how to handle it. Finally, as time grew short, they took out a piece of paper and under the pressure of the clock they produced a score. None of them really felt great about the result. You could see by their reactions that they were still frustrated and unresolved.

The presentations were just as dissimilar. The women started offstage (in a sense) in the parking lot adjacent to the site. From there, they nervously

Figure 126
The women hugged, laughed, and danced as they carried out their score.

Figure 127
The men's group struggled to reach consensus and found the score frustrating.

Figure 128

Although the manner of working together was different, both presentations worked. The valuaction at the end of the score focused mainly on the men's inability to work together in harmony.

and apprehensively climbed over a wooden stile to the site. The men followed them into the site and, led by the women, they climbed to the top of the hill and sat down as an audience. The women presented the site through a joyful, playful dance. They wound through the flowering lupine and climbed back to the top of the hill and handed each man a flower to smell, then patted him on the head. The men's performance primarily took the form of occupying the hilltop and not allowing anyone else to climb it. Although they seemed to want the women to climb up, anytime they did the men rushed off. This seemed to be quite the reverse of the women's presentation.

At the end of the score and performance, the differences were very clear. The experience had a strong impact and the men, particularly, seemed to feel frustrated and anxious about the revelations. The valuaction session that followed went on a long time, and I believe it generated a lot of creative thinking and appreciation for the power of the process of collective creativity (Figure 128).

After a week of such intense experiences at Sea Ranch it was time to return to San Francisco for our final days. The reentry challenge was to discover how to retain the new insights gathered and take them out into the real world, into life, as an ongoing inspiration. We gave the participants the following score: "Return home in any grouping that you wish. Pay attention to your feelings all the way home—including your leaving The Sea Ranch and its experiences and your re-entry into your normal environment. Be aware also of the difficulties you may encounter on your re-entry into real life."

When we reassembled at RoundHouse it became apparent how difficult the reentry process was for many of them. Several people admitted they had stayed with other group members rather than try to immediately explain the experience to their family and close friends while the workshop was still ongoing. One of the most important aspects of the workshop proved to be the interaction among participants and the reaction of the workshop participants to the outside world. I still hear from members of this group who say that this nine-day experience was a life-changing event. In some cases they introduced aspects of the workshop process into their future practice, in many cases they experienced profound personal insights that shifted their perspective about the process of design, and in several cases, it led to major shifts in professional goals.

FDR Art/Film/Report

During this RoundHouse period I continued working on the FDR Memorial. After a great deal of thought on the great themes and intensity of Franklin Delano Roosevelt's presidency, I had decided that my basic approach would be to tell a story about FDR and his twelve years in office. FDR's four terms of office represented a basic philosophy that led the country through the Great Depression and terrible years of World War II. His words were important not only to the people of our country but also to a world that was fighting dictatorships beyond our borders. I wanted a presidential memorial that would communicate all of this to future visitors. I didn't want it to be abstract but personal and emotional.

I reflected back on the special places I had experienced in my lifetime and how I had reacted to them. I looked for common threads between Ise Shrine in Japan, Delphi in Greece, and the Western Wall in Jerusalem. They all had a quality in common—that of taking me on a voyage through space that was choreographed and paced with meaningful stops along the way. The stops provide views and places to pause and sit with events and experiences of importance. Each of these places also evoked a sense of theater and often included sounds or other physical cues and signals. I remembered that the pathways in those places had significance and walking along those promenades produced emotions of their own that were often as powerful as visual sculptures.

Such thoughts took me back to my own relationship with FDR as a young boy. I recalled his fireside chats and how they affected me not only by their content but also through the sound of his voice, the slow vibration of his words and the measured pace. I know that I was changed by those experiences. This was what I wanted to provide in the design of the memorial. I wanted it to be unique and as much choreography as visual impact. I wondered how to capture that feeling and form in the memorial.

It was at this point in my process that I finally realized that sculpture would be vital and that I would have to find ways to include it seamlessly in the memorial. I wanted it to be absolutely integrated and emotional. I set off on a sculpture search, but several artists were already beginning to surface in my mind as I thought about the story to be told. I realized that I would need to justify the selection to the FDR Memorial Commission so I consulted with museum directors, members of the National Council of the Arts, and others. Soon I had a list of twenty-seven artists to consider. By refining the criteria I was able to shorten the list a bit before I set off on a series of interviews in July 1977.

The first artist on my list was George Segal. I recalled how his work often told a story and I was anxious to see if he was interested. At first George was reluctant to even talk about such a commission but gradually he agreed to meet for a walk up and down Fifth Avenue in New York. I explained what I wanted to accomplish in the memorial and I told him how much I appreciated the impact of his sculpture and its social values. I told him that I wanted to convey the same kinds of legends. We walked for several hours but George was still reluctant. I gathered he was concerned about the complexity of making sculpture for a public commission. The more we talked about the important linkage between sculpture and this memorial, however, the more I felt his enthusiasm grow and finally he agreed that he would think about it and let me know.

The interviews and interactions with the sculptors during the selection process were among the most interesting and provocative of my life. As we talked I expressed my concerns about working with sculptors who were used to designing objects for galleries and museums without the need to consider their ultimate spaces. I emphasized the need for the artists to understand the size and choreography of the memorial. I asked about their willingness to participate in a team effort and accept my role as the overall designer. I also explained how I intended to use my RSVP process to provide the understanding and consensus building that I felt was so necessary.

They, on the other hand, expressed excitement, concerns, and dilemmas I had expected as well as some that took me by surprise. Some worried that they would need to reinvent their entire working process, some simply felt it would be just too stressful and invasive to open themselves to the required review process, and several sculptors questioned whether they would even survive what they thought would be a three- to four-year project. Robert Graham, the youngest of the sculptors interviewed, was perhaps the most open to the expansive nature of the experience that the commission offered. It seemed that he was looking for a chance to change and grow in new directions. Leonard Baskin's name had come to my mind originally because of his beautiful calligraphy and the way he often incorporated it into his artwork. During our interview we talked extensively about how to capture FDR's words on the granite walls that formed our four great outdoor spaces. Leonard highly recommended the stone carver John Benson to work with me on the letter design and layout for FDR's inscriptions.

Eventually my recommendation to the FDR Memorial Commission was that we have a team of four sculptors. I proposed that each would be assigned one or two locations that would then be seamlessly integrated into the overall scheme. I proposed that the specific assignment of themes and locations grow out of their own strengths during several "Taking Part" workshops. The commission considered all of my recommendations and

added some of their own. In this way the list of four sculptors was finalized: Leonard Baskin, Neil Estern, Robert Graham, and George Segal.

The first workshop was held in November 1977. None of the sculptors knew each other at that point, and I remember their confusion and concern about the workshop that they all began to call a sculpture jam session. Upon being introduced to George Segal, Leonard Baskin commented, "I never thought to be the friend of a pop artist." George smiled at the strange compliment. Then I believe he spoke for the whole group when he said, "Every one of us is trained to stubborn individualism but the process sounds both pragmatic and idealistic. . . . I'll say yes." That exchange broke the ice and was the beginning of the real team building. We started by spending four intense days together in a huge warehouse at Fort Mason, alongside San Francisco Bay (Figure 129). A large-scale model of the memorial layout was spread out on the concrete floor. The RoundHouse office staff provided mechanic's dollies for the artists to lie on so that they could roll through the spaces at eye level (Figure 130). Then we began to work in an intense *charette* mode, getting to know one another as we immersed ourselves in the design.

The team became even more bonded as we viewed newsreels and began to reminisce about FDR and our personal memories of his presidency. Eventually this led to long discussions on who would take on what theme. Creativity flowed freely as we agreed on the themes for the four basic outdoor spaces and how people would encounter the sculptures as they walked through the rooms. I grew ever more excited about the vital role the sculptures would play as a counterpoint to the quotations on the walls and the abstracted sense of a growing intensity that was reflected in the changing granite surfaces and waterfalls.

By the time we finished with this first sculpture workshop (or jam session) it was time to get started on a comprehensive presentation of the memo-

Figure 129

Sue Yung Li Ikeda, Robert Graham, George Segal, Lawrence Halprin, Leonard Baskin, Neil Estern. At the beginning of the first artists' workshop we stood outside the Fort Mason warehouse in front of an outline that represented the twelve-foot wall that would serve as the spine for the FDR Memorial.

Figure 130

A large scale model of the FDR Memorial gave the sculptors a chance to "get inside" the design. George Segal looks from the entrance toward Room Two, where his three sculptures will reside.

rial design for the U.S. Congress. Because of the complexity of the concept, we decided that a short twelve-minute film accompanied by a formal presentation and report would be most appropriate. As the report and film were in process, each sculptor worked on in their studio developing conceptual maquettes, and when we met at George Segal's studio for the second workshop, in January 1978, we had a great deal to share (Figures 131, 132). The FDR Memorial film, produced by Glen Fleck for RoundHouse, was such a success that several times in intervening years people assured me that the memorial was already built because they had seen it. The fact that Glen Fleck was able to produce this belief in 1978 without animation or digital manipulation was a measure of his talent.

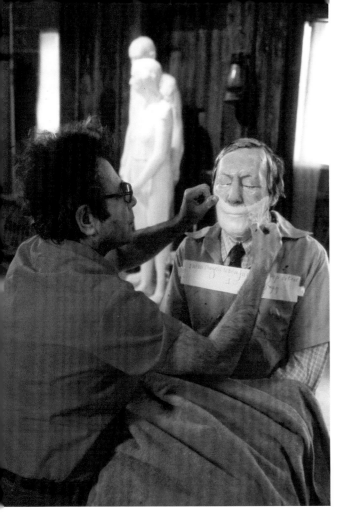

Figure 131

The second artist's workshop was held in George Segal's studio in New Jersey. In the background there is a mockup of a sculpture George proposed for Room Two of the memorial. In the foreground, George demonstrates his molding technique on Leonard Baskin.

Figure 132

Discussions regarding the manner in which to represent the horrors of war ended in tumbling down a wall in Room Three. It was decided that words from President Roosevelt's quote regarding war would be repeated on the fallen stones.

Figure 133

In my notebook I made sketches of the relationship of the Levi Strauss site to Telegraph Hill, Coit Tower, and the Filbert Steps. The plan for the development focused on this relationship.

have made their move ----

The context & environment impacts the design -- at the foot of traditionally bohemian Telegraph Hill - in an old warehouse district. The Hill anchors the design which opens up to it...

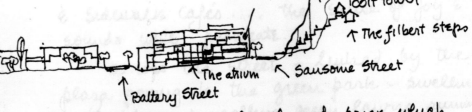

stepped Balconies

Coit tower

The filbert steps

The atrium   Sansome Street

Battery Street

The buildings are built of red brick which link them to the traditional warehouses of the neighborhood... balconies at each floor step down in all directions bringing the sense of the cascading of the hill down into the scheme.

Buildings are disposed around a great plaza

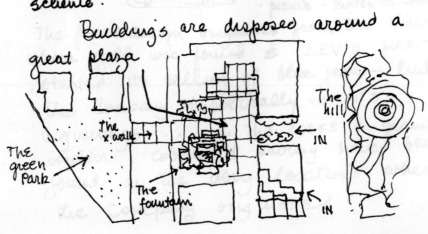

The green park

The x walk →

The fountain

The hill

IN

IN

Levi Plaza

That same year, I received a surprise call from Gerson Bakar, a valued friend and client, for whom I'd worked on a number of innovative and successful housing projects. Gerson said he needed my help with something and I invited him over to share an abalone lunch I was in the process of preparing. He hurried over and we started talking as I pounded the abalone. Then, with a straight face, he told me he understood I was no longer taking on new landscape design projects and asked my advice on what firm he should hire for an exciting new development he was planning right next door, the Levi Plaza project. This was my neighborhood, where the building I had owned with the partners at the office of Wurster, Bernardi, & Emmons for many years was located. I knew the Haas family who owned Levi Strauss and had even designed a small residential garden for Peter Haas. I already knew that this San Francisco company had a wonderful reputation and that the Haas family was renowned for their generous philanthropy. I needed a few minutes to take this all in so I suggested we walk right out and look the situation over on-site. I left the abalone soaking in the beaten eggs and when we returned I had the job. Gerson knew damn well I would be hooked.

I had not intended to stop the RoundHouse explorations or return to landscape design so soon but this was a major project I could not refuse. In quick succession the railroad evicted us in order to develop their site, I moved into an empty building on the Levi project site, RoundHouse closed, and I reopened as the Office of Lawrence Halprin.

I was excited about many elements of the Levi project. I was impressed that the Levi Strauss Company had realized that their recent move to a high-rise building in the Embarcadero Center had been destructive to their family-style working relationships. I was also pleased to hear that they did not want to move out to the suburbs to solve the problem. A number of businesses had recently done just that. The fact that Gerson Bakar had a magnificent, undeveloped site so close to the heart of the city seemed auspicious, and the proximity of Telegraph Hill and the San Francisco Bay provided a spectacular dramatic setting (Figure 133). In 1980 as the project was taking shape, I was interviewed by Levi's in-house newsletter and I was adamant about the future success of the four-acre project. I foresaw that the park, plaza, fountains, stream, restaurants, and services would draw adjacent condominium development and it would become a very lively place. I said that I thought this was the kind of multipurpose urban development that would be the future of the city (Figure 134). I was certain that the future was not the single-purpose office block development. For all those reasons and more I thought this was a damned important project.

Figure 134

While visiting quarries in my search for granite for the FDR Memorial, I saw this evocative carnelian granite stone. After being sawed into three pieces, it was loaded on train cars and shipped to San Francisco, where it became the water source for the main Levi Plaza fountain.

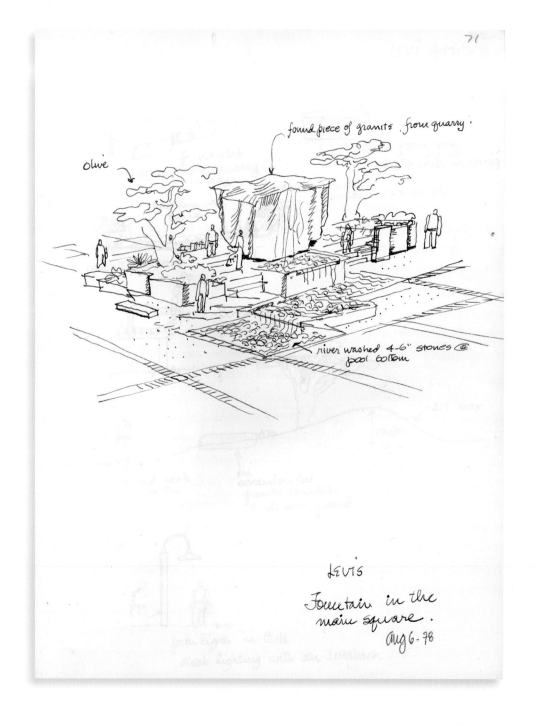

During the first few years of reestablishing myself as the Office of Lawrence Halprin I was constantly searching for new ways of structuring the office that would allow me to explore, be creative and productive, but also be flexible. I wanted to be able to take on just about anything but I did not want a large staff to manage and maintain. I wanted to have freedom without too much worry about the bottom line. I struggled to keep the office small and strategic—transforming it from a one-man operation for some projects to a larger entity when necessary—for workshops, competitions, or a short-term push to complete some phase of a project. For years we were also nomadic, moving from the railroad roundhouse, to the Levi project site, back to the building I shared with Wurster, Bernardi, & Emmons at the foot of Telegraph Hill, and eventually to an old warehouse south of Market Street, in the SOMA neighborhood. Somehow I usually managed to be out of the country or on vacation during all the moves, but I heard about them from Dee Mullen, who had become the management, administration side of the office.

While working in the nearly abandoned building that was soon to be demolished to make way for the Levi project my small transient teams and I were kept busy. One group was finishing up the report for the Berkeley CED workshop, another building a scale model of the FDR Memorial project, and some were working on the Armon Hanaziv

Master Plan for Jerusalem—a plan to protect a biblical landscape adjacent to and overlooking the Old City of Jerusalem. The Levi project was moving fast and needed project management and someone I trusted to turn my conceptual drawings into design development and construction drawings (Figure 135). This was a challenge that could not be met with an ephemeral staff; the task required stability and continuity. As I considered various options I remembered Willie Lang, who had worked in my office for a number of years. I knew I could work with Willy and I had heard he had opened his own office with George Omi. I called to see if Omi Lang Associates could provide the help I needed and become the associated landscape architect on the job. They suggested Paul Scardina, a recent graduate from Berkeley, to project manage. I questioned the ability of such a young man for this high-profile job but after an interview with him I agreed. The collaboration was a success and I realized that such an association could be a part of my small-office design arsenal.

As the design development phase of the Levi project drew to an end I decided to move back to the building I jointly owned with Wurster, Bernardi, & Emmons. By now my old associates from LH&A had moved on and I took over the fourth floor and mezzanine. This old warehouse felt like a comfortable old shoe although it was too large for

12

A Transitional Search

my current needs. As the move was taking place I took off for a long trip that took me first to Israel for ongoing projects and then to Japan to follow up on an intriguing invitation I had received in the summer of 1979.

The Japanese invitation provided an opportunity to test both my desire for exploration and the concept of a specialized team approach. The initial call had come from Dentsu, a public-relations firm. They said they had learned of our unique RSVP Process and its use in workshops that facilitated communication and participation within groups. Apparently some people within Dentsu had read my *RSVP Cycles* book and had spoken with Kazue Kobata, an insightful and talented young woman who had worked with me as a translator on occasion. They were contacting me on behalf of Tokyu, a subsidiary of Kintetsu, one of the largest companies in Japan. Tokyu were developers of modest-cost housing projects as well as office buildings. They owned railroads and even a Japanese baseball team. They wanted to improve the internal communications between their divisions and asked me to help them train their management personnel and staff. I thought it was an interesting challenge but I had some misgivings.

I had only been to Japan a few times since the war and those trips had not allowed much travel or exploration. The first time I was working

with Kenzo Tange, the Japanese architect, when he, Marcel Breuer, and I were commissioned to develop a six-hundred-acre sports complex in New York on the former site of the 1939 and 1964 world fairs. Later, Tange and I were also both involved in an early design for the Yerba Buena Center in San Francisco. During those early trips I had been kept busy working. I discussed the idea with Anna, who it turned out showed a great deal of interest in the Japanese invitation. She was intrigued with Butoh dance and knew Min Tanaka, a renowned Japanese Butoh dancer. She encouraged me to accept the invitation, but first I wanted to test the waters a bit, which was why I added a side trip to Japan onto my upcoming trip to Israel.

On my trip I held several planning meetings with the Dentsu representatives. I wondered how the Japanese would assimilate the idea of community involvement as well as how workshops could help resolve their internal corporate communication. I quickly learned that the usual methodology in Japan was from the top down. The approach was extremely hierarchical and it would be a challenge to apply a process that stressed diversity of participants and equality of input. The intensely organized structure of my visit and the evolution of my negotiations with the Japanese were in almost comedic contrast to the Israeli half of my trip. In Israel every decision was always open to being reconsidered

Figure 135
Even when the fountain was turned off during a drought, it remained a favorite spot for relaxing, visiting, and eating lunch.

and discussions went around in circles as new ideas were added or criteria were changed. In Japan there was no going back. Once something was decided, it became the foundation for the next decision. All of this became evident when Dee showed me the two trip files after I returned. My correspondence regarding the Israeli visit took up volumes while the Japan files were small, neat, and tidy.

Once I decided to accept Dentsu's invitation, my first task was to build a workshop team to take with me to Japan, and I began that process by asking Anna and our dear friend and colleague Jim Burns to join me. Jim, formerly a senior editor of *Progressive Architecture,* had joined my office years before based almost entirely on his intense interest in the workshop process. When he left LH&A, he set up his own office to lead workshops for small communities, often in collaboration with architectural offices. Anna, of course, would bring her own expertise, an emotional and expressive approach to problem solving through movement and collective creativity. Dai Williams, who had been with my office off and on since 1969, rounded out the team with his deep interest in diverse cultures and how they interacted with their natural environments.

I suppose it was inevitable that I would begin to question the task I had been asked to perform. My clients assumed that we would focus on the CEOs of the company and follow their hierarchical approach. They were confused by my request for more diversity—I wanted to include artists, sociologists, journalists, and anthropologists. I wanted to involve more women and young people in the workshop. As I restated my point of view, I became more adamant. I explained that if they wanted our involvement it had to be done according to our process—otherwise, it would not be a success, and I would not want to be involved.

In order to overcome these divergent points of view, I sent a representative who had participated in the workshop process. I hoped that he could personally explain our intentions and objectives and help them to understand the reasons for all of the elements we wanted to include. Kazue Kobata, our invaluable translator and cultural consultant, was also there to explore the types of artistic participants we might include in our proposed workshops in order to provide as much diversity as possible.

As a result of these negotiations we did eventually reach the following agreements: We would have two workshops, the first for creative, artistic participants (leaning more toward collective creativity) and the second for executives and staff members or "salarymen" (who would be more interested in the usefulness of the RSVP Cycles). In this way we were able to meet some of our objectives. We would be reaching a more diverse audience and presenting everyone with situations that were very different from their usual "Japanese way." It was not an ideal solution since it split the two groups so distinctly but it was a solution I felt would provide participants with new ways to interact with one another and potentially with Japanese community groups as well.

The venue for the first workshop for artists was at Lake Hakone at the foot of Mount Fuji. Everyone stayed at a hotel on the shore of the lake. We had beautiful views and a fine conference facility for the workshop—both indoors and out. I had been given to understand that the Japanese culture encourages everyone to fit in and does not encourage differences. I thought of the old saw about nails that stick up and thereby get hammered down. For that reason I wanted to start the workshop by having participants relate on an individual—not on a group—level. I began the artists' workshop with the following two scores.

Score #1 was held in a conference room at our lakeside hotel. I asked each participant to create a self-portrait. The portrait was to be not only a physical sketch or description, but also a self-history that explained who they were and how they came to be this person as a result of their background, their environment, their personal growth and development (Figure 136). I thought that sharing this portrait/history would not only introduce each person to the workshop group but also perhaps inform their future interactions within their families and communities.

Score #2, an environmental awareness walk, was held in a striking outdoor venue—a local Shinto shrine set in a crytomeria forest. I felt very at home in this location because the crytomeria are very similar to northern California redwoods and Mount Fuji's silhouette reminded me, by its quality and shape, of Mount Tamalpais, which I see from my own garden. For this exercise we blindfolded the participants and led them in single file through the area. They were told to focus on their senses (touch, smell, hearing, kinetics) and to use all the senses to experience their environment in a new,

Figure 136

Individual introductory scores were taken very seriously and we began to get a good sense of the workshop participants.

Figure 137

The second workshop group was quite different. These participants were employees and we moved the venue to the small town of Tamagawa, where we could encounter real-life development situations.

fresh way. Later, they shared their individual experiences with the group.

Our second workshop group, with Tokyu and Dentsu staff members, was quite different. The employees took a week away from their routines and were taken to Tamagawa, a suburban town south of Tokyo. Tamagawa was a typical small town built along a river. There was a railroad center, a shopping center, various small neighborhoods, and, of course, a public park threatened by development. This appeared to be a typical Japanese suburb

and represented the type of environment where these participants would later face real-life situations (Figure 137).

I felt this was a perfect site for the staff workshop since this group included management-level staffers who dealt with development-problem-solving issues on a daily basis. The reason I was invited was to help them understand my RSVP Cycles process, so this workshop started with a different type awareness walk through the environment. The participants followed their scores along the river, over several typical bridges and through fishing and recreational areas. They saw the inhabitants, especially the children, in their daily routines. This awareness walk was followed by a sequence of design and problem-solving scores that gave us a way of introducing the RSVP Cycles process. I was impressed with their incredible enthusiasm and the serious attention they paid to each score (Figure 138).

Following these scores, we moved on to a Tokyu department store in Tamagawa and began to move vertically to the roof of the building—experiencing the various clothing and food areas along the way. On the roof we found a small pet shop with large aquariums full of fish. I was charmed by the colorful koi with their fancy fins and watched them closely thinking that I might add some to my gardens. Suddenly there was a great deal of excitement in the tanks and the fish literally began jumping out of the water. I was enthralled and wondered at their behavior. Within a few moments, however, the meaning became clear as a strong earthquake began to shake the store. The fish had obviously sensed the quake well in advance. We all hurried down from the roof to the ground floor and scurried outside. I was impressed by the koi and felt they would indeed be a fine addition to any garden in an earthquake area. I felt that the score had been seriously interrupted, but I was told that such earthquakes are common in Japan and the participants felt no need to change our plans.

Near the end of this visit to Japan, Kazue, Dai, and I went out to dinner to discuss our experience and what we might do with the materials we

had gathered. Kazue suggested one of her favorite eateries. It was a remarkably comfortable and well-appointed little bar/restaurant where we were served on a handsome hand-sanded cryptomera plank banquette. Despite its small size, the owner managed to serve us ten delicious and surprising courses that kept us from our intended discussion for some time. The attention given to presentation was obvious and I still remember that they served a clear soup in a bowl made of kelp and a sea bass bone that arrived with only a few fragments of delicious meat still attached. Eventually we did get back to our intended discussion and we debriefed about the workshop and how to prepare our feedback presentation.

I took this opportunity to ask Kazue about comments I had made at the end of the first workshop when I was feeling extremely close to all the participants. I knew our process had been unusual for them and I wanted to thank them for their efforts to understand and participate fully. I also wanted to let them know how much I had enjoyed the experience. In my attempt to express the intensity of my emotions I mentioned that I had once fought against the Japanese at Okinawa and had suffered when my ship was hit, but now I was delighted to have changed my Japanese memories to ones that were warm and friendly. My comments were met by absolute silence and I was confused.

Figure 138

All participants approached the workshop with enthusiasm and were thoughtful even when faced with confusing and frustrating cultural differences.

A Transitional Search

Kazue then carefully explained to me that in the Japanese culture one is trained not to reveal feelings of shame in the presence of others. I began to understand how my comments had thoughtlessly crossed a cultural line and I recalled that Ned Hall, the anthropologist I met on the Doxiadis tours, wrote books about just such issues. This led to further discussion about other cultural tensions the workshop may have triggered. Our process asked for feelings and opinions that Japanese employees were trained to repress in a corporate environment. I began to realize and appreciate how difficult our scores had been—especially for the salarymen— and that sometimes a quiet comment takes a great deal of courage. After many cups of sake and lots more conversation I felt a greater sense of accomplishment, but when the bill arrived I was snapped back into the present. I was sure I was misreading it but our cultural interpreter assured me that $640 was not extreme for Tokyo.

Ode to the Not Built

As with the two projects I undertook with Kenzo Tange, during this transitional period I undertook a number of other exciting projects that were never implemented. Three of those unbuilt projects were important; at least, their memories remain so to me. One was in Jerusalem, another in Los Angeles, and a third in Florence, Italy. They provide good examples of why it is stimulating to take on big innovative challenges that can break new ground—they can provide inspiration along with the sense of loss.

The project in Jerusalem came about because of a desire to restore part of the Old City that had been badly damaged during the 1948 War of Independence. The area, known as the Jewish Quarter, needed more than just repairs, and in discussions with the city I said that we could meet their requirements (bus terminal, parking, sixty-five new housing units, distribution center, twenty new shops and cafes, an archaeological garden, and a series of plazas, courtyards, and walkways to connect the neighborhood) while at the same time protecting the Old City from the onslaught of modern transportation problems. I pulled together a small task force and invited Norman Kondy and Tom Aidala to travel with me to Jerusalem. I had worked with both of these men before and I respected their planning and architectural experience. Norman also worked with me often as an architectural illustrator and I greatly appreciated his unique ability. In 1980 I presented a design solution that included an underground entrance tunnel into the Old City. The tunnel would preserve the ancient city wall but allow tour buses, delivery vehicles, and private cars into an underground parking garage (Figure 139). From there, we proposed deliveries, tourists, and locals could transfer to small three-wheeled

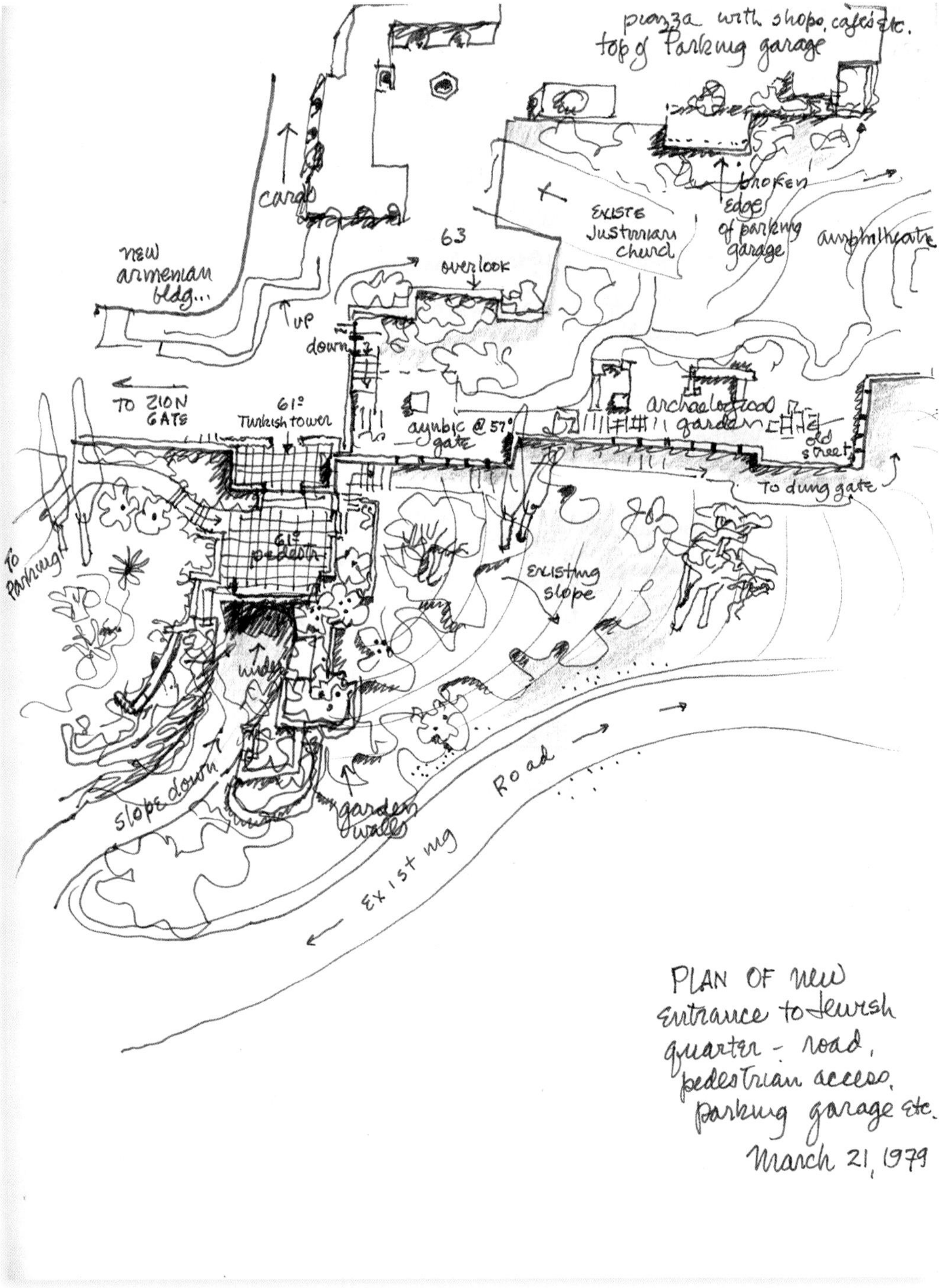
piazza with shops, cafes etc.
top of Parking garage
cars
new armenian bldg...
63
overlook
EXISTG
Justinian
church
broken
edge
of parking
garage
amphitheatre
up
down
TO ZION GATE
61°
Turkish tower
ayubic @ 57°
gate
archaeological
garden
old
street
To dung gate
To Parking
61°
pedestn
existing
slope
slope down
garden
walls
Road
Existing
PLAN OF new
entrance to Jewish
quarter - road,
pedestrian access,
parking garage etc.
March 21, 1979

Figure 139

I spent a great deal of time considering the concept of a tunnel into the Old City of Jerusalem. I felt that the parking garage could provide access and help to eliminate many modern-day transportation and delivery problems.

To Zion gate
& parking

car tunnel
into undergrd
parking....

column of
ayubic gate
reused

NO To Dung
gate.

PROPOSED: NEW Pedestrian GATE
TO Jewish quarter IN
Turkish tower & ON
axis with the ROMAN
Cardo...

March 21, 1979

Figure 140

On top of the tunnel, I proposed a new pedestrian gate into the Jewish Quarter.

carriers or walk to their destinations. The four-level underground garage was designed to bring pedestrians out into a new archaeological garden and serve new adjacent housing units, commercial spaces, and cafes (Figures 140, 141). The plan also provided access to important new excavations that had been revealed in 1977. Unfortunately, although there was a great deal of support for this solution, the city was never able to find the will and the funding required for such a complex vision.

During this same time frame Rob Maguire and his partner Jim Thomas asked me to join an impressive team competing for the right to develop eleven acres on upper Bunker Hill in downtown Los Angeles. The competition, sponsored by the Los Angeles Community Redevelopment Agency, included four office towers, a hotel, and a new Museum of Contemporary Art. Although Los Angeles was known throughout the world, it did not yet have a city center. Maguire Thomas Partners brought together an extraordinary team: Barton Myers, Harvey Perloff, and Edgardo Contini coordinated the master plan in consultation with

Figure 141

Our working model for the Rovah project made it easy for everyone to understand the relationship of the tunnel, four-story garage, housing and commercial spaces, as well as the outdoor amphitheater and archaeological garden.

A Transitional Search

Charles Moore, Cesar Pelli, and me. Charles Moore and I designed some fabulous open spaces—including the Angeles Steps, courts and fountains, and an urban boulevard on Grand Avenue (Figures 142, 143). Cesar Pelli, Robert Kennard, Ricardo Legoretta, Barton Myers, and Charles Moore designed the major structures. Hugh Hardy designed the approach to the Los Angeles Museum of Contemporary Art and Frank Gehry designed Angel's Place and integrated Angel's Flight, a historic funicular, into the project. The result was bold and exciting and received wide acclaim.

I enjoyed the buzz generated by this high-energy team and I especially enjoyed working closely with Charles Moore again (Figure 144). He was a good friend and our collaboration was effortless. We could silently work on the same drawing together intuitively understanding what the other intended. I felt that the concept, master plan, and individual design elements were exceedingly appropriate for the city of Los Angeles and the region. The presentation drawings and the book that was designed to document the proposal were elegant (Figure 145, 146). I had worked on the Crocker Center for Maguire Thomas Partners and I knew they were innovative and financially savvy. Apparently it was their inexperience with the political aspects of such a venture that undermined their submittal.

Figure 142 *(facing page)*
This illustration by Carlos Diniz gives an overview of the exciting eleven-acre development proposal Maguire Thomas Partners presented to the Los Angeles Community Redevelopment Agency.

Figure 143
Taken from a page of the proposal.

Figure 144

Charles Moore and I were good friends and enjoyed the times we could work together. In this case the Grand Avenue proposal was the focus of our attention.

Figure 145

This working sketch gives a sense of the richness and excitement the proposal offered at the street level.

In 1987, another fabulous and complex urban challenge came my way via the Italian car company Fiat. In 1983, I had been introduced to Fiat when the Italian architecture critic Bruno Zevi produced an international list of twenty architects to take part in a unique and exciting competition. At that time, Fiat was looking for innovative ideas for reusing their enormous, outmoded car factory in Turin. They treated the competition as a joyful opportunity to explore creativity and they invited all of us for personal tours of the facility, sent video teams to our individual offices to document our process, and pulled together an amazing exhibit and book that featured the proposals. I was therefore extremely pleased and honored when Fiat's representative, Alberto Giordano, called me in 1987

to ask if I would work with Fiat on another remarkable project—this time in Florence.

I had always loved Florence, its location along the Arno River, and the way that the bridges crossing the river have been converted to great streetlike experiences. It is a joy to walk and shop there and watch the views change as you shift from one bank to the other. Traffic and congestion is a problem, however, because the city was not built to accommodate modern traffic demands and the enormous numbers of tourists. Fiat hoped to alleviate some of these problems by relocating the governmental and administrative center of Florence to an old factory site they owned on the outskirts of town. During the Turin project Fiat had become aware of my collective creativity workshop process. They asked if I

Figure 146

Courtyards, fountains, and arcades provide a variety of public amenities in the Grand Avenue proposal.

Figure 147

When we began reviewing the workshop process with the architects in Florence, the air was heavy with tension.

would use it to coordinate planning for the whole Florence project.

I was concerned about how my American methodology would translate to a group of hot-shot European architects who had never been exposed to such a democratic design process. My Fiat client, as represented by Italo Castore and Alberto Giordano,

said they understood my concerns but felt that such an extremely talented group would find it challenging and interesting. Once again, Bruno Zevi was called upon and selected thirteen architects to work on the project. Ten were Italians, two were Americans, and Richard Rogers was from England. None of them had ever participated in workshops of this kind or tried collective creativity in such an expansive form.

I put together a small workshop team of trusted associates, agreed to a date in September for the first workshop, and took off for Italy. I started in my usual way to unveil a score that would explore our mission and reviewed the constraints of geography, transportation, housing, budget, costs, etc. As Italo Castore and I stood in front of this high-powered group and presented the format and score for the first day, I felt like we were facing a stone wall (Figure 147). I could feel the tension as we all walked out of the workshop space to examine the site. They felt that we were treating them like a bunch of school children and the air felt thick and unfriendly. By the end of the first workshop, however, we had defined fourteen points of consensus for moving forward.

The Italian architectural critic Giovanni Klaus Koenig acted as a witness for our three workshops and later wrote about the experiment: "Castore and Halprin had an idea—really tempting providence: supposing we tried to work collectively on the shape of the project with the contribution of all fourteen participants. . . . Above all else," he conceded, "the great danger is that of not being able to control the animus of creative genius."

In his article, Koenig captured all the feelings of intensity generated by those talented architects, who were being subjected to a kind of control they had never before experienced. It was clear on day one that they did not enjoy the control. This was the reverse of the usual approach that great architects insist upon. I absolutely understood that they usually insisted upon individuality and even egotism as part of their design processes. It was extremely difficult for me to face this form of resistance from designers for whom I held such high regard. The collective resistance was made up of lifetimes of insistence on self-indulgence in regard to design. We were asking them to follow a methodology that was diametrically opposed to their customary approach. Italo and I had to find a way to overcome their resistance in order to continue with the Fiat workshop. I wanted to use my process and they wanted to act individually. It was thirteen to one.

This conflict was not resolved quickly. Gradually, however, we overcame the tension by working together on an overall landscape plan within which each architect developed specific building plans. Working together in this way became more and more enjoyable—and increasingly successful (Figure 148). Finally, we arrived at an overall plan that pleased everyone, including Zevi and the client—Fiat. To my own great relief they approved the concept as the master plan for the project. In my notebook I comment that after each intense

Figure 148
Once the workshop group stopped talking and started drawing everything became much easier.

workshop, Italo, Alberto, and I spent a great deal of time in Harry's Bar drinking martinis.

Koenig refers to the plan that developed at the second workshop as follows: "With patience and good will it is still possible to launch a collective project whether town planning or architecture in which exploiting individual creativity to the full is compatible with the coherence of the whole." He also said, "I believe now that I witnessed a miracle just recently on the 9th and 10th of December, 1987 in Florence."

The Florence City Council approved the collaborative plan and everyone was greatly relieved. The Communist Party carried the majority at that time. I left for home feeling that all was well but on arriving home I received word that the National Communist Party in Rome was negative on the proposal for the factory site. I have never completely understood what happened except to say that I believe it was a political decision, not a planning one.

There is always a sense of heavy sadness when projects such as these are not implemented. Planners, architects, and designers know that not every competition will be won and not every innovative concept will be supported but if I had not been so busy I am sure I would have found myself terribly depressed over each lost opportunity. Luckily I was able to get caught up in other demands for my attention but I often think of specific losses, like the

tunnel into the Old City of Jerusalem, or the freeing of downtown Florence from tedious bureaucracy, and I like to think those projects would have added a great deal to the daily life in those wonderful places.

In my case, I often found that when I lost one competition or opportunity, another opened up in the same place or with the same client. During the eighties I completed a number of wonderful projects with Maguire Thomas Partners and several of them are on and around Bunker Hill. Although the historic Angel's Flight funicular was never restored, I designed a grand stairway to link the old downtown to the new development on Bunker Hill (Figure 149). It curves around a seventy-story building that I. M. Pei & Partners designed for Maguire Thomas. At the bottom of the stairs is Library Square, a project of such political and financial complexity I never did understand how Rob and Jim brought it all about; and somehow through it all they were able to save and expand Bertram Goodhue's Los Angeles Central Library. The new park I designed there provides an entrance to the newly renovated library, anchors the Bunker Hill Steps, and reinforces the link to the old downtown (Figures 150, 151). The park that Goodhue had built there many years earlier inspired my design. His park had unfortunately been demolished to provide surface parking. On top of Bunker Hill I also

Figure 149

This super-sized drawing for the Bunker Hill Steps was often used to explain the complex nature of the project.

Figure 150

The Los Angeles Library garden site had been reduced to a parking lot before Maguire Thomas Partners proposed a creative plan to resurrect it.

Figure 151 *(facing page)*

My design for the garden was inspired by Bertram Goodhue's earlier garden, although we had to reinforce the new role it played in an open-space network that led down Hope Street.

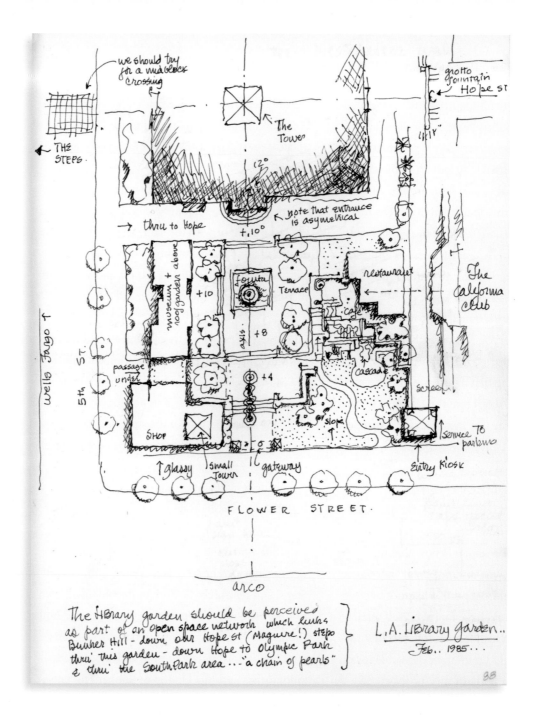

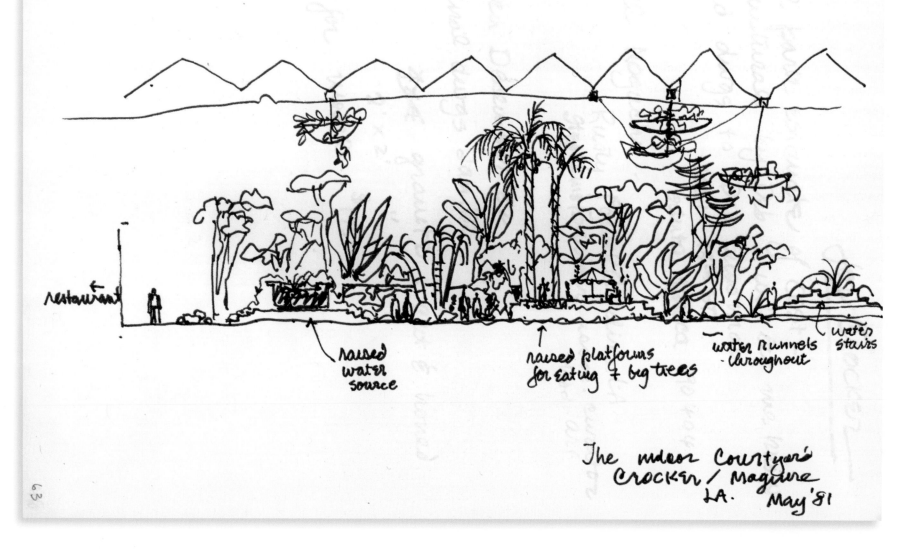

restaurant

raised
water
source

raised platforms
for eating + big trees

water runnels
throughout

water
stairs

The indoor Courtyard
Crocker / Maguire
LA.   May '81

designed an indoor atrium/garden to link the two Crocker Tower buildings that Skidmore, Owings & Merrill designed for Maguire Thomas Partners. I commissioned the sculptor Robert Graham to create centerpieces for the fountains, and the poetic sculptures and trinity of fountains produced an indoor fantasy garden (Figures 152, 153).

In Jerusalem, when the tunnel opportunity was lost, a concept from the Armon Hanatziv Master Plan gained attention. In that plan I had proposed a promenade meandering along the prominent ridge overlooking the Old City of Jerusalem. It was meant to protect the biblical character of the basin and provide everyone with spectacular views and an opportunity to hike and picnic. In the early eighties the Haas family offered to fund the central section of this promenade in the name of their parents and grandparents, Walter and Elise Haas. Because I knew I needed associates who were as committed as I was to Jerusalem and knowledge-able about the ins and outs of construction and bureaucracy there, I contacted Shlomo Aaronson, who had studied at Berkeley and previously worked in my office. Shlomo had an office in Jerusalem and I asked him to be my local associate. He in turn assigned Judy Green, a transplanted American landscape architect, to be my project manager. Once again history, experience, and timing provided me with just the team I needed (Figures 154–56). Soon after the Haas Promenade's completion, Shlomo's office was hired by a local donor to complete the second phase of the promenade as it moved to the west. This piece is known as the Sherover Promenade and it embraces much of the original design vocabulary. Then in the mid-nineties, Richard Goldman, another generous donor from San Francisco, came forward to finance the

Figure 152

I had never designed an indoor atrium but found the scale an interesting challenge.

Figure 153

Graceful, smaller-than-life-sized, bronze sculptures by Robert Graham became the centerpieces for three fountains. With a background of mature palms and lush plant materials, they helped me play with the scale of the courtyard.

A Transitional Search

Figure 154

The light fixtures on the Haas Promenade frame views of the Old City of Jerusalem.

more trees needed

The last niche

hold back 40± meters new recreation bldg base to be stone as on back wall of promenade

EXISTING PINES

Belvedere

new stairs to EXTENSION

add promenade lights on landings

TALPIOT

VIEW TO west showing location & vernacular of Plessner building & steps down to EXTENSION

♪?C - Sept. 26 · 87

89

completion of the promenade. For this final phase I associated myself with architect Bruce Levin, another alumnus from my San Francisco office who had moved to Tel Aviv. The Richard and Rhoda Goldman Promenade moves farther along the ridge toward the east, through a grove of pines and old olive trees toward a magical overlook (Figures 157, 158). On that point, where the view of the Dome of the Rock and the Al Aksa Mosque line up, we built an amphitheater and cafe. Locally, this whole area is known as the *Tayellet* and it fulfills a vision that Teddy Kollek had shared with me decades before. Teddy had long-range dreams for Jerusalem and during his six terms as mayor he shepherded many of them to fulfillment (Figures 159, 160).

Figure 155

Archways supporting the promenade are reminiscent of an ancient aqueduct that once transported water from Bethlehem to Jerusalem along this route.

Figure 156

The graceful curvature of the Haas Promenade provides much more interest than a linear walk.

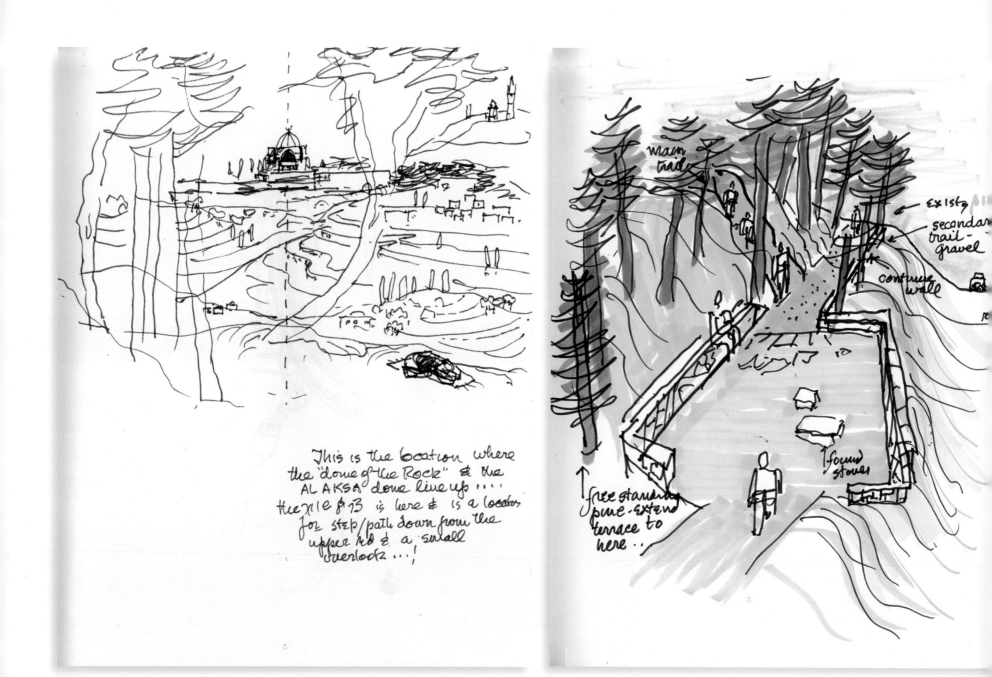

This is the location where the "dome of the Rock" & the AL AKSA dome line up ···· the π¹ e β₁₃ is here & is a locator for step/path down from the upper Rd & a small overlook ···¡

main trail

Exisᵗg secondary trail - gravel

continue wall

free standing pine - extend terrace to here ···

found stones

Figure 157

I was inspired by the alignment of the Dome of the Rock and the Al Aksa Mosque and we provided a small amphitheater and rest area here.

Figure 158

I felt it was important to save every pine tree on the site and meander the trails through them.

Figure 159

The dark asphalt worked well with the local limestone and rust-colored duff from the pines.

Figure 160

The Goldman Promenade passed below the site of the British consul general's residence from the days of the British Mandate (1917–48). I took the opportunity to enlarge upon their old rock garden and design this expanded rest stop.

Figure 161

Standing on a scaffold in the rotunda of the San Francisco Museum of Modern Art, Michael O'Leary and I took on the challenge of installing some super-sized drawings. My whole office staff put in lots of overtime preparing for the show.

Museum of Modern Art

Somewhere in the middle of this topsy-turvy period I received a call from Henry Hopkins, director of the San Francisco Museum of Modern Art. It was 1985 and he asked if I was interested in having a retrospective show the following summer, July–August 1986. He said I could have as much space and oversight as I required. The suggestion caught me off guard because it wasn't (isn't) my nature to look back. I would turn seventy that same year and I wondered if they thought I was getting ready to retire. I said I would think it over and get back to him. Dee, my office manager and sidekick, was immediately struck by the amount of work it would take and how disruptive it would be to our office. She pointed out that we were in the middle of some major projects and did not have time or staff to spare. I talked to family and friends and most of them reiterated the same concerns. They knew I would not sit back and let others choose the items to be shown. They knew I would want to be involved in every aspect of the show. We all knew that a year was not long enough to pull such a show together even if we didn't have projects under way. In the end, of course, I said yes.

We put a great deal of thought and effort into the major professional themes that best represented both me and my work. Our first task was to go through all of the notebooks I had been keeping since 1959, which at that time numbered eighty-three. We painstakingly looked through them all and carefully noted the constantly recurring themes that are evident in most of my projects. Seven themes surfaced: perceptions of nature, water, movement and choreography, networking, ecology of form, scores and workshops, and the RSVP Cycles. We chose the projects that would be most representative of my work and then unrolled thousands of drawings and opened up dusty boxes full of models and shadow boxes. The drawing boards, floors, and walls in my studio were overlaid with possible items for the show. It was a time-consuming experience and often required attention than I did not want to pull away from ongoing projects. I was constantly searching for a clear spot to sit down and make a new drawing.

In order to relieve myself of concerns regarding the installation, I suggested that the museum hire Frank Gehry to help with the design and layout for the show. The museum agreed and Frank designed a large structure for the rotunda that enlivened that vast space but required me to produce some super-scale drawings. It was a challenge to work at that scale and it required even more of my time but I found the process very interesting (Figure 161). Dee then suggested that we get some additional help in-house and tracked down several former associates who would help as liaisons, book designers, and editors. Throughout the whole process, Helene Fried, the curator for the show, made every effort to respond to my concerns. The show's catalogue took on a unique character as friends and former collaborators wrote chapters explaining how we worked together. The title for the show, however, remained elusive and deadlines were growing close. We couldn't all agree until a title came to me at the dentist's office one day while I was having a tooth pulled, perhaps emerging under the influence of some form of anesthetic. The title was *Lawrence Halprin: Changing Places*.

The MOMA show was time consuming in its preparation and it also required lectures, dinners, interviews, and tours. I enjoyed the show, however, and it provided a series of timely visits from family and old friends. After the show closed, however, I needed a rest and took off on my own for a week-long drive north along the coast and inland to sketch in the Richardson Grove State Park and camp along the Eel River. Shortly after I returned I began to get inquiries regarding the future home of my archive. Over the next five or six years I talked to a number of universities and after a visit to the University of Pennsylvania I was convinced that was the best place. Looking back it seems that the MOMA show was a benchmark. It marked a shift in the character of the office. After ten nomadic years I put down some real roots in the 444 Brannan Street building and the Office of Lawrence Halprin became more grounded (Figure 162).

By the mid-eighties my work on the FDR Memorial project picked up speed. All projects have highs and lows but this monumental project with its ephemeral schedule had highs and lows that could only be compared to a roller coaster. The federal appropriations process was the source of much of the problem. We could only move as fast as money was appropriated and this was a political process out of our control. Another part of the timing riddle was the approval process. If the FDR Memorial Commis-

sion of the Fine Arts Commission required a major change it could send us back to the drawing boards.

Back in 1978, for instance, I had pulled together a comprehensive and multifaceted presentation of the FDR Memorial design for my client, the U.S. Congress. There was a formal presentation with exhibits, a sixty-seven-page report, and the twelve-minute film that walked one through the entire memorial experience. It was well received but it would be about eight years before I was given the go-ahead to move forward, and when it arrived, I was told the 1978 construction estimate was still in effect. This news represented a major financial shortfall and rather than skimp on the heights of walls or quality of materials, I immediately began to look for ways to cut away major elements while keeping the essence of the design. The final built design lost four hundred feet in length as well as the fountains, artwork, and quotations that would have resided therein. It also lost an interpretive center that was meant to show old newsreels, broadcast fireside chats, and showcase memorabilia of the FDR era, as well as a café and dining terrace. It was painful to lose those parts of the design but in the years after its completion I came to believe that the primary message is just as powerful.

When I took the modified FDR Memorial design back to Washington for a subsequent presentation to the Fine Arts Commission, the exhibit

Figure 162

My office at 444 Brannan Street was in an old brick warehouse with a wraparound mezzanine. We cut a large hole in the floor to provide easy access to the basement, where we produced most of our models.

Figure 163

I visited Leonard Baskin in his studio in
Leeds, Massachusetts, to review changes he
was making to a bas-relief of FDR.

Figure 164

When asked to reorient the entrance experience, I
moved from a dramatic approach to one built on a
feeling of anticipation. Visitors must pass through a
transitional gateway to reach the sacred space.

materials spread beyond the meeting room and
extended back into the bowels of the administrative
office. All of the artists attended this session to present scale models of their sculptures for approval.
This was quite difficult for these artists, for in their
world, the art would be bought or exhibited without
any question of changing the scale or refining a
nose. I appreciated their position and was nervous
on their behalf. Some commissioners did in fact
ask that several of the artists reconsider aspects of
their proposals. They questioned the scale of Neil
Estern's FDR sculpture in Room Three and asked
us to reconsider the president's stance in Leonard
Baskin's bas-relief of FDR at his first inaugural, and
also to provide a larger-scale model of FDR's final
image, "The Apotheosis," in Room Four (Figure
163). The art discussions with the commission also
covered our decision that there would be no titles,
no descriptions, and no attributions associated with
the sculptures. Some members of the Fine Arts
Commission felt that it would be helpful to explain
the art and its historic relevance, but we did not
want the memorial to lecture or hammer messages
to the visitors. The FDR Memorial Commission, the
artists, and I all wanted the art to carry the underlying themes and engage the visitors in deeply felt
dialogues within themselves and with one another.

Then, turning their attention to the site plan,
members of the Fine Arts Commission asked that

I reorient the entrance to the memorial so as not to disturb the existing playing fields and provide a large opening in the memorial wall so that the unique quality of the peninsula site could be appreciated. I was caught off guard because the approach to the site and its isolation had not been questioned at the previous 1978 review. New members of the commission had been appointed during the hiatus, however, and they raised this new concern.

I had given a great deal of thought to the approach to the memorial. And I had located the entrance plaza on one of the major junctions of the 1901 McMillan Plan. I designed the approach so that the geometry of the mall would reveal itself subtly: From the entrance plaza one could see the Lincoln Memorial, and as one walked toward the memorial the contained axial view of the Washington Monument would be visible. I did not want to lose this dramatic quality. After some painful soul-searching, I realized that I needed to shift from a monumental concept to a more symbolic one that required visitors to negotiate a medieval-style gateway (Figure 164). Symbolically, this entrance cues visitors to the fact they are entering a "sacred" space and prepares them for the journey in quite a different manner. After negotiating the gateway they still encounter a magnificent view of the Washington Monument though it is a much different experience than the original design would have provided. When I was

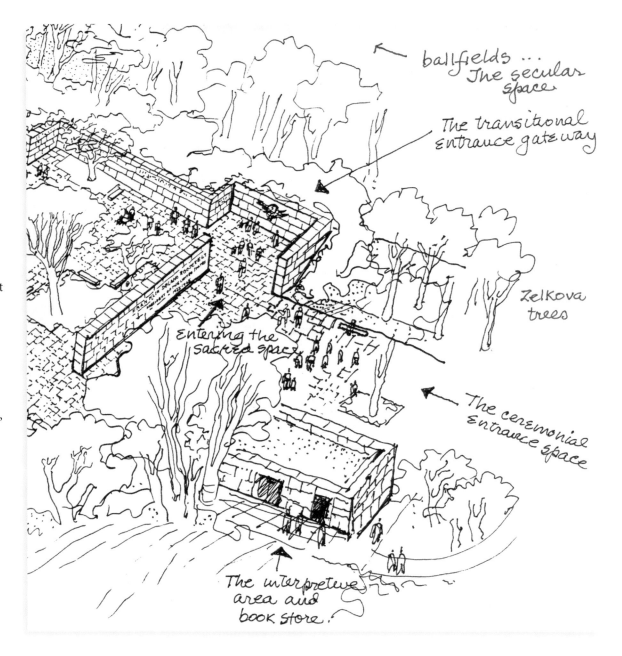

ballfields ... The secular space

The transitional entrance gateway

Zelkova trees

Entering the sacred space

The ceremonial entrance space

The interpretive area and book store.

confident that this new element in the progression would work, we made adjustments as needed to integrate it into the overall design.

The idea of creating an opening in the memorial to provide views was also hard to accept because, although I appreciated the desire for a view of the Potomac River, I did not want to make it possible to cut across the middle of the memorial. As soon as a shift in my perspective allowed me to envision the opening as a window with a bronze grate I was able to move forward and find the correct location and design for a view opportunity (Figure 165).

In 1989 we began our working drawings and hoped for a major appropriation that would allow us to move forward more or less nonstop. Congressman Claude Pepper, who had been a protégé of FDR and was now chairman of the FDR Memorial Commission, was committed to securing the funding (Figure 166). The eighty-nine-year-old chairman left his hospital bed and made his last official trip up

Figure 165

A bronze grate allows views out to the Potomac River and gives a sense of its relationship to the Tidal Basin and Cherry Walk. At this point, visitors can appreciate the overall landform of the peninsula site.

Senator Peppers office
after mtg with Sid Yates
re: FDR memorial
Washington — apr. 3 - 89

Figure 166

Claude Pepper served as senator and U.S. representative from Florida for decades. I visited with Congressman Claude Pepper in his office to discuss the specifics of our situation and he played a pivotal role in securing the funding we needed to move the FDR Memorial project forward.

to Capitol Hill to plead for the dollars necessary to move toward construction. His heroic efforts were successful, and we were finally able to move forward with a greater sense of immediacy and continuity.

It would still take an additional eight years, however, before the memorial was completed and dedicated. During those years the memorial was never far from my mind. In our converted 10,000-square-foot warehouse, we had room enough to build a large-scale model of the entire memorial and even larger-scale models of each fountain (Figures 167, 168). Two black boxes sat on our drawing files—they contained famous images of FDR, his quotations, and most historic moments. This "idea bank" was readily accessible during design sessions. Photos and mock-ups of the in-process sculptures were hanging on the walls. The entire office reflected our long-range goal.

My office remained in the Brannan Street warehouse space for fifteen years. The FDR Memorial was a constant presence there but I was also able to find time for ongoing projects in the Bay Area, a network of open spaces in Los Angeles, and designs for Lake Shore Drive in Chicago and the Goldman Promenade in Jerusalem, as well as workshops near and far including the one in Florence, Italy. The staff grew, but I kept the number under ten and often recycled staff members who went off to graduate school and then returned. I outsourced as

Figure 167

Integration of individual sculptures into the memorial design was an ongoing concern. The initial workshops provided a vehicle for us to work together but our collaboration needed continuity in order for us to produce an artistic whole.

Figure 168

The stone carver John Benson was an integral part of the artistic team. There was an important linkage between the sculptures and FDR's quotations.

needed and had a wonderful stable of consultants, many of whom I had worked with for decades. My project teams were usually made up of the same trusted friends: Russell Fudge at GFDS Engineering, Dick Chaix at CMS Collaborative for fountain work, Patrick Quigley of Patrick Quigley & Associates for lighting design, Ed Burger for architecture, and Norman Kondy for presentation drawings and illustrations. Omi Lang Associates continued providing working drawings for many of my projects. Paul Scardina, the young project manager whose youth I'd questioned on the Levi project, had opened his own firm, Befu, Morris, Scardina, with two friends and between 1989 and 1994 they completed the FDR Memorial working drawings.

Having this cadre of trusted associates was very reassuring and gave me the confidence I needed to continue taking on innovative and exploratory work. These professionals always kept a responsible eye on the big picture and kept me on point regarding all of the early sequencing required for FDR. The Army Corps of Engineers, for instance, had created the memorial site in 1887 by piling fill on a sandbar. Years in advance of construction, therefore, the memorial site had to be heavily loaded. Specified trees also had to be bought and grown for specific locations, and granite had to be cut during the summer and fall because the winter months were too cold to work in a quarry that lay on the border of Minnesota and South Dakota. During one winter visit to the quarry, a warming hut was transported out to give us an opportunity to view a mock-up. It was definitely too cold to stay outside long enough to cut and transport large slabs of granite.

In my SOMA office I continued to work in my own stubborn style. I sketched and my staff worked a great deal with storyboards, shadow boxes, and models. Then we'd transfer our information to drawing and report formats to document the decisions. The more I saw of computers the less I trusted them. Everything looked finished and refined on the computer screen even if it was just a preliminary idea. With computers there was a tendency to move too fast, not sleep on ideas or test them in three dimensions. We did, of course, have computers in the office but I looked askance at them and grew to resent the time that staff members spent staring at the screens while locked into headsets. I could no longer look over shoulders with a red pencil poised in my hand. I have never become comfortable with computers and for years they were kept out of sight in back rooms and basements.

By 1993, after almost twenty years, we knew that we would soon begin the actual building of the FDR Memorial. We also knew we had to restructure our office for the thirty-month-long construction process. We put out the word that we needed a contracts manager and found Susan Aitken, a thoughtful young architect who had the patience we sorely needed for such a daunting and detailed assignment. Paul Scardina and one of his partners, Dan Morris, agreed to come to work for me full time. Paul would project manage from San Francisco and Dan would move to Washington, D.C. The large fountain models were packed up and sent back to the construction site to help explain the complex arrangement of the fountains. It was a demanding time. I flew back often to check on progress, answer questions, make adjustments, and work with our clients. There were, of course, problems. A formidable old elm tree had, for example, been used as an anchor point from which we began our measurements. It was struck by lighting and came down just as we began staging for construction. Winter rains were unusually heavy the first year and the Potomac River was close to flood levels. All in all, however, the construction site was a happy place. Everyone working on the project was excited and honored to be part of the project. The construction teams were both professional and personal. They would often approach me to comment on the design or tell how their own families were connected to FDR. The work was carried out with pride, passion, and team spirit.

During this intense time friends encouraged me to produce a book about the long, complex process that had brought the memorial into being. I was told that it would be a unique opportunity for me to explain the choreography and design intent as I had done so many times to review boards, consultants, friends, and family members. Most of the material was already available in my office and I took up the challenge to engage in yet another aspect of the design process. It was rewarding to remember all that happened and record it in an organized way. It was also a good opportunity to thank many of those who were deeply involved. And, finally, I believe it was cathartic as it gave me one last opportunity to put down all the emotions that had gone into the twenty-three-year-long journey. I enjoyed writing that book.

When the FDR Memorial was dedicated in May 1997, I was overjoyed—it was the most overwhelming professional moment of my career. At the same time, however, I already knew that it wasn't over yet. As the opening of the FDR Memorial had drawn near, an unexpected challenge appeared on the horizon, and threatened to upset the opening, the design, and the composition of the memorial itself.

Over the years of planning, conceptual design, artist workshops, and multiple presentations to the FDR Memorial Commission and the Fine Arts Commission we had all reached a consensus on how to represent President Franklin Delano Roosevelt. As a group we recognized that, historically, FDR had spent a great deal of time and effort on keeping the results of his polio from the public. We wanted to follow his lead, be true to the attitudes of the time, and use approved images that were taken from the archives. In the first outdoor room of the memorial, FDR is shown enthusiastically waving his hat as he drove away from his first inauguration and in the third room he is seated in a large armchair specially designed for the Roosevelt family. The president's body language and attitude are accurately portrayed and his disability is underplayed, as was his preference. In Room Two and Room Four his presence is represented indirectly. In Room Two he is called to mind by a statue of a barefoot man sitting by a Philco radio and intensely listening to one of FDR's fireside chats. And as visitors enter Room Four they encounter the sad representation of FDR's funeral caisson surrounded by solemn mourners.

During the final year of the project's construction, however, members of the disabled community decided that it was important to make his disability more obvious so that the whole world could appreciate that a person with such a serious disability had led the country through one of its most difficult and trying periods. I resisted their demand for a number of reasons: a philosophical approach had been thoughtfully considered and decided upon, the artwork had been planned and carefully integrated into the walls and niches of the project, and an appropriate and thoughtful restructuring of

the design would be both extremely time consuming and costly.

In retrospect, I imagine that the demanding quality of such a singularly focused group played a hand in my reaction as well. The group seemed inappropriate and disrespectful in light of the time and efforts expended since President Roosevelt's death in 1945 and the 1955 congressional resolution that established the FDR Memorial Commission. The politics of the situation, however, were not in my hands. Threats to disrupt the opening ceremonies were taken seriously and the political decision makers decided to negotiate for a compromise. They promised to ask Congress to allow an additional piece of art to be added to the memorial, and so on May 2, 1997, the FDR Memorial was dedicated by President William Clinton (Figure 169) and on July 24, 1997, the same president signed into law an act directing the secretary of the interior to "plan for the design and construction of an addition of a permanent statue, bas-relief, or other similar structure."

I was in a dilemma. I did not want to go against the approach we had worked so hard to define. I wanted to follow President Roosevelt's wishes yet I feared that if I resigned from my commission the addition would be carried out in a manner that would destroy the integrity of the overall memorial design. I discussed my concerns at great length

Figure 169

On May 2, 1997, when the FDR Memorial was dedicated, I walked through with the president and First Lady. Ironically, President Clinton had taken a fall and had to attend the opening on crutches.

After the Show Was Over

Figure 170

The addition to the FDR Memorial acts as a forecourt. Before entering the official presidential years, you encounter FDR in his wheelchair. This placement acknowledges the fact that he contracted polio eleven years before he became president of the United States.

with John Parsons, who had acted as my liaison with the National Park Service and guided me through years of Washington protocol. John had talked me through many roadblocks and difficulties and I knew he would understand my concerns.

Finally I focused on the workshop process as a way for me to move forward. With John's help it was decided that the workshop should include a member of the Roosevelt family, members of the disabled community, a historian, architect, and landscape architect. Over the next three years this group met at various locations: on the actual memorial site in Washington; at Warm Springs in Georgia; at my office in San Francisco; and eventually at the artist studio of Robert Graham in Venice, California. As usual, over time the workshop format developed a group awareness and vocabulary. The initial meeting in Washington, D.C., focused on the criteria that were used for the original design and we arrived at an agreement regarding the need for careful integration in regard to siting and materials. Part of the original criteria was that the memorial unfolded chronologically. This focused our attention on the appropriate location for a new sculpture. FDR, after all, had contracted polio eleven years before he became president.

By the time that the group reunited in Warms Springs we were in agreement that the location for the enhancement should be at the entrance to the memorial, just across from the bookstore. It is in effect a forecourt. We also agreed that the criteria for the new sculpture should be the same as for other sculptures in the memorial: chronological, historic, bronze, on or adjacent to walls, and integrated with an appropriate quotation, and that we use one of the previously selected and approved artists. With these agreements confirmed, the committee went on to decide that we should approach Bob Graham to take on the commission for the new sculpture (Figure 170).

In April 1998, the Franklin Delano Roosevelt Memorial Committee reconvened in San Francisco. Robert Graham was invited to meet with the group and hear their mandate in person. By this time, the criteria had been expanded at a second meeting with disability activists in Washington, D.C. They wanted a sculpture that was life-sized, in the round, and at grade. Their main goal was to have a sculpture that would allow visitors to approach in wheelchairs—they wanted to be able to look directly into the face of FDR and have their pictures taken with him.

As Bob Graham worked in his studio to develop a scale model for presentation, work continued on finalizing contracts, fund raising for the new addition, choosing an appropriate quotation, collaborating with the stone carver, John Benson, and providing architectural drawings to accompany the presentation to the Fine Arts Commission

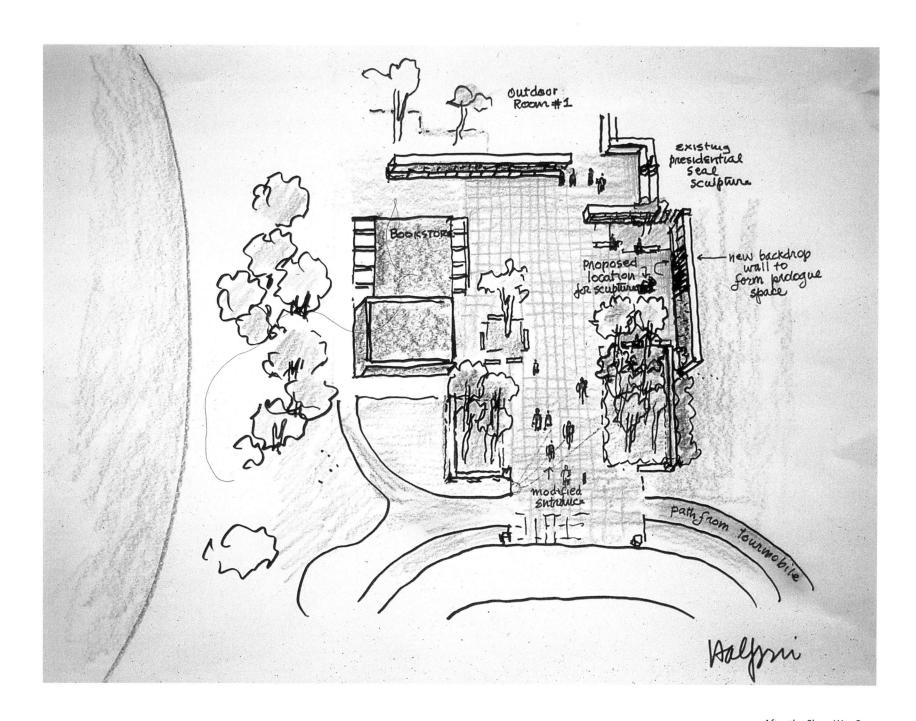

Outdoor Room #1

existing presidential seal sculpture

BOOKSTORE

proposed location for sculpture

new backdrop wall to form prologue space

modified entrance

path from tourmobile

After the Show Was Over

scheduled for May 18. If all went well, construction was scheduled to start up in July 2000. Two criteria had been modified—the image of FDR was not archival but one envisioned by the artist, and the quotation was not one of FDR's but one from Elea-

nor: "Franklin's illness . . . gave him strength and courage he had not had before. He had to think out the fundamentals of living and learn the greatest of all lessons—infinite patience and never-ending persistence" (Figure 171).

Figure 171

When the new statue was installed at the FDR Memorial, it provided visitors with an opportunity to pause in the forecourt, view the image of FDR in his wheelchair, and read Eleanor Roosevelt's insightful quotation.

By the time that the new FDR Memorial Forecourt was dedicated we had entered a new millennium and moved our office back to Levi Plaza. The move was initiated by the Loma Prieta earthquake that hit San Francisco at the start of the third game of the 1989 World Series. The quake underscored the fact that unreinforced brick buildings—like the very one we were occupying on Brannan Street—were dangerous. The city began to consider new rules and restrictions, and a time line for building repairs was developed. It took nine years, but finally in 1998, we had to leave Brannan Street and found space available back in my old neighborhood. This time I planned to avoid the move by taking off for an August vacation. First, however, I decided to deal with a neck problem that had been plaguing me and so signed up for the quick elective surgery that I was told would relieve my spinal stenosis. I expected a two-day hospital stay but ended up in the intensive care unit for six weeks. I am told I died twice during that cloudy period when things went terribly wrong and an emergency tracheotomy was left in place until I left the hospital. Following were months of recovery and rehabilitation when I had to relearn speaking, eating, writing, drawing, and walking. By the time I returned to work, my new office at Levi Plaza was already well established.

Doctors were amazed at my recovery but I was simply focused on getting back to work. In 1996, as the FDR Memorial project had neared completion, I had been offered an extraordinary opportunity. Bob Hanson, executive director of the Yosemite Fund, asked if I was interested in designing the fifty-four-acre approach to Yosemite Falls, an icon of the National Park system. This was a perfect transition from my work on the memorial and it could not have come along at a more opportune moment. I had wondered what I would do after finishing a project that had claimed so much of my attention and energy for what turned out to be twenty-six years. The invitation from the Yosemite Fund represented a return to the high Sierra wilderness and I was anxious to revisit a place that had helped define my personal value system and design philosophy.

The Yosemite Fund and the National Park Service were interested in my "Taking Part" workshop process as a way of gathering input from the numerous diverse stakeholders who all felt deeply committed to Yosemite National Park. Soon after our initial discussions we began planning the workshops and defining the variety of participants that would need to be involved. Adjacent communities, Native Americans, environmental groups, disability advocates, concessionaires, climbers, hikers, park rangers, historians, and designers all had concerns and worried that their perspective would be overlooked. The purpose of the workshops was

14
The New Millennium

to develop a consensus of what we were trying to accomplish and the specific elements that should be included.

It was a wonderful and expansive feeling to return to Yosemite. This was the place where I first came to understand the difference between designing in order to make places for a predetermined purpose and designing as the result of nature's wild and powerful processes (Figures 172–74). That discovery had given me the ability to think and create in a profoundly new and enjoyable way. From my point of view neither way is absolutely better than the other. It is really a question of appropriateness, and I promised the Yosemite Fund and the National Park Service that in Yosemite the design would feel as if it had emerged organically (Figures 175, 176). I did not intend for the area to feel designed or manufactured but rather to feel like it had evolved through the forces of nature.

Very shortly I received another phone call that offered an opportunity to express the other design approach at Stern Grove, a parklike setting located on the outskirts of San Francisco. In 1931, Rosalie Stern had given the land for the park to the city, and she had initiated a tradition of offering free public concerts there every summer. In a number of ways, Stern Grove is the reverse of Yosemite Valley. While both are canyonlike, Yosemite is in a remarkable wilderness area surrounded by

Figure 172

There was some immediate consensus in the Yosemite workshops. It was agreed that we needed to remove the parking lot and outdated restrooms that blocked the view corridor. There was also consensus that Yosemite Falls needed a wider approach with places to step aside for rests and photo opportunities.

Figure 173

I incorporated existing boulders and trees into the design. Additions had to reinforce the organic sense of place and feel as though they belonged.

Figure 174

The idea of a natural amphitheater to serve as a meeting place was incorporated into the Yosemite Falls entrance experience.

Figure 175

The smaller trails that loop back to the main road from Yosemite Falls have a feeling of their own. Narrower pathways meander through the trees, boardwalks cross braided streams, and dramatic views catch visitors by surprise.

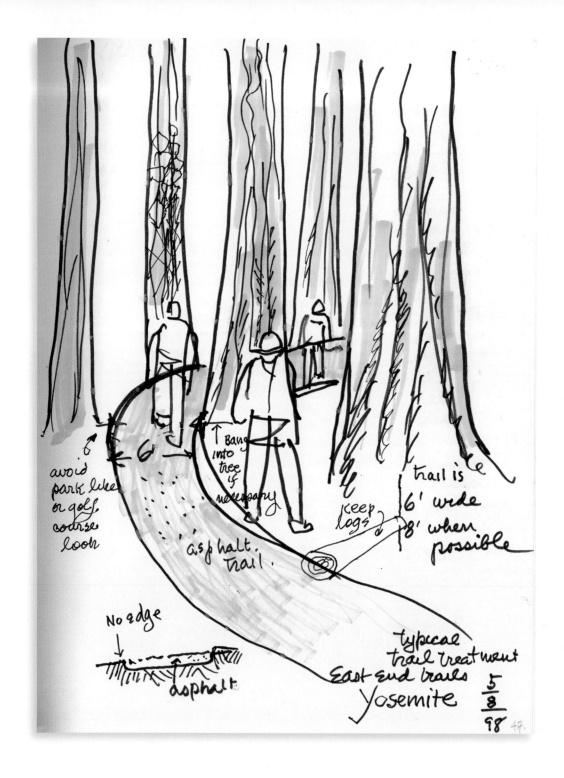

avoid park like or golf course look

Bang into tree if necessary

keep logs

trail is 6' wide 8' when possible

asphalt Trail

No edge

asphalt

typical trail treatment East End trails Yosemite

5/8 98

high-sierra mountains. It is wild in character and full of great waterfalls, enormous granite domes, and wilderness trails. Stern Grove is in an urban neighborhood near the city's edge. It is surrounded by a rigid grid of housing, is quite close to the University of San Francisco campus, and is close to sea level.

Doug Goldman, president of the Stern Grove Festival Association and great-grandson of Rosalie Stern, had heard that I'd made a quick sketch for site improvements on my box lunch container during a concert there. He wanted to follow up on the concept I'd been illustrating, and I knew that if he was serious we could develop a wonderful

Figure 176

It took two pages for me to draw this niche in my notebook. I wanted it to acknowledge or pay tribute to the natural placement of the central boulder.

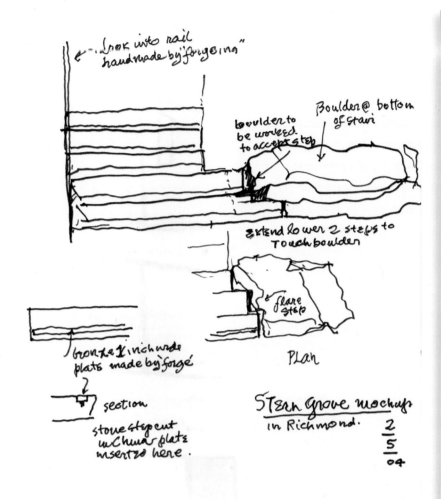

"look into rail handmade by forgeing"

boulder to be worked to accept step

Boulder @ bottom of stair

Extend lower 2 steps to Touch boulder

flare step

PLAN

bronze 1 inch wide plats made by forgé

section

stone step cut in China plats inserted here.

STern grove mockup in Richmond.

2/5/04

Ziggurat 1

Typical

Ziggurat type 3

stern grove ziggurats 10/27/03

theatrical amphitheater. The park is located in a deep, magical, chasm and the steep slopes form a natural canyon that drops some one hundred feet below the street level. Summer performances included symphony, ballet, ethnic dance, and music from a variety of cultures. The performances were wildly successful and drew large crowds but the venue was suffering from overuse and was in need of a major intervention.

With Yosemite and Stern Grove unfolding in the same time frame I was able to embark on two different approaches to design simultaneously. Yosemite's design appears to be the result of organic processes while the Stern Grove design is carefully worked out and the man-made decisions are obvious and powerful. The design differences are perhaps made more interesting and apparent because granite was the dominant building material in both projects. The stone used in Yosemite for seating, paving, and walls was local while the stone used at Stern Grove's amphitheater was quarried and worked to specification in China. Yosemite is easygoing and naturalistic in its character, as though it emerged from the natural forces of gravity and water. Stern Grove follows thousands of years of formal amphitheater designs and is more rigid and urban in character (Figures 177, 178, 179).

Since granite played such a primary role in both of these amazing projects it was important

that I had a trusted, local consultant to collaborate on all aspects of the stonework. I first met Ed Westbrook, and his firm QuarryHouse, in the mid-eighties while working on a small garden for a friend. For twenty years I had turned to Ed to provide me with information regarding the characteristics and sources of stone worldwide. His crews were knowledgeable and took great pride in their work. As the Yosemite and Stern Grove projects evolved, crew members rotated from one project to another bringing their special talents to play as needed, identifying, harvesting, transporting, reinforcing, shaping, and refining the granite textures (Figure 180).

Incredibly a third great project came to me during this same time period. It was equally fascinating and exciting as well as controversial. The seeds for this unique endeavor had been planted years earlier when a thoughtful and proactive group of San Franciscans petitioned to have the Presidio military base transferred to the National Park system if it was ever decommissioned. They assumed it could be incorporated into the adjacent Golden Gate National Recreation Area (GGNRA). In 1996, however, when the transfer finally came about, the U.S. Congress added a new twist. The Presidio was required to become financially self-sufficient by the year 2013. At that point, Nancy Pelosi, the current Speaker of the House, took up the challenge and

Figure 177

The Stern Grove amphitheater seats and steps were carefully designed. The topography did not lend itself to symmetry and the design had to take the cross-slope into consideration.

Figure 178

From the beginning of the design process, I envisioned large granite ziggurat configurations in the concert meadow. In addition to serving as seating for concertgoers, they also provide wonderful focal points and accentuate the fall of the slope.

Figure 179 *(facing page)*

In the springtime, cherry trees and azaleas add a touch of color to the hillside.

Figure 180

The scale of the boulders is powerful and exciting. The meadow is perhaps best appreciated when there is not a concert in progress.

helped to set up the Presidio Trust, a new entity developed to administer the undertaking. Special criteria evolved to meet the congressional mandate and that was how certain areas of the fifteen-hundred-acre Presidio were designated for development. The goal was to meet the financial needs while complimenting the park setting.

One of the areas opened for development by the Presidio Trust was a twenty-three-acre parcel that was geographically and historically exceptional. Located near the entrance to San Francisco Bay and the Golden Gate Bridge, it commanded magnificent views. It had been the location for the formal entrance to the military fort, a venue for the Panama Pacific International Exposition, and home to the Letterman Army Hospital. A number of select development teams were competing for this prime location and I was asked to join the team that wanted to build a San Francisco campus for filmmaker George Lucas.

As I mentioned, the competition site was magnificent and the views were world class. Since 1969, however, it had been the home of Letterman Army Hospital, a ten-story reinforced concrete building surrounded by acres of surface parking lots. I was delighted by the prospect of both transforming the massive military facility and joining an exceptional design team. There were, of course, other worthy developers and teams who were anxious to win, but I have always appreciated a good competition.

George Lucas's winning scheme was driven by concepts that arose at our very first team meeting when it was decided that we had to find a way to convert the site to a car-free pedestrian zone. We also determined that we had to protect the existing mature trees that defined the edges of the site, and we needed to showcase and enhance the views. We felt that if we could accomplish these three goals the site would be transformed into a spectacular and welcoming entrance for the Presidio and the GGNRA. It was obvious that the only way to reach these goals was to put all the cars associated with the development underground. As project manager for the design team, Glenn Isaacson gulped at the cost implications but immediately said, "Wonderful idea, let's present it to George." We did that at our next meeting and George said, "Of course, we should do that. How much will it cost?" I had no idea but I made what I thought was a very high guesstimate and George never blinked. He said that was what we would do and I've never been able to determine how right (or wrong) I was about the actual costs associated with the underground garage. I like to imagine that the underground parking that corralled all the cars and left the site open and green was a major determining factor in winning the competition.

Once the competition was won, the team had to evolve a strong, environmentally correct design scheme, full of opportunities that would serve all park users. The Presidio and the GGNRA are very unusual units within the National Park system because of their proximity to a major urban center—both are tightly woven into the fabric of the San Francisco Bay area. The approaches to the Golden Gate Bridge pass over, under, and through the park; Alcatraz Island is a pivot point in the San Francisco Bay; and the Presidio has a fretted border that meanders in and out of quiet neighborhoods and busy traffic corridors. Our site offered further challenges because an urban park offers visual delights that are similar to but also different from those of a natural park. In this case, along with magnificent natural vistas such as the San Francisco Bay and Mount Tamalpais towering above the rolling hills of Marin County, equally spectacular man-made icons also surrounded us. The site offered views of the famous prison landmark, Alcatraz Island; the graceful dome of the Palace of Fine Arts, designed by Bernard Maybeck for the 1916 Panama Pacific Exposition; and the Golden Gate Bridge, one of the world's greatest masterpieces of engineering (Figures 181–84). All of these had to be considered as we sited the buildings for the new campus to be called the Letterman Digital Arts Center (LDAC).

Neighborhoods adjacent to the LDAC site presented another interesting challenge. The project needed to connect the newly designated park space to the adjacent neighborhoods and to the city beyond. To accomplish a surface connection, I proposed a pedestrian street in the form of a promenade. This design gesture invites the San Francisco neighbors in, and the long sweeping arc of the promenade gives a sense of enclosure to the park. By wrapping around the meadow, the walkways pull your eye into the center of the park rather than drawing it into the distance.

The surprising drop in elevation, fifty feet from the upper edge of the new LDAC buildings to the lower edge of the meadow, offered yet more opportunities and challenges. We took advantage of the slope to create a cascading stream that meanders down from the promenade through a great meadow to a lagoon. Then we faced the next challenge. It was vital for all visitors to be able to travel comfortably throughout this area and for the guidelines established for disabled access to integrate smoothly. Because we had constraints regarding cross slopes and special ramps, I was concerned about the overall impact on the form and shape of the pathways. Linear pathways would have severely limited the shape of the great meadow. That is why we chose a curvilinear pathway that reinforced the wonderful slopes and curves. These slopes and

Figure 182
The scale of the Palace of Fine Arts could not be ignored even from the lower elevations on the site.

Figure 181
Striking views, both natural and man-made, were the most obvious resources to be considered at the Letterman site in the Presidio. Views of the Palace of Fine Arts were as dramatic as those of the San Francisco Bay.

Figure 182
The scale of the Palace of Fine Arts could not be ignored even from the lower elevations on the site.

curves in the landscape had the added advantage of inviting young children to roll and play on the lawn. Besides allowing visitors comfortable access to the site, the paths also directed the eye to the vistas surrounding the San Francisco Bay.

From the very first design meeting all of the buildings for the LDAC project were purposely sited to provide large visual corridors. The project architect, Kevin Hart from Gensler & Associates, totally supported the idea and was a great collaborator. The generous openings between the buildings maintained wonderful views of the Palace of Fine Arts for anyone driving by or arriving at the campus from the upper entrance. These wide view corridors also provided opportunities for semiprivate garden areas where small and mid-size groups could meet, visit, and picnic while enjoying the site.

Although I envisioned those semiprivate gardens from the beginning, they proved to be more difficult to achieve than I originally anticipated. We had chosen mature, multitrunked olive trees to form spatial edges, cast shade, and provide natural sculptural forms for these meeting niches. We had also found enormous moss-covered boulders for benches and picnic platforms. Although the concept was straightforward, it was not easy to accomplish. A great deal of thought went into techniques for limiting the overall weight load on the garage below and locations had to be carefully

The New Millennium

Figure 183

As I walked the site I was constantly aware of where I could catch a glimpse of the Golden Gate Bridge.

Figure 184

I designed a decorative arcade at the bottom of the Letterman site, near the end of the lagoon. It draws visitors down through the meadow and then presents them with a new perspective of the Letterman campus and the views beyond. The British call such attractions follies.

calculated for placement of the extremely large and heavy trees and boulders. Scheduling was also difficult because the passageways weren't ready to accept these final elements until the buildings were finished. Then, an enormous crane with a gigantic reach was needed to tenderly lift trees and boulders over the buildings and place them delicately where we wanted them. Long, exciting days were spent spinning these trees and boulders in the air before settling them in their proper orientation. We had to hold our breath when gusty bay breezes caught at the branches of the trees and swung them around precariously close to the newly glazed windows. One day a large tree was blown out of balance and in slow motion leaned out of its cradle. The crane operators always worked at a snail's pace and as the tree slipped they slowly lowered it so that the landing was moderately soft. The tree was examined and deemed healthy enough to take its place in the garden. It survived beautifully and today anchors a corner of the passageway. As I walk through these garden corridors today I enjoy reliving the memory of those amazing days when I could command such mechanical giants.

All three of these projects basically started in 1997 and formed my professional bridge into the new millennium. All three were complex and required years to unfold. They required multilevel approvals and had to wend their way through budget cuts and setbacks yet they all opened with a bang within weeks of one another in the summer of 2005. Opening ceremonies began in Yosemite while there was still snow on the mountain peaks. Participants from the 1997 workshops were invited to celebrate the results of their input. Weeks later the Stern Grove Festival summer performances began and the new buildings and amphitheater were showcased. The project was almost miraculously constructed between the final performance of 2004 and the first performance in 2005. Shortly thereafter I drove across the Golden Gate Bridge to sit in the great meadow at the new Letterman Arts Digital Center. It was a beautiful day and as crowds enjoyed box lunches and live performances I walked along the meandering paths and watched children explore the stream and roll down the green slopes.

Now, as I look back from my nineties, I can clearly recognize the luck or blessings that provided me with the resources that set the course for my life. I was born to parents who strongly influenced my character, the quality of my interest in the arts of painting, architecture, and design, and an appreciation of cultural diversity. I also had the good fortune to have an uncle who was close enough in age to fill the role of big brother and provide advice and counsel throughout my life. I was given a sound foundation for future success.

From that sound beginning I continued with good luck to acquire friendships and colleagues who led, pushed, and prodded me along my route. There is no doubt the trajectory of my life would have been quite different without them for I always seemed to meet just the friends, mentors, and role models I needed at certain times whether it was during travels in Israel, at preparatory school, or at university. Such friends were not always in close proximity but they surfaced time and again in my life both personally and professionally.

I have had much the same luck and good timing with many of the clients I encountered in my career. There is not enough said in the design world about great clients. You can have enormous talent but without great clients you cannot realize important designs. I have had some exceptional clients during my sixty-year career and they provided

challenging assignments, unique demands, insightful solutions, and ongoing encouragement—as well as difficult program requirements and budget constraints. Great clients are true collaborators.

I absolutely can't imagine how my life would have evolved without my partner in life, Anna Schuman. We were drawn together by a love of the arts and similar social values that somehow enabled us to create a unique life together. Our Jewish cultural heritage provided us with a philosophical outlook that helped us weather life's rough and sad moments. With the addition of our daughters, Daria and Rana, our lives were fueled by additional purpose. The family provided me with the humanizing roles of husband, father, and grandfather. Through my grandchildren, Ruthanna, Levanna, Jahan, and Micah, I came to appreciate even more the importance of the love, stability, and continuity that my family has provided.

Being able to work creatively with Anna, at both our home in Kentfield and our Sea Ranch retreat, added a vital and exciting dimension to our family life. Our early workshops at the Sea Ranch translated into the RSVP Cycles and the "Taking Part" workshops that I used to gather input from communities. These processes were emotional and psychologically charged and they empowered the average citizen. Over time they became part of the design, environmental, and even political

15
Reflections

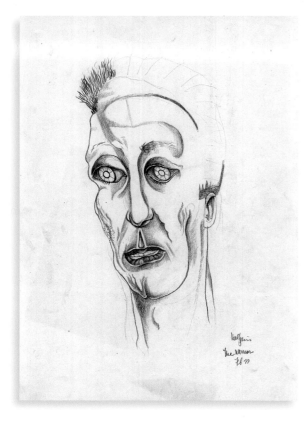

Figure 185

Figure 186

vernaculars. Though I feel that some institutions have learned to manipulate them, overall, I believe they added a great deal to the field of design. It was important to open the planning and design fields up and encourage input and creativity from all members of a community because everyone, absolutely everyone, needs to take responsibility for what happens in our environment.

Throughout my life, the act of sketching kept me grounded (Figure 193). Much of my sketching is obvious and throughout this book you have seen examples of how I recorded family, friends, and events and studied nature. Sketching facilitated my ability to visualize solutions to planning and design problems, to explore sites and designs with a pen or pencil as I searched for the locations and compositions that spoke to me. I often covered my drawings with explanatory notes as I grasped the lessons they were revealing. It is, in fact, hard for me to explain anything without a pen or pencil in my hand.

In 1981, my friend Jimmy Burns wrote an essay for a book based on many of my project sketches. He explained the uses of sketches much better than I ever could. As a highly literate man, Jim wrote about sketching with allusions to Leonardo Da Vinci and William Blake. He quoted Shakespeare, T. S. Eliot, and the Japanese artist Hokusai. Jim described how he had mined a number of my sketchbooks covering a twelve-year period and

edited them down to one volume published by MIT Press in 1972. Then he went on to describe how drawing can allow emotions, concepts, and experience to make a "metaphysical leap"—he described how some artists use their sketches to "find without searching." Whether one calls this automatic writing, doodling, or daydreaming on paper, it is a process that has served me well.

It has also been suggested that I draw to exorcise my demons. Caricatures and cartoons of military bureaucracy, horrific war images, frustrating clients, and management conundrums spilled out of my pen during the war and for years after (Figure 185). Later I pinpointed and explored mental, emotional, and physical pains in hundreds of self-portraits. Earaches, headaches, toothaches, hip replacement, spinal stenosis, and other ailments were all explored with as much technical accuracy as I could muster (Figures 189–191). Depressions, anxieties, anger, frustration, fear were also transferred to paper (Figures 186, 188). Did it help? My long-time associate Dee Mullen apparently thought so because she would sometimes suggest I perform such an exorcism before I went into a particularly difficult meeting, presentation, or medical procedure. In 1998, I believe sketching had as much to do with my recovery from the operation-gone-bad as any other form of therapy (Figure 192). I was able to write and sketch before I could talk. I used it to communicate and record my

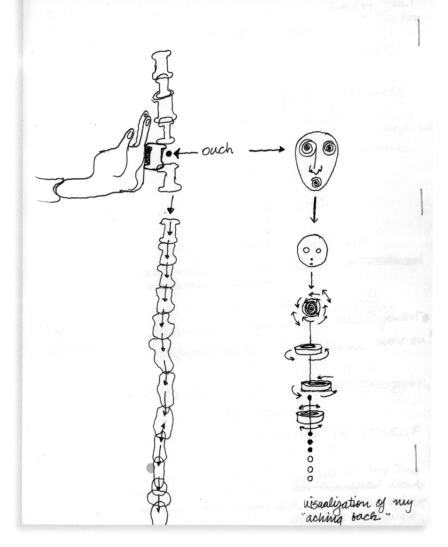

ouch

visualization of my "aching back"

Figure 187

Figure 188

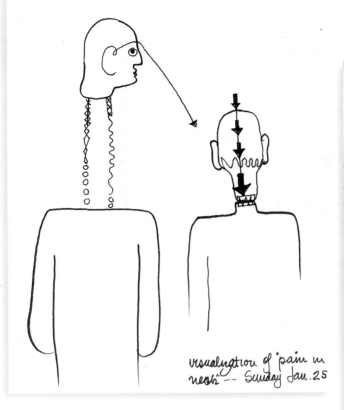

visualization of "pain in
neck" -- Sunday Jan. 25

Figure 189

Hair "in pain"
gout..
10/27/93

Figure 190

Figure 191

after allergy attack
2/7/95

surroundings, and as my sketching ability returned so did my drive to get back to my creative life.

I have always been a great believer in talent, but in writing this autobiography I have discovered how much of a part genes, luck, timing, and intuition have played in my life. These ephemeral elements gave me opportunities, experience, and social values. Those in turn guided me to a number of special places and projects that gave me an overriding sense of purpose and great satisfaction. And as I helped give those places life, they did the very same for me (Figure 194).

Figure 192

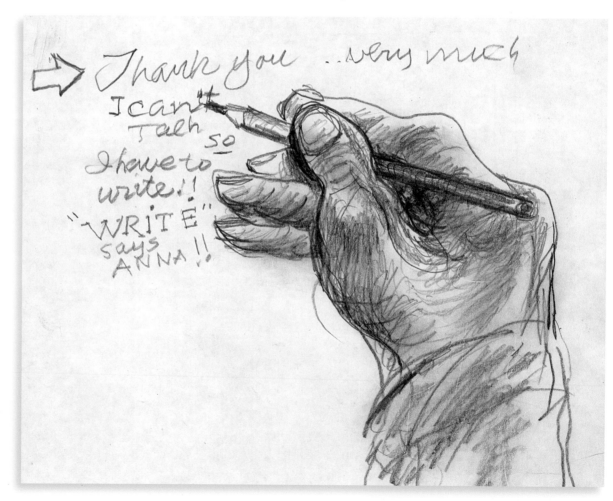

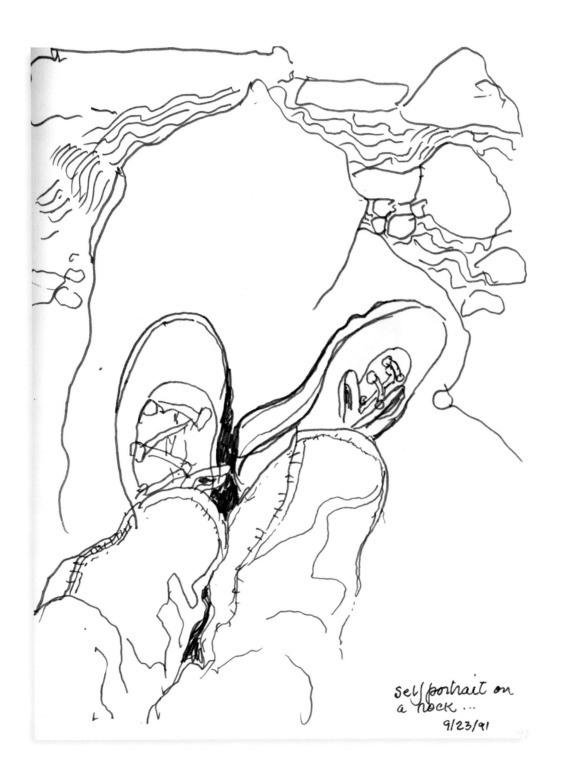

self portrait on a rock ...
9/23/91

Figure 193

Reflections

Figure 194

Index

Series Editor's Note

It is apt that Lawrence Halprin's memoir *A Life Spent Changing Places* is published by the University of Pennsylvania Press, as his archives were deposited with the Architectural Archives at Penn. The manuscript was written and finalized by Halprin before his death, and it has been seen through the editing and proof stages by his former colleague, Dee Mullen.